War and Revolution

WAR and REVOLUTION

by Nicholas S. Timasheff

EDITED WITH A PREFACE BY
Joseph F. Scheuer

SHEED AND WARD / *New York*

© *Sheed and Ward, Inc., 1965*

Library of Congress Catalog Card Number 65-20856

Manufactured in the United States of America

To my former students
who encouraged me to publish this book.

ACKNOWLEDGMENTS   First of all, I wish to acknowledge my deep gratitude to Professor Joseph F. Scheuer of Fordham University for his editorial work on the MS in general and especially for his worthy suggestions as to chapters on social causation and the theory of conflict, as well as his continuous encouragement throughout the various stages of this work.

I acknowledge also the help of my daughter, Mrs. Tania Bobrinskoy who has typed the early versions of my book and collected some information for me.

Last but not least, I wish to thank the Humanities Fund, Inc., New York City, for generous grants without which this book never could have been completed.

N. S. TIMASHEFF

Preface

THAT OUR WORLD consistently exhibits a recurrence of certain events, has and probably always will intrigue the understanding of men. *Ab esse ad posse,* the ancients argued—from the fact that it has always been, it can always be. Yet, there is really no great evidence that nature *must*. Yes, it has always been. But need it always be?

Logically, this seems to be the basis for the pursuance of the scientific inquiry into the nature of things. And even though faith may give the scientist one set of assurances in this matter, and his philosophical convictions may warrant the same or another set of assurances, he will still seek to know for himself in ever new forms.

Part of the great scientific effort in our generation has been the development of the social sciences. The almost ceaseless questioning of sociologists like Pitirim Sorokin, Talcott Parsons, Charles Loomis, etc.—to say nothing of historians, psychologists and anthropologists, and other specialists—has marked the twentieth century with an intellectual productivity to rival our technological and industrial affluence.

Indeed, a major portion of this intellectual labor proceeds in a manner not unlike that of mass production with its technological systematization. Large philanthropic foundations and government grants, immense university bureaucracies and teams of intellectuals, are mobilized in the quest for "new insights" which will furnish the basis for contemporary formulation of public and private policy.

In 1932, Pitirim Sorokin began the research which eventually led to the publication of his truly magnificent *Social and Cultural Dynamics* (New York: American Book Co., 1937). One of his twenty American and European collaborators in this monumental work was Nicholas S. Timasheff, a specialist in law. However, Timasheff's long experience as a teacher, journalist, and lecturer marked him in Sorokin's task force for another remarkable assignment: the highly specialized study of some 1,622 revolutions.

The fruits of his work quickly became an integral part of the Sorokin masterpiece and it spurred Timasheff's own interest in sociological theory and research. This research has led him to formulate his own observations and conclusions about those social processes leading from peace to war and from order to revolution, and back again. The fruits of this work are contained in this present book.

The case studies presented here are not the chief concern of this work. Competent historical works, many of them quite standard, contain the record of men's conflict with other men. But the reader will find here a particular kind of reasoning, the development of a particular kind of *logic* about the social phenomena involved in the human processes related to war, revolution, and their opposite, peace. This is Timasheff's contribution. This is the *raison d'être* of the study.

Timasheff has never formed what some might call "his own general, systematic theory" of society, culture or personality. There is no "school of Timasheff," as one might point to the school of the ecologists—followers of Spencer, Park or Burgess. Nor is Timasheff concerned with building "models" for analyzing social phenomena. Basically, a Timasheff analysis is refreshing. It is refreshing because it is free of such built-in myths and images as occur in discussions which view human experiences in *terms of something or other,* in a perspective in which they never happened in the first place.

Timasheff's analyses are elegantly logical analyses. He observes the social system, its processes, its dynamics, without any predeterminants in his own mind other than the principles of identity, contradiction and analogy. These are the only tools with which he observes, thinks, and finally makes a judgment. To do less than this is not to think. To do more is to over-step the limits of rigorous science.

War and Revolution contains many case studies of the phenomena it is intent upon understanding more fully. It also contains eminently logical discussions on causation, political systems, conflict, violence, and prediction—discussions which make war and revolution understandable.

JOSEPH F. SCHEUER

ix

Contents

xi

Contents

War and Revolution

1/ Understanding
the Recurrence of War
and Peace

THE RECURRENCE of a beat, a theme, or a rhythm has always engaged the interest of man. Whether that beat is in the music of an orchestra, in color on a canvas, in the turning of a season, or in the flow of a life; whether it appears in the speed of electrons, or in the swift orbit of the planets, the man stands transfixed, and the mind, in genuine wonder, asks "Why?" Equally wonderful is the human mind's ability alternately to attribute these recurrences to nature and the universe, to its own creative power (or weakness and selectivity), or to a combination of both a real and a mental reality, working in parallel, or in an organic and vital interrelationship, or perhaps even by accident.

3

Poets, philosophers, and bearers of revelation have had opinions and insights, gained by grace or effort, into these questions. Most lately the scientist, with his own disciplines, methods and techniques, has been a powerful source of further probing of the regularities—or the lack of them—in the workings of man and nature. In the social sciences, in particular, recent advances in history, psychology, anthropology, and economics have sparked new interest and given new focus to these old problems that the human mind has always faced, rarely solved, but has always succeeded somehow in rising above, or struggling through.

Not the least important of these rhythms are those expressed as fluctuations from peace to war, from social order to revolt. No other century possessed the vast amount of information about these phenomena that is available to the twentieth.[1] And this, among other factors, may explain the growing scientific interest as well as social concern in dealing with the questions of war, revolutions, order and peace.

The magnitude of wars and revolutions varies greatly. They may be short or long, lasting a few days or years and even decades. Wars may be waged against weak enemies, mighty foes or coalitions. Likewise, revolutions may be purely local, affecting one city, or a particular district; and again, they may involve the entire nation. They may be concerned with relatively small social problems, or they may involve issues affecting the entire social and political order.

The generalized findings of Pitirim Sorokin and Quincy Wright, supplemented by other investigations, allow a careful observer to draw several judgments which have great importance for orientating our study.

1. War and revolution have occurred in the history of all

4

human societies which have evolved above the primitive level.

2. War and revolution are more frequent than commonly assumed, but are less frequent than periods of peace and order.

3. In the movement from one phase to another, from peace to war and back to peace, from war to revolution and back to order, there is no periodicity.[2]

4. There is no general trend observable relative to the frequency or the magnitude of wars and revolutions. In other words, there is no experimental basis for a judgment that mankind is or has become or will become more or less peaceful, more or less law abiding, more or less war-like, or more or less revolutionary.

Problems of Definition

We can see already the need to define our terms further. In common-sense terms, war and revolution are not hard to identify. But, for example, if one simply states that war and revolution are violent conflicts, he is not supplying a proper definition. There are obviously many violent conflicts which men do not identify as wars or revolutions: gang violence, race riots, or open violence between unions, are conflicts not generally regarded as wars or revolts. This suggests our first specification: the identity of the *parties* to the violence (the *who*) must have something to do with the definition of war and revolution.

In the case of war, there is no problem identifying the parties involved. They are states (nations) or groups of states if the war involves coalitions. For this reason, a clear grasp of the nature of war requires the understanding of the nature of the state—or at least those properties of the state which are relevant to war.

Peace will now of course come to mean simply lack of conflict between states or nations.

Another element must be explicit in the definition of war. When states enter conflict, they bring into motion *specialized organizations* called armed forces. In terms of these preliminary specifications, war can be defined as the clash of the armed forces of two or more states.

This is a realist's definition of war and it is made independent of legal prescriptions, e. g., those of international law. If every violent conflict between states which is manifested in the clash of their armed forces is war[3], then no violent conflict is war except one involving the clash of the armed forces of two or more states. However, assessments of a situation on this basis do not always coincide with the judgments of reality. Why this discrepancy?

In terms of international law certain clashes of armed forces do not produce the legal consequences of an outbreak of war. For example, the rules of neutrality or of the treatment of prisoners do not enter into force. A lawyer would deny that a war is going on. Such was the situation that obtained between Japan and China after the Mukden incident (1931), and again after the Peiping incident (1937). This latter was the signal for fighting between the armed forces of China and Japan. Contrariwise, from the legal point of view, war continued between the United States and Japan until September, 1951, and between the United States and West Germany until 1954, although the armed forces of Japan and Germany had been annihilated. Even when they were restored they were not used

6

in combat, so that there was *actually* no war, although legally
a state of war was in force.

The presence or absence of the legal consequences attached
to war may be relevant in many regards. But legal formulae
cannot affect the basic fact nor efface differences of real situations: one, when armed forces are only trained for fighting,
and two, when they actually do fight.

War is violent armed conflict between states. Accordingly,
if one of the parties is not a state there is no war. This means
that colonial expeditions against tribes living in pre-political
conditions are not wars by this definition. (Pre-political tribes
are those having no government groups specifically differentiated from other groups in the tribe). By a similar reasoning,
military actions against rioters or rebels are not wars. Obviously, it is not our meaning of war to speak of conflicts between
two tribes, or any two groups of people who are not *organized*
as states. To do so would be to identify a species of violent
conflict (war) with its genus (violent conflict). Incidentally,
Sorokin commits this confusion, identifying war with murder.

Several simple refinements of the definition of war will
eliminate from our observations insignificant incidents such
as the following. A border incident takes place when a pla-
toon belonging to the army of State A has trespassed the
boundary of State B. The sentries of State B shoot. Events of
this type may be conducive to war but more commonly do
not start war. Payments of indemnity, diplomatic apologies,
renegotiation of boundaries—or similar actions—usually take
place without the violence taking on larger scales.

It is inadequate to think of such incidents as war because
they either happen by accident or are void of significant consequences. The line between "an incident" and war may be

delineated by the following. War is actual when the clash of armed forces is induced by the agencies of the central government of at least one of the parties involved. If the armed violence originates locally, the supposition is that war exists when the government agencies approve it (and thereby confirm it), making the original outbreak of armed violence the starting point of further clashes. If it appears from later developments that the clash was merely the expression of a local and temporary conflict, not confirmed by government representatives, it is not classified as war.

Revolution

Revolution is also violent conflict which involves the state, differing specifically from war in that it is violent conflict *within* a state. Of course, there may be simultaneous revolutions in two or more states, or revolutions in several states produced by a kind of contagion. But in all these instances there are as many revolutions as there are states affected.

In a war, the parties are all (or both) equally states. In a revolution, *one* party is normally a state, or a centralized government, but the other party is a more or less organized (and hence more or less disorganized) group by comparison with the central government. Sometimes the revolutionary party is a totally disorganized mob, but one strong enough to challenge the government. Or the revolutionary force may appear with some organization, e.g., a political party. Other times it may appear suddenly, led by a prophetic leader; or it may appear as a secessionist movement, once part of the organized political structure.

In whatever form the revolutionary force appears, it may be

distinguished from certain social processes which are called revolutions by simile and metaphor. A case in point is the "industrial revolution" which engendered many social conflicts, and even some genuine revolutions, but was (or is) merely rapid social change. It is as improper to extend the idea of revolution to social change as it would be to extend the concept of war to a violent conflict between two individuals. Rapid social change, carried out in institutional forms, and admitting no disruption of power positions in government, prevents revolution in the proper meaning of the term.

Then there are those phenomena involving violence against which the government has to use force. Race riots, violent labor strikes, or when there are national food shortages, raids against granaries or warehouses—these and similar actions have a serious, violent character, and hence may look like revolutions. Confusion is heightened by the fact that racial, or inter-ethnic clashes, or hunger marches, begin as clashes between non-political groups, i. e., as clashes between groups that have no formal existence as part of the relatively permanent governing bodies of the state. However, since these groups almost inevitably come to grips with some part or parts of the political structure, e. g., the police, only the *metaphorical* term "revolt" seems proper to these cases.

There are still other phenomena which must also be excluded from the analysis of revolution. In countries where the *pronunciamento* or other such upheavals are almost institutionalized—and often even named "revolutions"—one could easily be misled and include them in a study of revolution. The typical *pronunciamento* is limited to a change in some *part* of the governing personnel in a country. Usually a sequence of generals, majors, captains, or even non-commissioned officers, does not come within the meaning of the term revolution. If a *pronunciamento* should replace a democratic government by a dictatorship, or a dictatorship by a democracy (even through delayed action), it would properly be a revolution. By the same reasoning, convulsions at the top of a dictatorial pyramid, not accompanied by spectacular changes of policies, are not considered revolutions. Item: the elimination of L. Beria (Moscow, 1953), although accompanied by a display of military force, is not considered a revolution. Neither would the assassinations of monarch, president, or other leaders of state necessarily indicate revolution.

Coups d'état are another phenomena that we must consider in this context. Usually a *coup d'état* indicates a serious mutation in the form of the political system, but no great disorder. In fact, the *coup d'état* normally involves the use of already existing political power to effect change in the political structure with little or no resistance on the part of the governed beyond the verbal protest. A *coup d'état* implies that an overwhelming force already in existence has violated the law. But every crime is a revolt against the law. It is noteworthy that an attempted *coup d'état* stopped by bearers of political power ordinarily results in the trial of the unsuccessful usurpers for crime.[4]

One would not consider that there was revolution in France when on December 2, 1852, President Napoleon Bonaparte proclaimed himself Emperor Napoleon III. There was no revolution in Russia when on June 3, 1906, Emperor Nicholas II of Russia on the advice of Prime Minister Stolypin signed a new electoral law issued contrary to the dispositions of the Fundamental Laws in force.

The definition of revolution proper to this study, therefore, comes to be a violent conflict between the government and an opposition engendered by the incompatibility of generalized goals of the two parties to the conflict.[5] The term "generalized goals" logically eliminates from observation the *pronunciamento* and conspiracies discussed above; it similarly eliminates cases where mob action is aiming at a concrete demand, e. g., in the case of a riot, or a strike. The term would not eliminate situations like the following: the government rejects a change in the law demanded by the opposition and the latter carries out acts of violence or preparations for them; or the government enacts a law which in draft form already meets strong opposition and the opposition proceeds to violence. These cases may be minor revolutions, but they are still revolutions (e. g., the July, 1830, revolution in France).

There may still be cases when the classification of a concrete process might be dubious. A race riot may, to a certain extent, aim at the improvement of the social status of an oppressed group; a violent strike may develop into a revolution-like movement aiming at the overthrow of the social order. But this only demonstrates how, even after precise definition, some phenomena will always appear as residual. This need not deter the scientist.

Social Processes

Since wars are conflicts between states, and revolutions are conflicts within states, there are many points of similarity between them. Obviously, since we are viewing them both under the common term "conflict," they must logically appear similar, but what further concrete similarities may be found from more extensive observation?

Conflict is by its nature intermittent; sooner or later it must end.[6] This is characteristic of conflict as a social process. Unlike the processes of cooperation and competition, which are relatively continuous both between and within societies, conflict does not endure. Hence the continuous fluctuation of societies between peace and war, order and revolution. Societies cannot *remain* in the state of war and/or revolution, while they can and do remain, in principle, in the state of peace and order.

Second, wars and revolutions are *violent* conflicts. Other social processes may also be observed in degree, i. e., in forms of more or less violence, more or less apathy. As we shall demonstrate in another place,[7] this has special significance when investigating the question: Why do men resort to war and revolution when attempting to resolve *some* of their conflicts?

Third, peace and order, the opposites of war and revolution, are commonly regarded as "normal" states of society. This appears to have a double meaning. First, peace and order are deemed desirable, although there may be groups and perhaps even whole societies which would prefer war and/or revolution. Second, peace and order represent the state of "maximum probability," i. e., peace and order occur more frequently than war and revolution. Data collected on the frequency of war and revolution[8] would verify this. This is especially true when one uses smaller units of time in which to perceive or observe periods of war and revolution. In other words, if one counts not the number of years in a century during which wars and revolutions occurred, but the number of days they lasted, peace and order are much more "normal" than war and revolution.

As deviants from normalcy, wars and revolutions are disturbances. When their intensity is high they become social calamities,[9] and are experienced much as severe famines, widespread epidemics, floods, and severe economic crises are experienced. When the intensity is strong enough, a return to a state of normalcy is no longer possible. The government involved breaks down. History tells repeatedly of states disappearing after unsuccessful wars and the Boer republics in 1902, and the Austro-Hungarian monarchy of 1918, are conspicuous examples. Several Italian principalities were destroyed by revolutions (1859-60), unsuccessfully aiming at their union with Piedmont to form a unified Italy.

Fourth, war and revolutions conflict with processes running in the framework of the political organization of society. As such the conflict brings face to face states, or the central core of the state (the government), and its antagonists, led by a virtual government.

Fifth, war and revolution are related to the two basic functions of the state: self-assertion, and the maintenance of law and order. War is an expression of self-defense and, eventually, of aggression against other states. Revolution is a challenge to the maintenance of law and order. It is significant that there are no other functions of the state which can give rise to war and revolution. Assume, for instance, that the people emphatically demand a reform of the system of education or a drastic change of foreign policy, and the government denies the demand. The people would not attack the educators or the diplomats. If they did the government would interfere, using its armed force when necessary. If the parties persisted a situation of revolution would emerge.

It is possible for something more than similarity to exist between war and revolution. The two may become one and when this occurs, civil war emerges. Examples are the American Civil War, 1861-64, the Russian, 1917-22, and the Spanish, 1936-39. The War of Independence (1776-81) is often called the American Revolution.

How does it happen that this perception of identity is possible? On the one hand, a revolution may be successful in one part of the political structure, and unsuccessful, or even non-existent, in another part. In the sector where the revolution has been successful a new and centralized power structure emerges—the revolutionary government. Legally, it does not exist; but the fact of its existence as a political structure is enough to put it at odds with the older or legitimate government. There is a clash of two armed forces, each directed from a center which undeniably exerts supreme power. Although this would not yet, in international law, be classified as a war, it is *de facto a war*. On the other hand, in the same case, one of the centers challenges the government which ruled all sectors of public life prior to a disturbance, and has been resisted by force. This is revolution; logically, revolution and war are now merged into civil war.

There is sometimes a causal connection between war and revolution. Wars, especially unsuccessful war, may provoke revolutionary movements against governments. The defeat of Russia by Japan in 1904-5 resulted in the so-called Abortive Revolution of 1905-6 in the Russian state. The defeat of Germany and Austria-Hungary in the First World War resulted in the revolutionary overthrow of the monarchy in the two states. The defeat of Italy in the Second World War was reflected in the overthrow of Mussolini's dictatorship; the puppet governments established by Germany in Norway and Czechoslovakia had to quit when Germany was defeated.

But then revolution may provoke war. A twenty-three years period of war, 1792-1815, began when Austria and Prussia declared war on France because they would not tolerate the success of the French Revolution. The Communist revolution in Russia provoked the so-called intervention of Russia's allies in the Civil War which was then going on in Russia. Of course, this was war between Russia, headed by her new government, and her former allies who were helping a "counterrevolutionary movement."[10]

One may therefore *think* of *periods of wars and revolutions*. In Europe such periods have been the years 1789-1815, 1914-26, and 1939-48. It is interesting that, after painstaking tabulations, Sorokin finds the incidents of wars and revolutions to be quite independent. In other words, the periods of maximum belligerency in a particular state or states does not coincide with periods of maximum revolutionary activity.[11] This means only that the causal background of war differs from that of revolution; and that, in concrete cases, war does not engender revolutions, and that revolutions do not cause wars.

The Sociological Interpretation of War and Revolution

The many similarities between wars and revolutions, the possibility of their merger into civil war, and the possibility of causal relations between these phenomena, allow us to make an initial judgment: *these are kindred or related phenomena*. A study of these phenomena as related (or interrelated) phenomena may lead to their more precise and deeper understanding.

This is ultimately the only justification for yet another study.

Since ancient times wars and revolutions have been the special interest of historians. And, until perhaps the nineteenth century, history was studied and written predominantly from the political viewpoint. War and revolution, reform, changes from monarchical to democratic forms of government, and similar *events* loom large as the subject matter for such research.

The historian is expected to reproduce the sequence of events as faithfully as possible, and eventually explain them. He tries to make them understandable by establishing cause-and-effect relationships between some of the preceding and some of the subsequent events. He knows that the events he deals with will never recur: there will never be another Trojan War or another American War of Independence. The historian seeks causal relations in all their concreteness and specifications as they occur, but as they will also never recur.

Using the same data, and relying heavily upon historians' research, a sociological interpretation seeks the generalizing principle in human events. The sociologist's interest now turns not to events in all their concretion, but to the patterns that appear and reappear, and patterns that may even be predicted. The sociologist will seek to find what, in general, causes societies to move from peace to war and back to order again. His judgments in this will contain no references to individual wars and revolutions, to individuated points in time or in space, although these are presupposed in his judgments or conclusions.

How is this achieved? It supposes, as we have suggested that the sociological study have basic data and information from historical sources. The conclusions must be empirically verifiable. But they must also be *scientifically reliable*. This is another way of saying that the sociological interpretation involves and is based on a scientific model of causation. This is not exactly the same as saying that the laws of nature (the laws of biological organisms, or chemical substances) are always identical. Everyone knows that they are not. But we do claim that a *science* of something or other (atomic energy, or human action) does have a logical consistency about it. There are rules and specifications about causes and their effects, which while they may not be *absolutely* universal in our universe of contingency, are nevertheless quite necessary and useful if nature and the things of nature (e. g., human behavior) are to make any sense—if they are in any way intelligible.

In this context an indispensable preliminary step in our inquiry is to state the problem of causation—social causation —since it is the model for our generalizations. The nature of the political system must be elaborated since it is this that suffers war and revolution or exists in peace and order. Finally, we need precision in our thinking about the nature of conflict, especially *violent* conflict.

2/ Perceiving Cause
in Social Phenomena*

WITH THE APPEARANCE of Karl Pearson's *Grammar of Science*[1] some seventy years ago it became fashionable in the social sciences to replace reality with "routine sense impressions." What Karl Pearson did not foresee was the next fashion in science: the replacement of routine sense impressions by routinized concepts. Conceptualism is, of course, one of many possible philosophical or metaphysical positions, just as realism or idealism—moderate or extreme. Conceptualism, however, unlike realism, or idealism, argues that since there can be no causal relations between concepts, there can be no causal relations between things, and the modern "conceptual model"

* This chapter quotes substantially from my article, "Order, Causality, Conjuncture," in *Symposium on Sociological Theory,* edited by Llewellyn Gross. Copyright © 1959 by Row, Peterson and Company.

18

used in the social sciences predictably ignores the concept of cause as outmoded, and irrelevant.

Idealism versus realism, conceptualism versus realism, etc., are important and fundamental questions. But they are questions whose discussion is possible at a level beyond the level of science, i. e., that of metaphysics. And while it is true that one's metaphysical preferences will almost invariably be reflected in one's observation and theoretical orientations in science, it is easy to distinguish between them. Further *logically integrated* theory is possible at all levels. Our preference metaphysically is the *moderate realist* position. And it is within the assumptions of a moderate realist position that our logically integrated system is consistent. Viewed from the extremes of any other metaphysical position it will, of course, appear out of step.

There are other fashions in modern scientific thought to which this view of logically integrated theory will not seem appropriate. It is quite *avant-garde* in some circles, for example, to avoid the term *cause,* or at least to deny that cause implies sequence in time. Terms like "asymmetry" are substituted when, for example, B depends on A, but A does not depend on B, according to H. A. Simon, a proponent of the new "meta-language." Nonetheless, it is surprising to find the term cause *in common use* among scientists; and he himself often speaks of "causal ordering," "causal relationship," or simply "cause," and finally when drawing meaningful conclusions from the manipulation of concepts in his new style ends in largely common-sense causal judgments himself.[2]

Logically integrated theory in the moderate realist position assumes that there are invariant and real relations between phenomena recurring or succeeding in time, and when these relations are consistently observed as recurring and succeeding in time, they are properly and proportionally perceived as causally related.

Since the formulation of the *principle of indeterminacy* by Heisenberg, and in view of many and rapid developments in quantum mechanics and microphysics, the manner of understanding "cause" in relation to real relations of phenomena has undergone considerable reinterpretation.[3] That phenomena are really related, and that there are real causes between them is not so much in doubt. The problem is the *nature* of that causal relation or relations independent of the observer and the tools, conceptual or otherwise, by which he perceives it. Quantum theory since Heisenberg postulates relative (or relational) real relations between phenomena, rather than the older simplistic theories of universal causal relations. There is no evidence, in the nature of the phenomena observed, and there is no logical necessity for more involved in the postulates of the principle.

In social sciences, as in the natural, there has always been a serious difference of opinion between the universalists and the relativists. Comte emphasized that social laws were more flexible than the laws of physical nature, a judgment much more in accord with modern relativism. Spencer, and most if not all of his school, insist upon a universalist conception based upon an unequivocal cosmic evolution. Many of the classical eighteenth and nineteenth century political economists judge their phenomena in terms of a universalist position, as for example, Ricardo in his famous iron law of wages. Neo-positivists today, like Lundberg,[4] implicitly at least, postulate a universal in their judgment of reality as capable of understanding in terms of frequency distribution and probability. Adherence to a more relational position is evidenced in the work of such men as Sorokin, Gurvitch, and others.[5]

Whether one accepts the logic of the universalist or that of the relativist will also have bearing upon his acceptance of a determinist or a relational concept of *order*. The question now is not whether or not there is order in the world and in the phenomena the scientist observes. Implicitly or explicitly this is what the scientific search is all about. And not only in science! Men act on the basis of order quite generally. They assume that water will boil when sufficiently heated, that water will flow down from higher to lower ground levels, that the duck will be killed or wounded if an arrow or a bullet pierces its body. Socially they assume that men will honor their formal obligations, that within an area of peace they will not be attacked, that men will reciprocate insults and injuries. Here there is no difference between primitive and advanced societies; the primitive knows less, specifically, about the order around him, but insofar as he knows, he acts.

In advanced society highly complicated technological processes are unthinkable when one doubts the consequences of specific manipulations of matter and energy. The economic processes and the industrial organization upon which they depend are unintelligible without assumptions of standardization and predictability of order. Legal processes are impossible without routinization of cases. Medicine is meaningless without something more than random treatment.

The question, then, is not whether or not there is order, but rather whether order is universalist and absolute, or whether it is particularist and relational. Our position on this question is clear and unequivocal: in the sciences, whether natural or social, order is particular and relational. Why?

21

First of all, the experimental observation and the scientific generalization to which it is directed deal with and arise out of limited and defined (by the observer) phenomena. No scientist claims that he is observing universally. Repeated observation and experiment have confirmatory weight, but can guarantee the same conclusions from the same data (reliability) only with increasing degrees of probability.

Secondly, the observer or experimenter can be concerned only with the *relations* between the phenomena, and their *variance*. Logically this excludes the observation of *natures* as such or *essences,* except insofar as these are *probably determined* by *relationship*.

Order, therefore, in science can be conceived only as a principle operative within certain limits, i. e., the limits implicit in experimentation and the limits implicit in relationship.

Order in this conception may be either static or dynamic. Here again this is more a matter of the logic of the observer than the logic of the thing observed. In physics Einstein's formula: $E = mc^2$ (the quantity of potential energy is measured by its mass times the velocity of light squared) can be thought of or viewed in both a structural and a dynamic sense. Similarly in the social sciences: for example, Sorokin's theorems, establishing the esthetic, ethical, legal, economic subsystems from a culture's dominant system of truth.[6] Viewed in one time dimension the independent variable appears static and its dependent varibles accordingly static; viewed as processes, in time, the independent variable (now itself a dependent of the time perspective) changes and so do its dependent variables, the subsystems.

Properly the concept of causality is meaningful only (logically) in the time dimension.[7] The scientific judgment that a causal nexus exists (is observable) between two (or more) phenomena implies points of time. Put another way, the judgment that A causes B implies in the judgment a temporal sequence. If A, as often as it is observed, is connected with B following, the scientific judgment correctly assumes that B is caused by A. Further, and in still other words, we assert the (at least probable) existence of a causal nexus if we know that the combination of conditions (antecedents) A.B.C. . . . N is invariably followed by the effect(s) (subsequent) $X.x_1.x_2.$, etc.

This is not to imply a certain kind of reversal of the process involving the temporal sequence. It is highly fallacious to argue, in other words, that *because* a thing or things (phenomena) have followed other things (phenomena) in a temporal sequence, they are, *therefore,* the effects of the phenomena prior in time. "Tom," my cat, is here, *because* his mother gave birth to him; but I cannot reverse this, saying that *because* "Tom" is here his mother gave birth to him. His being here, in other words, is not simply the *cause* of his mother's being a mother. Of course I may *infer* now since he is here that "Minnie" *was* his mother.

One may readily grant that it is perhaps due to some of these logical difficulties (if not subtleties) that the fashion of ignoring problems of *social* causation have been side-stepped, more often than have the proportionate problems in the natural sciences. And there are historical and traditional habits of thought which do not make its exploration any simpler.

Social Causation

Perhaps the most evident confusion, historically, lies in the tendency to identify scientific method and theory with a determinist position at the level of metaphysics and morality. The confusion here is logically transferred as an identification of order in physical and biological phenomena, and order in personal and social phenomena where (or when) concepts, measures, and experimental controls proper to scientific method are used to analyze nature simply.

Subjected to the scutiny of science, natural order is no longer simple. In terms of social order and freedom, the simple reference to metaphysical freedom (of the will) no longer suffices either.[8] Some human choices, e. g., decisions, may have a strong effect on social phenomena, such as Hitler's decision to attack Russia, or the decision of President Truman to resist the North Korean aggresion against South Korea. Such phenomena may seem to be dependent on a force or forces not covered by any postulate of order, and therefore, will seem to be outside the view of any causal interpretation.

But in actuality every human choice is made in the framework of definite observable conditions known to affect these decisions, limiting the number of possible decisions, and making some decisions more plausible and probable than others. Further, human order and its processes are a concatenation of human acts. Looked at simply, each may be considered a relatively free act; but viewed as many they converge into a composition of forces which in turn puts into motion actions of men which are not the simple matter of free choice, and which are clearly covered by the postulate of order.

On a free market, buyers and sellers individually make free decisions to buy or to sell and at what price. But the analyst of the market situation can *predict* the trend of these decisions and prices; he can do so because he knows the "law" of supply and demand which governs the composition of forces (wills) involved when individuals transact on the conditions established by the market.

Nobody admits to wanting inflation. Nobody admits to actions aiming at inflation. But in situations which a science of economics describes as "inflationary," most people if unchecked make decisions which, by their very necessity as individual decisions, are observable as social phenomena causative of inflation: demanding higher wages, imposing higher prices, spiraling the economic system out of proportion to its real wealth and ability to turn credit into cash. This is inflation. No *one* caused it. But the social composition of forces of wills did.

Similarly no one wants war. But the same ones who do not want war *when acting* and choosing within the framework of their political system commit sequences of actions which lead to war. The political process is full of developments in which the resultants of the composition of the forces of individual wills have little in common with the individual wills and decisions of the individual *as such*. On the eve of America's entrance into the Second World War pacifists suggested a constitutional amendment which would make the declaration of war dependent on a plebiscite. They knew that the direct composition of forces expressed in the individual answers to the question of war would yield a negative result whereas the composition of individual forces expressed in the political process did fall in favor of a positive answer.

What we intend to say is explicitly this: the model of social causation implies neither the assertion of, nor the denial of, judgments concerning individual freedom of choice. It considers social phenomena as something more than merely the resultant of individual wills,[9] and capable of logically consistent analysis independent of consideration of individual freedom of choice.

A model of social causation must logically also enjoy a similar independence from the natural science model involved in the analysis of natural phenomena. There is a trend of thought which assumes that a model of causal analysis useful in the study of plants, animals, or the stars and planets, is *equally* useful in the study of human affairs.[10] Because of the very great advance of human knowledge in the use of these models in studying the universe, they have often been simply transferred to the study of human actions with sometimes disastrous conclusions.

A reaction to this extreme identification of natural and social science models appears in some of the works in another extreme form. Pitirim Sorokin, for example, tends to identify social cause with properties that unfold in what he calls the "sociocultural system."[11] The properties themselves are part of the system. Parts of the system, therefore, cause the system. This is a theory of immanence. In Sorokin's analysis there is no longer anything other than pure *equivocation* between natural and social sciences in terms of cause.

There is something of middle ground between these extremes in the position formulated by Robert MacIver.[12] The judgments made by MacIver recognize the category of cause in all the realms of phenomena, natural and social; but these judgments also recognize that the invariable relations obtaining between physical phenomena, and the invariable relations obtaining between social phenomena, while similar, are also very different. In one word, cause, like order, can be used logically only *in some proportion* or *analogically*. The precision of the proportion is dependent upon the methods used.

26

The Thought Model of Causation

The thought model is formally the same whether in natural or social sciences; the differences are in the content and the demands this makes upon the interpretation of the model.[13]

To clarify this position two considerations must be discussed in some detail: a) the model of causal analysis in the natural sciences; and, b) the limits of its transfer to behavioral systems.

There are five errors commonly made by social scientists in the transfer. They may be stated this way:

1. The natural scientists do not ask the question "why" but only the question "how." This is the error of substituting operations for natures. It is an error found in Comte and has become the position of many, if not most, neopositivists.[14] It is often stated as an impossibility of there being an active agent whose very action engenders something in a passive agent; it is also stated as: "laws of nature are ultimately sense impressions in sequence; as such, they are established as statical, concomitant variations."

2. Causes and effects are basically only functions, or functional relations, without any distinction between the two. Many modern functionalists replace causation with *asymmetry*.

3. The laws, propositions, or scientific judgments of the natural scientists can all be tied into one logically consistent system; when the work of science is more advanced, all laws will be deducible from one law, or one supreme generalized system. This error is very explicit in Spencer, Ward, and many contemporary theorists whose intent seems to lie along the line of extending the biological analogy of Spencer or his principle of "survival of the fittest," often expressed as Social Darwinism.[15]

27

4. All the laws are basically equations, or forms expressible in mathematical symbols, and capable of the manipulation implied in the logic of such symbolism. Basically nature follows the laws of probability.

5. The *laws* expressed by rigorous natural science inquiry allow of no deviance or exceptions.

Michotte, in *La perception de la causalité,* indicates that men perceive differently simple sequences, and sequences in which there is a transfer of energy or movement. He emphasizes that in the latter perception there is a correspondence in the perception to an objective reality, which he calls "the conservation of energy."[16] In a fascinating study of *Mathematics of Plausible Reasoning,*[17] Polya continually refers to human behavior in illustrating *why* the mathematics of probability in scientific induction works the way it does. The often repeated notion that the scientist is not interested in the "why" but only in the "how" simply does not represent the interest of scientists.

The physical sciences recognize the processes of nature as reversible and irreversible. Few of them give any evidence of problems understanding causal sequences in viewing the latter. In reversible and circular processes they also make clear-cut distinctions between cause and effect. In the Boyle-Marriott law according to which the volume of a gas varies in inverse ratio with pressure, the law means simply this: if there is change in volume, change in pressure will ensue; if pressure is changed, there will be change in volume. Change either, and in either case, cause and effect are discernible.

In social science analysis there is a proper analogue. A "circular" relationship exists and has been often noticed between racial prejudice and the legal, economic, and educational status of oppressed groups; racial discrimination lowers status, and lower status begets prejudice. This can obviously be interpreted as a two-way cause-effect relationship and not simply "a functional relationship" in which cause and effect allegedly disappear.

The improbability, indeed the impossibility, of a supreme law or model of law governing the whole universe, and to which all other laws will relate inductively, is becoming quite clear in science. There are definite discontinuities in nature. The properties of atoms are not simply reducible to those of the electrons in the atom, and vice-versa. In chemical compounds the properties of the molecules are irreducible to those of the atoms of which they consist. Biologists have not succeeded in deriving the properties of life from the properties of inanimate matter. Their hope to do so is not a proportionate answer for the facts standing against the probability of doing so. Early in the beginning of this century Emile Durkheim developed the concept of the *social fact,* insisting that there are reasons to assume that out of purely individual behavior one will never account for social order and culture. Social facts are not simply reducible to the facts of individual.[18]

Sciences use mathematical and statistical models and symbols. Patterns of causal relationship may be expressed in this and other fashion.[19] The "laws" correlating the pressure of gases with volume and temperature, the "laws" of Mendel on heredity, the principle of indeterminacy expressed by Heisenberg,[20] are all expressed or confirmed by use of quantum theory and calculus. All these "laws" refer to masses, universes, populations, whether molecules, electrons, genes or people. Not one of them refers to the individual units in the experimental unit. In other words, scientific laws stated mathematically or statistically are not statements or judgments about the probability of an individual subsequent, but about the invariant relations between two states of masses, one following the other under the impact of a causal agent.

Moreover, laws stated statistically are true only in proportion to the relations (variables) inherent in the phenomena behind them. The laws of heredity allow one to predict the biological composition of a later generation only if one knows the *real* biological composition of the previous generation and the *real* mode of the selection of mates (i.e., the limits of endogomy). The prediction of hereditary traits is reliable because genes unite in patterns (order) following the patterns of mathematical probability. They do this *en masse* really; and the mathematics of probability is reliable as a predictor only where phenomena occur *en masse*. Obviously, the statistical probabilities do not cause the genes to pattern themselves; but because they *causally* act in the pattern, the laws of statistical probability can validly and reliably represent to the observer what is phenomenologically happening.

In a similar way, death rates, birth rates, marriage rates, crime, delinquency, migration, and a great variety of social phenomena, are determinable and predictable in terms of mathematical probability. These are phenomena of masses, or statistical universes. But such mathematical formulae will never predict who will die, who will marry, who will go deviant to the moral norms of the society and become criminals and delinquents. That there are people *really* doing these things, however, must be true before the statistical manipulations become valid and reliable.

It is true that in terms of pure logic the laws of nature do not allow exceptions; if they do they are not real laws. The sciences are replete with judgments like the following: if A, then B. But if C intervenes, then D follows instead of A. If the first judgment (if A, then B) is applied to a given set of phenomena with no regard to *other* laws which might be equally applicable, then the appearance of D instead of B as an exception is possible in perception. In reality, it is no exception, but evidence of not one but more than one law in operation under the same postulate of order.[21]

The analogous case appears in the social sciences in the study of criminal behavior, or in the case of juvenile delinquency. The chances of children growing up in slums to become law offenders is much greater than in the case of children growing up outside of the slums. The probability of delinquency is, therefore, high, unless balanced by other forces working against delinquency such as good parent-child relationships, adequate guidance of a teacher or clergyman, membership in a play group oriented toward standard values, etc.

The Model of Logical Causality

It is a truism to say that the scientist in studying causal relations (or any other relation) must abstract. In other words, he does not study *all possible* relations, but only those which come into the terms of his observation. Already this implies a choice, a choice determined by his interest, by the terms of his science, and perhaps by many other conscious and unconscious elements.

The point is that this choice already sets up a *relatively closed* system. The scientist abstracts out of everything possible of study something which he makes, in his consideration, relatively independent of the rest of the world as far as his particular study is concerned. The physicist who studies this or that movement of molecules in this or that gas; the sub-atomic physicist who studies the properties of the electrons, protons and neutrons; the geneticist watching the transfer of inheritable traits from one generation to another, e.g., in fruit flys—each of these must choose to abstract his phenomena from all possible phenomena in the universe into a relatively closed system. He knows that in point of actuality each of these abstractly closed systems operates in something more, including the earth's gravitational system, the movement of the solar system, etc.

In his relatively closed system the scientist observes change, i.e., the difference between an initial and a final state of the system. He does so by comparison of the two states. By repeating the observation, sometimes modifying the conditions, the scientist establishes:

(a) the relevant traits of the initial state of the system;

(b) the operator, or the precipitant which when added to the system in its initial state puts it into motion (change) towards the final state.

Operators can be either internal or external. They are internal if they are engendered by the operation of the system. For example, some glands in living organisms are internal operators. Increases of the population of an area may become an operator bringing about emigration, shifts in the economic system, perhaps war or revolution. Or the operator may be external—influencing the change from the outside of the system—as in the case of extreme heat from the sun in the earth's atmosphere setting the body's blood circulation to compensate keeping the body within a relatively narrow range of temperature compared to the temperatures outside of it. Or

32

cultures widely different may meet, effecting changes in each.

It must be stated explicitly that time and space themselves are never operators. Change occurs in time and space but time and space are not causally related to the change in the systems perceived as contained in time and space. It is apparent that time and space may be used logically as reference points for marking change; and that change in systems (say a clock or a yardstick) may be used to mark time and space. This amounts to a rejection of univocal immanent causation. A seed, it is sometimes asserted, *must* of itself grow into a plant. Obviously it can change into nothing else. But in order that it does develop there must also be at least light, heat, food—all operators external to the system.[22]

Are operators really different from the relevant traits of the system in its initial state? In each particular case they are. For when operator O has been added to system Λ the system moves to a new state, A_1. From a more abstract point of view, however, there may be perceived an exchange between operators and the relevant traits. For example, if operator O is introduced into system A, B, C, the system become A, D, F. It may appear then that if a C is introduced into a system A, B, O, the system also becomes A, D, F. This may be demonstrated in the case where an organism lacking a specific immunity may be the bearer of germs of a contagious disease; but since resistance is strong, the system does not change, i.e., it does not move from the state of health to the state of sickness. But if, for some reason like catching a cold, the organism's resistance is weakened, sickness develops. The weakening of resistance is here the operator in place of the introduction of germs which is the more common expectation.

The apparent possibility of exchange (logically) between

33

operators and the relevant traits of a system at a level of general abstraction seems most important to us in understanding causal relations in social phenomena. It indicates how one might make sense out of long lists of eventual causes of specific phenomenon. Such lists, as for example, the lists of causes of war,[23] of crime, of divorce, or business depressions, etc., commonly contain operators interchangeable with some traits in the initial system. Consequently, a definite phenomenon, e.g., crime, will seem to be caused this way, and then that way, and on a third occasion in still another way. On the surface of the particular phenomenon, it will appear impossible to logically attribute causality to anything.

In reality it is still possible to find sets of conditions which, when concurring, cause the phenomenon under observation. Assume that there are N conditions, and that N-1 are present. The phenomenon expected does not appear. Then the -1 condition shows up, and the phenomenon occurs. Now the postulate of order goes unoffended. The expected invariant relations are there. When the set is complete, change occurs.

But, it must be remembered, the postulate of order does not predicate something about each and every concrete phenomenon in the total aggregation of phenomena. Further, the postulate of order does not predicate the sequence of the appearance of the relevant conditions at its level of abstraction. So it appears to the observer that the last trait to appear in the system plays the part of the operator pushing the system into motion.

When the relevant traits of the system in its initial state and the corresponding operator have been determined by observation and/or inference, the scientist is enabled to make a judgment of cause. Its form is logically always the same: "If A, then B (follows)."

However, the logical simplicity of the form must not blind the observer to the complexity of the reality it assumes to be judging. A, by the necessity of its being a phenomenon, is complex, involving at a minimum, a typologically defined situation (itself consisting of a juxtaposition of traits), plus an "operator" or "precipitant," something added to or subtracted from the situation.

Much better may be the formula: "If conditions N, P, R, are present, effect B follows." Now N, P, R, = A. As has been suggested, cause will never appear in reality as simple as its logical formula makes it appear. Cause will always be the concomitance of two or more factors. Taken separately each may appear as creating a "causal tendency" in a total field, but neither yet causing. If the chances of the realization of the possibility is measurable (statistically), we call it probability.

In every situation many causal tendencies are present. Logically, none of them necessarily must act. Dependent upon which final tendencies appear, different effects will follow. In other words, logically, any given situation may develop in one or more ways; or, relative to any one situation, two or more possibilities (eventually probabilities) may be asserted to exist. Judgments in these terms are possible not only on the level of anticipation (often in the form of choice between two or more courses of action), but also at the level of retrospection. One may plausibly assert that any situation X might have developed differently than the actual course of events had a different set of causal tendencies been present in the original situation, or had the final tendency to appear, throwing the situation into change, been different than it was.[24]

The logical causal model here stated is designed for *relatively closed systems,* where the perception of the observer is focused upon:

a) an original or initial state of the system, including all its relevant traits,

b) a final state of this same system, and

c) an operator eventually interchangeable with at least some of the traits in the initial state of the system.

In the case of the analysis of the movement from peace to war and from peace to revolution, and their movements back to peace, the political system, or the system identified as the "state," is involved. With regard to this system we have now to establish the relevant traits to appear in the initial state, and the adequate operator, and to establish whether or not they are interchangeable.

3/ Political System and Process

SOCIAL PROCESSES occur in the context of many systems, and in many respects the political system is, while not the smallest, one of the simplest.[1] For this reason, it seems best to understand it first.

The State is a Social Group

This is only another way of saying that a state is, after all, people. But it is not just people. There is a kind of order among the people who comprise a state, which while it is true of each and every person in the state, transcends the individual person.

Persons are citizens or subjects in a system which is something much more than the addition of each to every other one, and this something gives meaning to the otherwise independent co-existence of each member of the system.

We can demonstrate this on a common-sense level in a variety of ways. The members of a group like the state speak and think of themselves as "we" (e.g., the Americans), and designate the others as "they" (e.g., the Canadians). The outsiders recognize the real unity of a group; a foreign state, e.g., China, might challenge the United States by issuing an "ultimatum." Further, groups are capable of group action: the state wages a war, or makes a law. The group, or the state, resists attempts from inside or outside to destroy or even interfere with its equilibrium: the state punishes a criminal or retaliates against an outside aggressor.[2]

People forming a state are limited by certain territorial limits and within these limits the state does not tolerate activities of another state. The state does not act outside of these limits except under very special circumstances. The distribution of territory may very frequently vary, and is often a central issue in wars or less violent forms of conflict between states.

The power of the state is one of many kinds of social power.[3] In general, power is observable when the persons of the group divide themselves into a relatively small center or nucleus from which orders and commands emanate, and a relatively large periphery where these orders are received and obeyed. The existence of social power is tantamount to a lasting and dependable composition of forces deployed over the members of the group. This gives it structure, and without such structuring any one individual alone will have little or no effect socially, as an embodiment of power. The composing of individuals into ordered relations becomes incomparably stronger than the diffuse force of simple individuals. Further, through such structured relations the forces of individuals can be directed toward selected instead of diffused goals, and the chances that individuals nullify one another in their efforts to achieve given ends are minimized.

Power structures can be observed in many ways: in the family, in schools, in business, in labor organizations. There is even a power structure in a baseball game where the umpire is seen as the chief authority in arbitrating disputes, and in carrying out the rules of the game. In fact, any group that is really operating as a group toward goals will manifest this phenomenon of power.

Political power differs from other forms of social power in its possession, in principle, of a kind of monopoly of coercion. That is, it is sovereign. This means that the use of strength, physical or otherwise, of men against men, is invariably limited to the interference of political power. The policeman arrests, the prison warden forcibly holds a sentenced criminal in jail, the executioner deprives him of his life, or until recently in many countries, he also inflicted corporal punishment. Such persons are exercising political power—the power of the state. If they were acting without such power, the state would interfere to prevent them from acting.

Of course, this is absolutely true only in the abstract, logical ideal. Experience will show many deviations. Individuals may be found who violate the monopoly of coercion, and use force not proper to them with the consequences we have just indicated. Or political power may grant certain limited amounts of coercion to be exercised by non-political groups: domestic and school discipline, even physical, may be permitted within

39

certain limits. But the limits of non-political power are set by the political power, and can be quite unilaterally changed by the state.

The supremacy of political power, or its sovereignty, is its outstanding characteristic. On the level of direct human experience the power of the state is subordinate to no other, not even another state or combination of such states.

The supremacy of political power is functionally related to the coordination and direction of common affairs. Ordinarily this necessitates a reciprocal process of centralization and decentralization. Centralization is seen in the existence of a capital in every state. Geographically, the capital symbolizes central power. But dependent upon the center are also other *loci* operating in the interest of central authority, but delegated by it to perform some of its functions. In one way or another these are arranged into a system based on a hierarchy so that central direction will prevail over local; in other words, we are dealing with a system of systems, or organization within organization. Supreme power belongs to the entire system, though properly it is seated in the top level.

An exception to this appears to be the existence of federal states where political power seems to be divided between two or more levels. A traditional example of this is the United States where power is distributed between the federal or national government and that of the states. Those who call themselves "States Rightists" jealously guard the rights of the individual states against "encroachments" from the federal government. The seeming exceptional nature of this case can be resolved if one conceives of the United States as a system of systems, where the national government *is* the system created out of the systems which are the individual states. It is to the complex system itself that the plenitude of power politically belongs.

The Functions of the State

Every social organization has definite things to do, ends to achieve, goals to maintain. These are its functions.[4]

The main function of the state is to coordinate the activities of individuals and groups living in its territory. This is achieved in two ways: negatively, by preventing and eventually resolving conflicts; positively, by directing these activities not only to the goals envisioned by those acting, but to those which transcend the interests of all.

The coordination and centralized direction is effected by assigning to individuals and to groups definite social status, each possessing a specific set of rights and duties. Behavior conforming with the assignments is eventually enforced by coercion since the power nucleus (the government) disposes the forces of individuals possessing and acting in the set of statuses assigned. In this way order, or negatively, the absence of conflict between citizens, is assured. Such order in interpersonal relations is a necessary condition for the advance of culture.

While such coordination is necessary even in the most simple societies which consist of a very limited number of identical groups (families or clans), it comes into heightened importance in multi-group societies, or societies which are in change and becoming multi-group societies,[5] where individuals are assigned highly complicated tasks, and work in groups whose specialization and differentiation of tasks have become very intricate. Such a society cannot exist without a power structure indicating to individuals and their groupings the limits of their competence and the activities which they may perform. This is why political organization, or the arrangement of men into states, emerges concomitantly with the transition from simple to multi-group society.[6]

Centralized direction emanating from the power center (the government) must be obeyed by all. This is true in democracy as in every *form* of government as expressed in the first part of Lincoln's famous definition contained in the Gettysburg Address, "government of the people." In normal situations obedience is present, and order, in contradistinction to revolution, ensues. Obedience is based not only on the anticipation of coercion, mentioned above, but also on inner acceptance of the government and its orders on the part of the people. Inner acceptance is solidly grounded in the belief that the government is *for* the people.

In addition to the function of coordination, every state performs the function of self-assertion. This is a function dependent upon the fact of coexistence of many states over geographical space who more often than not display a tendency to aggrandizement at the expense of their neighbors. At its *best,* self-assertion is protection from the outside. At worst, it is aggression.

There are many bases for this function, but one of them deserves special attention. The majority of states have risen in small areas, smaller than those inhabited by ethnic groups, or people sharing a particular culture, areas smaller than "natural provinces," either geographic or economic in character. Since time immemorial the tendency has been operative in human affairs of politically unifying an ethnic group or natural provinces; in other words, the tendency to make a state coextensive with closely related ethnic groups or natural provinces is a prime condition for creating power centers. This is often achieved by peaceful means, but more often it can be achieved only by war.

On the other hand, the basic function of coordination technically requires wider areas than those in which the state is originally conceived. To reach the goal of ethnic unification, the smaller political structures have to be knocked out. In this way, the cultural tradition becomes enriched by another trait: military virtue and the prowess of conquest (e.g., *la gloire* in France, the cult of the army in Germany). Once arisen such a trait may become the dominant fibre of a culture and its national character. And the greatness of the nation through aggrandizement becomes a commonly recognized and highly ranked value.

A similar result may be achieved on the foundation of glorious and successful resistance to dangerous aggressors. As in the former instance, once arisen, the trait displays a tendency to persist.[7]

The state also commonly performs many auxiliary functions: educational, public health, trade and commerce, housing, transportation, industrial. These are extensions of the instrumentality of the state. A strongly centralized power structure is first operated to satisfy two basic needs as described above; later it appears that this instrument is also well fitted to satisfy other problems arising in human association. The transfer of activities and operations from private means to public or state, seems logical and consistent.[8] Of course, time and again men will withdraw from the state functions so assigned. Industrial and religious protection have been prime functions to be state supported and then withdrawn from state support in the course of human affairs.

The Coalescence of Functions

Wars and revolutions, as we will demonstrate, arise from abuses of these basic functions of the state. But to see this more clearly, we must demonstrate that logically and realistically what we have designated as the two basic functions of the state cannot be performed except by the one agency: the state. In other words, the two functions are one in the basic character of the state.

It will be quite apparent that neither coordination nor self-assertion can be carried on by individuals as individuals. This would assume that there is no coordination of the activities of men organized by non-territorial power A with the activities of men organized by an equally non-territorial power B. If the functions occurred, it would have to be on raw chance. The case is, of course, imaginary and logically abstract. But a close approximation to it appears where the state comprises an important ethnic minority, and across its border, there is another state where the corresponding group forms the dominant majority. This was the situation of the Sudeten Germans in Czechoslovakia after the morbid exacerbation of German nationalism under Hitler. Even less could two organizations (A and B above) grant their members adequate protection against aggression on the part of an outsider. This is why the state is territorial in its very nature.

It will be equally apparent that the two basic functions can be fulfilled only by an organization possessing power overwhelming the power of individuals and of other organizations existing in the territory. Self-assertion often requires sacrifices on the part of individuals and their groups. Coordination often meets resistance or evasion: both must be broken or there is no coordination. Assume that the state would not be endowed with supreme power. Approximations to such a situation can be seen in cases where in modern, technologically advanced society, certain economic power groups (either of management or of labor) become *de facto* stronger than political power. Such was the Weimar Republic before the rise of Hindenburg's veiled dictatorship. The 1959 steel strike in the United States indicated to many Americans they were advancing along a similar dangerous path. Negatively, such cases well demonstrate that the state must be supreme or sovereign.

On the other hand, the two basic functions always appear together. Both require the existence of an overwhelming power in a given territory. Assume again that in the same area there would appear two such powers; one so to speak, military, exerting the self-asserting function, the other civilian, exerting the function of coordination. So long as they would cooperate, everything would be in order.[9] But should cooperation fail to be continuous, as is quite probable, disruption would immediately appear. Dissent is almost certain to appear between the two powers, and each will try to force the other to yield. The territory would soon be a house divided against itself, and an easy prey for outside invaders. The ascription of two functions to one organization is one of the rare social constants; exceptions can be found only in instances where states are in early stages of development. The examples of American Indian tribes who had different chiefs for times of war and peace are relevant.

Finally, the functions of the state, the two basic ones as well as the auxiliary ones, may give rise to abuses.[10] To the co-ordinating function there corresponds the abuse of arbitrariness contrasted to the "rule of law"; to the self-assertion function, the abuse of aggression; to the auxiliary functions, totalitarianism. Logically the three abuses are separable, and in fact, many arbitrary regimes have not been totalitarian, nor have some totalitarian states been notably aggressive. But especially in recent European politics, the three abuses have tended to form a syndrome, as in Hitler's Germany, and in Russia under the Communist Party. When this occurs, peace and order, as internal or external conditions, are in jeopardy.

Power and Its Potential Danger

The abuses are real as the power in back of them. And for this reason, the state may become a dangerous instrument in the achievement of human ends.

Social power in general, political power in particular, is ranked by men as of high value. They strive for it in itself sometimes and quite often they seek it or seek to maintain it without being aware of why they are, or even that they are, doing so. They like it.

Further, power is highly instrumental. Other things equal, power gives prestige and access to wealth, and oftentimes gives great opportunities for sex gratification. Power, wealth, prestige, sex—these are major targets for which men compete in society.

There are acceptable ways for the accession to political power, like an election campaign or high administrative efficiency and promotion. There are also disorderly ways, like bribery, or collusion exerted by power already achieved. There is also the way to power through sheer audacity and the display of complete lack of moral inhibition. The way to revolution is along this way.

Further, the functions of the state (both basic and auxiliary) are fulfilled in the main by government decisions and orders. Often enough these decisions are problematic enough due to the diversity of interests involved, ideologies, interpretation of the "charter," and the competition in society of predilected plans of action. Government action is very frequently compromise action, and always in flux. To maintain a state in equilibrium requires great art—the art of politics.

Compromise always involves the neglect if not the outright repression of some views and interests. These then continually form danger spots. To overcome neglect and eliminate repression, there must be social movements and reform organizations. Prophetic leaders may emerge attracting larger and larger masses to the existing movements and organizations and giving them more and more momentum. This is the pattern out of which revolutions arise, governments are weakened, violently attacked.

The recurrence of revolution in a given territory and the positive record of some of them often result in the glorification of revolt, and the formation of a revolutionary tradition. France, Spain, and Latin America have or have had such periods. In Russia, prior to 1917, many intellectuals worshipped revolution and spelled the word with a capital "R." In the United States and England, despite the fact that each of them has had revolutions in their history, no such tradition of glorification of revolution ever occurred.

Finally, government, like all major social structures, is

also a social process constantly differentiating itself. There is always a special military branch, and a police department. Both coordination and self-assertion make these requisites. They also become well articulated, highly autonomous within the state, developing *esprit de corps,* and techniques of self-perpetuation.

During times of war the armed forces prove themselves valiant, and in victory the tendency toward greater aggressiveness is elaborated. Armies attract strong men, men with high dominance, and the danger is implicit that the military group will come to display more and more domination, engulfing if possible the entire state. This is the root of militarism. It is also the root of the *pronunciamento* pattern found in many Latin American countries, and lately in the Arab nations. Military men exalt military virtues and consider that war must be permitted to recur again and again. Equipment, and organization, and men must be tested. Scientists, technicians, engineers, and politicians may join them. Ideas are invented to vindicate war, and propagandize their power throughout the nation. A kind of war complex infiltrates and then penetrates the culture. The barriers between peace and war are substantially lowered, and war may break out for even trivial reasons.

A similar case can evolve as regards the role of the police within a state. It can happen relatively easily that they begin to interfere deeper with the endeavors of citizens than is really necessary for the maintenance of law and order. Perhaps the police force may want to expand its duty rather than become unneeded and obsolete. The arbitrary and unnecessary supervision of activities and ideas is begun, and soon there is the ferment aiming at revolution. Both military and police, through the overstress of goals for which they may have to strive legitimately, may endanger peace and order and defeat the very purpose of their existence in the first place.

Paradoxically, the state is necessary if the affairs of a large number of men are to be advanced; but in the very human means for advancement, are the potentials for great evils.

The International Community

Just as individuals, by their knowledge of one another and *through* knowledge, form structures, reciprocally interacting groups, or political systems, so states or families of nations arise through mutual awareness of each other's existence, and are influenced in their actions by this knowledge and by the actions of other members of the community. Even though the relations between nations may be antagonistic and hostile, insofar as they are in human contact and interaction, states may be conceived as forming a community.

In the twentieth century the community of nations is tantamount to the totality of nations on earth. This is a novel development. Two thousand years ago the Roman and Chinese Empires were in coexistence as great powers, each hardly knowing the other. Only one hundred years ago Commodore Perry forcibly introduced Japan into the family of nations, and only a few years before that, Great Britain and France fought a war against China opening her gates to the West, though China and Russia had then been in contact already.

Strictly speaking the family of nations must be classified as an unorganized and decentralized community. It is a community rather than an associative society because it exists as a "given," not as an intentionally created group designed to pursue specific ends or objectives.[11] It is decentralized because there is no central, formal power existent, able to give binding orders to the members and capable of enforcing them. The League of Nations and the United Nations—which themselves are associations, not communities—have amounted to loose confederations, but far from being world governments. World government, while always possible and perhaps desirable, is not likely to appear soon.[12]

The community of nations is largely unorganized though there are forces at work at the present time working toward other ends. But international law, the one governing order to rule relations between nations, is still quite vague, and above all, difficult to enforce.

The lack of organization and the decentralization present in the community of nations is quite explainable. Organization rests on the foundation of solidarity, a particular "we feeling" and conviction which unifies men and *wields* them into larger groups. But solidarity grows mainly through opposition and differentiation of roles and functions. We have not arrived at the time when this has turned into an actual fact among the nations of the world.

Consequently, the state of international relations is analogous to that between individuals or families in pre-political society. Informal, customary rules were *in force* controlling mens' behavior, but there was no organized authority enforcing these rules. Violation put into motion vengeful action on the part of the victim and/or his kin, which it its turn could become a stimulus for revenge on the part of the former. The result was an interminable private feud.

The unorganized and decentralized family of nations can be considered as a system of forces in dynamic equilibrium, each of the component forces corresponding to an individual state. What does this mean? The majority of the corporate actions of the states do not involve other states or their members. Some do. Since the family of nations is decentralized, the forces of the individual states acting in the common field of force, i.e., the family of nations, are not checked by an organized force superior to theirs. But reciprocal check is possible and actually exists: in their self-assertive actions the individual states meet resistance of other states whose interests are also involved. This resistance inhibits any state from going too far, as it could and would were it completely unchecked. In this way a kind of equilibrium is created.

This equilibrium—let us call it "existential"—is dynamic, or ever changing. The magnitude of the forces of the individual states and the direction of their actions are constantly subject to change. The magnitude of the changes depends on many factors, including population, migration, economic development, military progress or regress, the fluctuations of morale in each of the member states. The direction of the changes depends on fluctuations in policy: particular goals are selected or abandoned, aggressiveness increases or decreases, and so on. At any particular time, the states may form peculiar configurations, somewhat analogous to the structure of complex molecules. Great powers appear as centers of crystallization, with satellites and protégés about them. The centers of crystallization are sometimes tied together by alliances of stronger or weaker types; sometimes they form hostile camps.

But the analogy to "fields of force" in mechanics is far from perfect. Since the states are not subject to the vascillations of the individuals who compose them, their relationships and equilibrium may be substantially modified by the acceptance of some principles of behavior expressed in international law and morals.

The order that obtains is of a special type. It is not enforced from the top, as in the case of the ordinary political system, the state, but from the very midst of those who are under it. More often than not, a state follows the directions of international law. But if it so wants, it may break away, and enforcement, on the part of the other members of the community, is possible only by means of war.[13]

Nevertheless, the impact of the acceptance of international law and morals is tantamount to an additional inhibition of the self-assertive actions of the states. A nation wanting to remain at peace cannot change the state of the system by unilateral action against objectives of another nation. But, according to international law, if bilateral modes of change fail (attempted by negotiations and treaties), the state can choose the residual mode of war. War is terminated by a peace treaty, and the new treaty (superseding the others) binds the parties involved. The same international law which prior to war prescribed a pair of states to respect their reciprocal rights on level A (e.g., along a definite boundary), now prescribes them to respect their reciprocal rights on level B (e.g., along another boundary). The *lack* of peaceful, but binding procedure imposing change from A to B, or from B to still another situation C, makes international law basically static, sanctioning a kind of normative equilibrium, in contradistinction to the existential equilibrium expressed in the actual strength of the states.

The clearest manifestation of the rigidity of normative equilibrium and its discrepancy with existential equilibrium is this: at any given time, all the existing boundaries expressing relationships between states as territorial groups are founded on treaties reflecting existential equilibrium at the termination of the last conflict. Thus, the boundaries of the European states in 1938 expressed the equilibrium of the years 1918-21, with Russia and Germany exceedingly weak, France and her satellites strong, while on the existential level, Germany and Russia had recovered their earlier strength and France was exhausted in her efforts to maintain the equilibrium of the earlier years.

In a similar way in 1914 the boundaries of European states reflected the existential equilibrium achieved at the end of the Napoleonic wars (1815) with partial modifications engendered by the wars of unification in Italy and Germany (1859, 1866, 1870-71). At the outbreak of the Mexican war the boundary between the United States reflected the existential equilibrium as it existed at the time of the Louisiana purchase, partly modified by the secession and later annexation of Texas by the United States.

War is, to a large extent, therefore, an instrument for adjusting normative equilibrium to existential equilibrium. It readily follows that in an unorganized community of nations, the temptation is great to take advantage of a favorable change in existential equilibrium and to impose a change in normative equilibrium by all means available, eventually war.

But war is evidently the *ultima ratio*. The art of the statesman in international politics consists in gaining advantages by efforts short of war. Because of the real and strong interdependence of the members of the community and of the awareness of possibility in various combinations, the actions of leaders are analogous to a sharply conducted game of fencing. The line of action of the leaders is by no means predetermined, though obviously it is limited by objective conditions opening only a small number of reasonable choices. The leaders rarely execute any definite and immutable plan which traces far in advance the steps to be taken. More often than not, alternative plans exist fitting various eventualities, depending on the increasing or decreasing strength of a competitor, changes in alliances, etc. At any particular time, the leaders choose and put into effect the plan which seems best under the conditions.

To cushion the shocks which necessarily obtain in the course of the game; to prepare conditions under which the efforts of the individual will be most effective; to gain as much knowledge as possible of the intentions and actions of competitors, and to promote cooperation which is also operative between the states, an old and venerable institution exists, called diplomacy. This is a great art. And it depends on the skill and efficacy of its practitioners whether war is to be avoided in ominous situations, or allowed to break out against the true will of the parties.

Through diplomatic means many wars have broken out on the basis of change in existential equilibrium unaccompanied by change in normative equilibrium. By repetition they produce a war tradition in the community of nations. This has happened in all the communities of nations that history has recorded. It is another sociological constant.

A theory has been formulated which emphasizes this constant. The theory states that war was invented in Egypt around 3000 B. C., and has radiated from that center.[14] It is obviously an inadequate theory, since war has been invented "independently" many times, and in many "communities of nations."

Naturally, the existence of the culture tradition for war is not the cause of the war, but it does make war possible and perhaps even probable to greater or lesser degrees. The culture tradition is more general but less intensive than the militaristic tradition evolved in some simpler political systems. Further, the culture tradition for war makes men aware of the possibility of war, both aggressive and defensive, and correspondingly, influences the decisions of the political leaders. But militaristic tradition impels them towards the fateful decision of actually launching war.

The emergence and maintenance of the culture tradition for war among nations forming an unorganized community is almost inevitable. But this need not imply the inevitability of war. Every dynamic tendency can be checked by another and stronger tendency as displayed by the occurence of long periods of peace. In terms of our general thought model of social causation, this proposition can be stated as follows: *Among the relevant conditions of the movement from peace to war, the existence of war tradition is one thing; but, to provoke war other conditions must also be present, among them the absence of strong inhibitions against war.* The presence of war tradition, therefore, is only a dynamic tendency which, if unchecked and not reenforced by other tendencies, may be *ineffective as a causal element.*

Just as the structure of the state was found to contain certain dangerous features eventually making war and revolution possible, so also in the family or community of nations. The problem will always be that the dangers are part of the very essential traits of the community. It may be eliminated only by replacing the unorganized community by an organized association in which the states would transfer the right and means of war to one sovereign world state and thus really abrogate war. We will return to this notion in the final chapter of this volume.

4/Conflict and Violence

WAR AND PEACE, and order and revolution are states of the political system. The presence or absence of *violent conflict* in the system is critical, but the identification of conflict and violence is not absolute. Their differences and similarities, their merger in war and revolution, form the logical matrix of our analysis.[1]

Conflict

Like all human interactions, conflict is basically not simply one kind of act, but a concatenation of actions meaningfully intertwined. These actions (processes) start or cease, depending on the presence, emergence, or disappearance of certain social situations. These social situations are definable largely on the basis of the participants' goals, and the relationships that obtain between them as they perceive and react to goals.

Goals may be common to all in the sense that all share them. To each individual the success he feels is the success felt by every individual in the group; each wins, or each loses. This is designated as a simple solidarity situation, and human interaction in such solidarity is recognized as cooperation. Transporting a common heavy load, helping a child with his homework, playing a game as a member of the team, are illustrations of solidarity situations where the human processes are cooperative.

At the other extreme goals may be incompatible—the possession by one means the exclusion of the other. The participants may strive for the same objects (the possession of a rifle, the love of this girl), or the achievement of objectives which cannot be simultaneous (playing a game of chess or going to a dance). The situation now involves not solidarity but antagonism. Conflict is now possible.

There is still logically the third alternative: goals may be both common and antagonistic in the same situation but from different viewpoints. The situation is now one of equilibrium, but the processes which flow are neutral. One may create any number of species in this category. We might call one species contractual, based on a kind of give-and-take: the relations between capital and labor, or between buyers and sellers in a free market. Each of the participants achieves part of his goal, but seldom, if ever, all of it. A given wage is high enough, but not as high as desired by certain employes;

or these prices are low enough, but not as low as certain buyers might like. But the wages and prices are proportionate to the balances necessary to keep productive work going, and an effective market operating.

The fact that human interaction is of this mixed or neutral type rather than simply cooperative or antagonistic, is more clearly recognized by modern minds than by those of a century ago. In the middle of the nineteenth century, the relationship between the "capitalists" and the "proletarians" was analyzed in almost purely antagonistic terms. The Marxist saw an inevitable and intrinsic struggle between capital and labor which manifested itself in the struggle between classes until the proletarian must defeat the bourgeois. This notion implies a too simple logic and interpretation of history. The English version of this same idea is called Social Darwinism.[2] But this version puts the antagonistic process forward on a biological level as the sole determinant of human interrelations. These doctrines reflected the attitudes dominant in the two classes and tended to reinforce them, the "capitalists" denying the laborers anything above the survival level, and the "proletarians" dreaming of exploding the old order in the name of a similarly dangerous Utopia.

The spell of these pessimistic doctrines was broken only in twentieth century America. Ford's initiative, guided by no particular doctrinaire position, helped to reconstruct American capitalism into the necessity of recognition of the meeting of the interests of both capital and labor in generally increased production and rising standards of living. "Most American unions recognize their dependence on the survival of business."[3] And the counterpart, recognition by "management" of its dependency upon a prospering labor class has been embodied in the legislation of the New Deal and every political administration since.

In Europe, the existence of neutral processes was recognized by many students and observers of social affairs. The earliest systematic treatment was probably that of L. von Wiese.[4] But it took time—and the years of experience with Communism and Fascism—before the European leaders of industry and labor accepted the idea. Practically all European socialist parties this side of the Iron Curtain have revised their programs, abandoning the idea of wholesale nationalization of the means of production.

Our emphasis upon a correct understanding of the neutral processes in the causation of war and revolution will appear in later discussion. For the moment we are faced with the problem of establishing *conflict* in its logical connection with the neutral processes. The problem deserves emphatic clarification, since in the literature on this topic facts are often interpreted in a faulty and fallacious conceptual scheme where conflict is identified as a species of antagonistic process. This "genus" species relationship can be misleading.

Simmel, a pioneer in the study of the social processes, and L. Coser, a contemporary, have tried to formulate exhaustive theories.[5] Coser checks and develops Simmel's propositions, and distinguishes "realistic" from "non-realistic" conflicts. The first arise from the frustration of specific demands which cannot or hardly can be satisfied by alternative means; the others arise from the need of at least one of the participants to release tension.[6] To some extent, Coser was preceded in this distinction by A. Johnson who singled out conflicts which arise exclusively from aggressive impulses and those which do not.[7] The aggressive impulses are almost identical with Coser's non-realistic conflicts.

Coser continues his discussion by saying that non-realistic conflicts are not occasioned by rival ends existing between the antagonists but by the need of tension release. This position not only removes the whole discussion and analysis of conflict from the realm of goals (as in our position), but puts it in the realm of psychological phenomena. It simultaneously refutes itself and the idea of unrealistic conflict. For if A, in the state of nervous tension and needing release, tries to achieve the release by beating B, and if B would not be inclined to let A do this (namely, beat him and he probably would not let him), and B would thereby perform acts diametrically opposed to that of A (namely, not allow himself to be humiliated and beaten by A), then A would be back where he started, with simply the need for tension release, but logically incapable of it.

A more realistic and logically consistent treatment of conflict, in our view, is to locate antagonisms along a continuum. At one pole is antagonism in the sense of pure or "fair" competition; on the other pole is "violence." In the "center" of the continuum are modes of antagonism which combine elements of the extremes. This gives us a logical "stick" or matrix calibrated in terms of the intensity with which antagonists expend effort in deviating themselves, or leading the antagonists to deviate, from goals.

Instances of fair competition may be found between neighborhood grocers, or between students striving for a restricted number of scholarships, or between two boys courting the same girl. Several traits characterize this mode of competition. The goals are incompatible, i.e., not every actor seeking the goal can achieve it, although all have a hope. And each participant seeks the goal without directly interfering with the similar efforts of the other, although the presence of each competitor limits the chances of the other's achievement. The competitors may or may not be conscious of these traits. The element of *force* is notably absent.

By contrast, modalities of competition more toward the "center" of the continuum involve something of "unfair" competition. While the main effort of each competitor is still expended toward reaching the goal, part of it is also directed toward immediately impeding the other competitor from achieving. Instances of such competition would be underselling by one grocer of another, or using outside sources of information in an otherwise "secret" examination. Often this mode of competition is exercised verbally: opposing parties heaping insults or disparaging remarks rather than "telling the truth." Or this middle modality may appear by withdrawing cooperation in situations where it is expected, e.g., two men stop recognizing each other and break off their friendship, or two states sever diplomatic relations.

The other extreme appears as "violent conflict," conflict involving the use of force as the means of achieving the goal. However, very close to, but not properly the extreme, are modalities of conflict which stop just short of violence. In a marital quarrel, husband and wife may temporarily adopt extremely hostile, non-speaking postures toward one another, the purpose being to see who will hold out longer against the other and thereby determining who is actually the stronger. This is "eyeball to eyeball" conflict, just short of physical violence. Two hostile states may take initial advances toward one another, perhaps even intimidating steps. Strikes and boycotts commonly occur in race relations, or in industrial relations, and they stop just short of shooting or fisticuffs. Some large scale political strikes also belong in this category. In the great Belgium strike of December, 1960, and January, 1961, the executive committee of the Socialist Party stated: "Since the government (a coalition of Catholics and Liberals) wants a trial of strength, it will have it."[8] Envenomed debates, even in learned and scientific societies, may also possess traits of all but violent conflict. In past centuries the papal interdict took this form; its purpose was to oppose spiritual power to secular power and to demonstrate the superiority of the spiritual.

In extreme, violent conflict, besides the use of actual, physical force—and because of the employment of this force—there is a temporary relegation of the original goal to a secondary position and substitution of the force itself in its place. The elimination or substantial weakening of the opponent, the breaking of his resistance, becomes the immediate goal. Obviously, since this is temporary, the attainment of the intervening goal is sought as a means for achieving the original goal.

It should also be clear that in violent conflict the goal substitution is much more complete than in other forms of conflict; contrariwise, the features of a mixed or neutral process, perceptible in non-violent conflict, are conspicuous by their absence in violent conflict.

It is now possible to state the social function of the antagonistic or competitive process. In fair competition, "the best man wins." Who he is in particular depends for its definition on the nature of the goal; it may be the most intelligent, the most skilled, the fastest runner. In the intermediary modalities on our continuum he wins who combines the required trait with the appropriate technique without resorting to force. In the extreme, in conflict, it is the strongest.

But in any modality of competition the process functions to sort incompatible goals into those which will be realized and those which will not. In Simmel's thought, conflict is designed to resolve divergent dualisms; it is a way of achieving some kind of unity.

Logically there are very few ways, probably only three, of resolving conflict regardless of its intensity. One is negotiation which involves simple give and take, or equal exchange, or rearrangement of goals. Another way of resolving conflict is conciliation, or the employment of a third party to whose final judgment the conflicting parties previously agree. If this party is superior to the parties in the dispute and can impose his decision on them, the procedure is adjudication; if it is not superior, the procedure is mediation or arbitration. The third possible means to conflict solution is the test of relative strength, or fighting.

It is worth noting that negotiation assumes reference to social norms, legal or customary. Conciliation assumes more explicit forms of social norms as the basis on which the judge or the mediator can determine who is right and who is wrong. Fighting is based on the totally amoral maxim: "Might is right." The goal of the party who proves to be stronger will be achieved.

When conflict is terminated through any one or combination of these means, and comparison is made with goals achieved with goals aspired to, only one of three possible conclusions may be stated. The termination will be:

1. A return to the *status quo ante*. Neither party to the

conflict possesses the goal sought, and both accept the situation.

2. One party wins; the other loses. *Vae victis!*

3. Redefinitions of the relationships to the goals, or the goals themselves, are accepted by the parties. Each gains something, but also loses something. By inner necessity the redefinitions will involve conflict being replaced by neutral processes, perhaps even the replacement of antagonisms with cooperative processes.

Violent Conflict: Cases and Types

The movement of political systems from peace to war or from order to revolution (and back again), may be observed and predicted only if we can empirically identify the conditions by which simple conflict becomes *violent*. "When do men fight?" This inquiry concerns those conditions (traits) of groups in which violence occurs. As before, our procedure will be to move from simple forms of fighting to the more complicated, drawing the proper generalizations by inference.

Inter-personal Fighting

The most basic case of violence is the fist fight. It is extended when a tool is used instead of fists: club, knife or pistol. Such fights occur everywhere, in every time, in every culture. To attempt to find generalized forms from particular cases at this point would be impossible, but two observations may be made without fear of error.

First, two men do not come to actual blows without some opposition between them, without there being some perceived opposition in their goals. The child has a toy, another wants it. Two boys court the same girl: one demands that the other stops, the other refuses. One man aspires to become the leader of the gang, and his rival appears having the very same ambition. This man claims that the other has cheated him of money, the other denies the accusation. In all such situations an antagonistic process is in motion.

Further, the actors in the process ascribe some importance to the goals involved; men do not fight for trifles. And most important, what is a trifle, and what is not, is defined by the participants' value systems. In turn, these value systems are determined by their respective cultures. Persons reflect the value systems of their cultures.

Most culture norms forbid fighting. One of the basic principles of every ordered society is the intent to prevent, and eventually to eliminate, every kind of fighting among individuals. Political organization appears in ordered society for this end. When striving for incompatible goals men are allowed to argue, but not to resort to insults. In many cases they can go to a court where a third neutral party decides what is right and what is wrong. Or they may resort to mediation through friends; or they may agree to disagree and leave matters at that, and the situation becomes that of persistent non-violent conflict. But if they fight, they expose themselves to unpleasant sanctions, such as arrest, trial, fine or some other such punishment.

Nevertheless, men do fight. Obviously, the decision to fight is tantamount to overcoming the corresponding social inhibitions, i.e., the anticipation of possible punishment, the condemnation for amoral actions, and the various informal sanctions which might be imposed by one's fellow men. This assumes the weakening of social norms, especially in the virtual aggressor, since legal and customary norms against fighting are not applicable to actions taken in the interest of self-defense. The weakening of social norms commonly takes place in one of the following situations. The individuals are members of certain sub-groups where the social norms against fighting are weaker than they are in the larger society.[9] Fighting among youngsters is judged mildly by adults. Among persons of lower classes, fist fights are not considered degrading. In criminal gangs, the intensity of the pugnacious attitude may upgrade one's rank. In addition, there are occasions when serious emotional stress, or intoxication, result in what appears as a temporary desocialization of the personality, and the conflict becomes violent.

Men more commonly use other means for resolving differences before resorting to fighting. They argue, use intimidation or subterfuge—even lie. Or they negotiate, or go to court, or use other forms of mediation and arbitration. But where such means are not available, or are mistrusted by the parties in conflict, fighting becomes an obvious means. A conflict between leaders for gang authority cannot be brought into court for the same reasons than it cannot be solved by peaceful means: the display of physical strength is part of the scale determining the "right" to run the gang. A dispute, pure and simple, for a girl's affections does not go before a court because affairs of the heart do not fall within the competence of a court. In cases like these, fighting comes to be a residual or vicarious means of conflict solution, standing parallel to the peaceful means both in frequency and social esteem.

Again, each of the participants chooses to fight with the assumption that he has a fair chance to win. He sees himself superior in physical strength, or commanding greater agility or skill, or possessing better weapons or allies. Even though chances of winning may be blurred in judging such items of prowess, rapid and unconsidered decisions to fight may still be made on the basis: "Somehow I will win."

If the chances of victory are conspicuously lacking, a fight will not occur. If the aggressor feels the weaker, he will delay. If the defender feels the weaker, he will yield.

In summary, we can say that a system composed of two or more individuals moves from peace to violence if these conditions are all simultaneously present:

1) There exists a situation where high values are represented as incompatible interests.

2) At least one of the parties in the conflict suffers a weakening of his inhibitions to fight.

3) At least one of the parties has lost hope of winning without fighting.

4) Each of the parties assumes reasons for having a fair chance of winning.

Any one of these may act as the precipitant, or operator, changing the situation from peace to violence. The change is normally attributed to that trait which appears last in the change from peace to violence. Antagonistic attitudes appear throughout the system, but their seriousness may be suddenly quickened. For example, disparaging remarks made by A about B might not really hurt the latter, but if outsiders start calling B a coward, the specific value called honor may be suddenly activated, and this would appear as a precipitant of fighting. Or the relevant conditions can be put into motion by a sudden weakening of normative inhibitions, or the set may be completed by the loss of the hope of victory short of fighting, or the increase, subjectively or objectively perceived, of one's chances to win.

In other words there is always an operator distinguished from the initial condition of the system. But when searching for the start of violent conflict from the viewpoint of abstract cause, the operator appears to be interchangeable with any one of the relevant traits of the system in its initial state. This is why the causation of interpersonal conflict seems to defy any valid formulation. Events provoking a fight in some cases do not provoke it in others; and even when they do they seem not to be covered by any postulate of order.

It is not permissible, however, to ascribe to any segment of reality causal significance *per se* outside the total situation. A concrete precipitant is seen as causing a fight because its appearance completed the set of necessary and sufficient conditions.

Race Riots

Race riots raise the level of our perspective on fighting from the level of individuals to mobs, or at least groups of people. Race antagonisms can be expected where two racial or ethnic groups live together with one dominant, i.e., one imposing an order of racial or ethnic relations, and the other subject, reluctantly accepting this order.[10]

Does one find in the open conflict between races conditions similar to those of informal, inter-personal fighting?

Legal and social inhibitions against the race riot are present since it is prohibited by law, and both legal and customary pressures are strong against such outbreaks. However, vicarious means of solving conflict are almost totally absent. The lack of organization in racial or ethnic groups has the corollary void of a central agency responsible for the actions of the group members. Negotiations or arbitration is impractical. Court action is usually impossible because the social norms involved are mainly non-legal, but customary. And if they are legal, they probably protect the privileges of the dominant group against the subject. What is more, the subject group does not believe in adjudication since it is at the disposal of their oppressors. Eventually the dominant group considers that its own mechanism of adjudication is too slow or too lenient. If the subject group is allowed to develop leadership, which is by no means always the case, and if the leaderships of both the dominant and the subject group hold inter-racial or inter-ethnic peace in high esteem, there is hope. Cooperation between leaders, and their admonition of the rank-and-file members is the best means to avert a threatening outbreak of violence.

A fair chance of victory is commonly given to the dominant party so far as it has at its disposal the political apparatus of coercion; the chance of victory is especially high if there are reasons to believe that this apparatus which, after all, must interfere with any violence, will be slow and complacent.[11] The chance of victory decreases significantly if the political apparatus is above the passions temporarily possessing certain strata of the dominant group.

In the subject group, the chances of victory seem to approach zero, at least in the long-range. In the short-range there is only the possibility of killing or injuring a few representatives of the oppressors and destroying their property. Since race riots are mob actions in which emotions prevail over reason, the short-range perspective may become decisive.

The pattern of reward and punishment is clear. For the dominant group, excessive oppression in the form of violence may provoke a reaction which, if successful, may result in mass extermination and a reversal of the social order. Such developments took place in the ancient world, but also in the West Indies and in the United States during the temporarily successful Negro revolts. For the subject group, a defeated insurrection commonly results in most drastic sanctions and the deterioration of group status. These are mighty, but not insuperable brakes, against the lifting of inter-racial or inter-ethnic tensions to the level of violent conflict.

The causal background of race riots may be summarized in this way: the dominant group resorts to violence if an accumulation of incidents makes probable the disruption of the *status quo*. The subject group resorts to violence if an accumulation of incidents displays the danger of a significant deterioration of their status, or further blocks their advancement. If the apparatus of legal coercion is not exceptionally efficient, violence may seem feasible to the subject group. This is also the case if there is a fair chance of achieving *now* some short-range goals, or of achieving in the long-range, a degree of retreat by the dominant group who have been intimidated by the withdrawal of cooperation. The resort to violence occurs in the absence of wise and conciliatory leadership.

As in inter-personal fighting, operators and precipitants are interchangeable with one or more of the relevant conditions in the system. Most commonly there is sudden aggravation of some element in the antagonistic situation; or it may be the weakening of the law enforcement agencies, or the vigilance of the leadership.

Strikes

Industrial strikes are a third type of antagonism useful to this survey. Like race riots, they involve a group or groups rather than individuals; but unlike riots, these groups are more organized, and less informally motivated. Further, while race or ethnic eruptions involve groups differentiated by national or biological characteristics, strikes involve groups distinguished largely on the basis of class position, or occupational interest. Strikes, moreover, are good evidence of situations where antagonisms may be resolved by measurement of relative strength without resort to open violence. In other words, strikes are evidence of solutions to antagonistic situations without resort to violence.[12]

Antagonisms in the classic strike may refer to goals as different as higher pay, better labor conditions, or their opposites. Concrete disputes about wages, or the length of the working day, or the conditions of work must assume some importance, at least subjectively. But it occurs more and more frequently that labor leaders, pursuing greater prestige for themselves, come to inject a more or less artificial importance into the goals sought.

Situations prior to the outbreak of a strike are roughly analogous to those existing before the outbreak of a race riot: opposing parties participate in mixed types of relations where the incompatibility of goals is neutralized in the interest of keeping the plant running in order to earn wages and gain profits. But when the neutral equilibrium finally breaks, the solidarity involved in the process weakens, and antagonisms come to the forefront.

Normative inhibitions against strikes are weak. In free

society as a rule, there exists no legal means to coerce parties to work or not to work on conditions not freely stipulated by them. As a consequence, there exists no general legal inhibition against strike; the parties can resort to it when they disagree on the terms of the labor contract. This configuration is, however, susceptible to change: a few advanced societies of the democratic type make arbitration compulsory, or provide for the imposition of labor conditions by special courts.

Moral inhibitions against strikes are also very weak. At best they forbid strike when other means of resolving labor conflicts are available. And customary inhibitions against strikes have never evolved. On the contrary, today, in contrast with days before industry developed, there is more of a tradition to strike than not to strike under certain conditions. Employers and employes both know that in the framework of a free economic society, strike may be resorted to, and this knowledge motivates decisions to do so. This tradition is functionally connected with the structure of society acknowledging the principles of free labor and free enterprise.

The residual character of strike is conspicuous. More often than not the parties to an industrial dispute first try to come to terms through negotiations. In many cases they pass through the procedures of mediation or arbitration. In some cases this is imposed upon them; in others, they freely choose to do so either on their own initiative or on the initiative of a third party, sometimes the government. But where there are no legal rules by which courts can adjudicate the conflict, striking parties cannot go to court.

As in inter-personal conflict, strike is chosen when the chances of victory appear fair to each of the parties involved. Management expects that the strike will break down because the workers' means of subsistence will be exhausted; labor expects that management will yield lest its profits should go to others.

The residual character of the strike and its dependency on favorable estimates of the chance of victory reflect the presence of the mechanism of reward-punishment. If labor loses a long strike, not only has it to accept the conditions offered by management, but savings are gone and other heavy losses are often incurred. If management loses, not only has it to pay the increases, often retroactively, that are demanded by labor, but it has also lost to competitors in the market.

Violence in strikes today is relatively rare. It was not so a few decades ago when strikebreakers often appeared on the scene and were attacked by regular workers, or when picketing workers were attacked by ruffians hired by employers. Furthermore, violent strike is opposed by strong legal and moral inhibitions, and in advanced industrial society, by more and more customary inhibitions. Labor and management consider violent strikes against the best traditions supported by utilitarian reasoning: if a plant is destroyed or heavily damaged, so is the opportunity to work.

Violence will appear only when high values are at stake, or when a peaceful strike has not yielded the expected results. And even then only when all other means have failed. Its residual character is clear.

Several leading generalizations are possible when we now compare these three types of fighting: the inter-personal, the race riot, and the strike.

1. In all instances one finds situations defined by incompatibility of goals, differences of values, which are therefore tense in their antagonism.

2. Normative inhibitions are present and strong against individual fighting and against violent strikes. But such inhibitions are ambiguous in cases of race riots, and almost absent in nonviolent strikes. In some of these cases one may even speak of a specified cultural tradition demanding that at times men resort to strike in order to establish their relative strength. The presence of this cultural tradition affects the conduct of persons who might be involved in the conflicts.

3. The residual character of individual fights and strikes is clear; it is rather weak in race riots.

4. Fair chances of victory must appear to the parties in conflict.

5. The mechanism of reward-punishment must be present.

6. Operators or precipitants are equivalent to one or more traits of the initial system.

These generalizations can now be used to guide our inquiry into the relevant states of political groups prior to the outbreak of war or revolution.

5/The Movement
from Peace to War

IF OUR BASIC JUDGMENTS regarding conflict and the conditions under which it becomes violent are correct, and if our propositions on social causation and their extension to apply to political systems are correct, we should be in a position logically to travel still further, and seek an answer to the question: "Why do wars occur?"[1]

Inter-State Conflicts

In every community of nations there exists a cultural tradition for war, stronger in some nations, weaker in others. Men

76

know that they can achieve certain objectives by resorting to war. They also know that war can be imposed on them by their neighbors against their desires.

The processes involved in the relations between nations are, by and large, of the mixed type. There is always antagonism present because of the self-assertive tendency of every state and because of the scarcity of many objects desired by them. Solidarity between states is also present, partly because more often than not the nations prefer peace to war and partly because their leaders are aware that important objectives can be achieved through cooperation with other states.

But under certain conditions this solidarity can be destroyed. Then the latent antagonisms are loosed, and they may reach the level of violence. In this respect, war is quite similar to race riots or strikes.

The presence of the culture tradition of war and of the possibility of the release of antagonism through repression of the solidarity component are sociological constants. As such, they are always present and cannot explain causally the movement of the system, consisting of several nations, from peace to war. They form, however, the necessary background for the understanding of war causation which must be achieved by scrutinizing more precisely the traits which necessarily obtain in the system before it moves toward war.

First of all, a situation must be present involving concrete incompatibility of important objectives of two or more states. The range of values must be obviously related to the essential traits of the states as social groups. The following inquiry based on this assumption will therefore differ significantly from the so-called "list approach" which proceeds by simple enumeration of various antecedents of as many wars as possible.[2]

The state is, first, a territorial group and land is limited, i.e., scarce. Scarcity situations are likely to develop into conflicts, if and when two or more pretenders to a specified area appear on the scene. Territorial antagonisms[3] form therefore the primary type of inter-state conflicts, one of the most frequent "causes" of war.

These antagonisms appear in different varieties. State A claims or covets a territory possessed or occupied by state B; a subvariety would be formed by the case when state A would covet the whole of the territory of B. State B is likely to resist. Or states A and B simultaneously claim or covet a territory possessed or occupied by state C, or not yet belonging to any state. Then, every step of A or B in the direction of C is frowned upon or even resisted respectively by B or A.

The state is also a concentrated power structure. Another class of antagonisms corresponds to this trait of the state. Quite a few modalities of such antagonisms may be discerned. The first type is formed by disputes concerning themselves with "spheres of influence": a state is sovereign in its area only, but may exert influence outside of it more or less informally. These radiations of dominance may interfere with one another, engendering antagonistic situations. "Power politics" designates the tendency of mighty states to dictate their will to neighbors or even to remote, but rather weak, states.

Another type of antagonism arises from questions of prestige. As a power structure, the state cannot tolerate an ostentatious decrease of prestige. This happens, however, when state A humiliates or insults state B or commits an action which state B declared in advance to be inadmissible because of its rights or interests.

The third type is connected with the general tendency of

social groups and subgroups to persist; more especially, the holders of high positions in the individual states strive to maintain their position despite changes in the objective situation which demand changes in structure or personnel. Experience shows that one of the means to restore, or even to enhance, the vanishing prestige of a government is to gain a victory in external affairs, be it diplomatic or military. Under such circumstances, an antagonism may be intentionally brought about by a government with the specific purpose of improving its internal status. Such an effect may be achieved only by debasing the prestige of another state and its government, and since every state is likely to resist pressures of this kind, antagonism almost necessarily emerges.

A fourth type involves primarily not the government as such, but the armed forces. Their leaders may reach the conclusion that the prestige of the armed forces is fading and, consequently, their own position is deteriorating because for a long time their valor and efficiency has not been tested in action. If they are able to exert strong pressure on the top of the government (of which they are part), they may push it toward provoking an antagonistic process conducive to war and thus perhaps give new brilliancy to their arms.

The state is, however, much more than a territorial power structure securing order in a certain area. It exerts many auxiliary or welfare functions varying in time and space and, exerting them, it is exposed to the pressure of many groups embodying interests which are not primarily political. The modern state becomes more and more an economic unit, an organization of the economic interests of the population or of some of its influential groups. Such economic interests may be incompatible with one another, and this incompatibility may be assimilated with territorial conflicts. This is not always so. Two or more states may shift from the symbiotic relationship to antagonistic processes of various intensity, because one demands exclusive or privileged access to some source of raw material, or exclusive or privileged dominance of certain markets; or, perhaps, admission to sources of raw material or to markets dominated by another state. Economically, lines of communication with the outward world are of great importance. Hence, antagonisms involving problems of access to the sea or, more specifically, to the open sea (in contradistinction to landlocked sea) are possible. Disputes about the command of the sea, i.e., availability of uninhibited navigation, belong to the same modality of antagonisms.

Further, the state may become the standard bearer of nationalistic aspirations of ethnic groups. This commonly happens in the following background. In state A, the ethnic group X is dominant; but, across the boundary, members of the same group live, forming repressed groups in states B, C, etc. In the framework of the ethnic group, a movement may emerge demanding its political unification, and the government of state A may reflect this movement by including into the number of its objectives, "the redemption of enslaved brethren." Naturally, the governments of states B, C, etc., resist. An antagonistic situation emerges.

In some cases, at least as an intermediary measure, it is not the reunion of the brethren which is demanded, but alleviation of oppression—actual or alleged; this is again resented by the corresponding governments which see in such demands intolerable infringements of their sovereignty and prestige, with similar consequences. The history of the nineteenth and early twentieth centuries is full of such situations.

Conspicuous were the cases of the Italian *irredenta* (prior to the First World War) and the movement for the unification of the German people; Prussia took the leadership and achieved that goal, though not completely, through three victorious wars, of 1864 against Denmark, 1866 against Austria, and 1870-1 against France.[4]

Also, the state may come under the pressure of religious groups which may use the political organization of their members to alleviate the persecution of their brethren outside of the political boundaries. Or they may even use political power forcibly to convert non-believers to their faith. In a similar way, a state may become the bearer of a secular ideology. The mechanisms put into motion are quite similar to those just discussed. The Islamic conquest, the Crusades, Russia, Great Britain and France's intervention in the Greek insurrection (1827), numerous wars waged by Russia to liberate her Orthodox brethren in faith in Serbia and Bulgaria (also in Armenia, though the Armenians are not Orthodox), may be cited. The aspiration to impose the secular ideology of the French Revolution onto neighbors provoked antagonisms which resulted in a long series of wars. In our day, the cold war between the United States and the Soviet Union is caused mainly by the clash of the secular ideologies of the two greatest powers in the world.

Finally, an antagonistic situation of whatever origin, in combination with the existence of the culture tradition of war, tends to develop into a generalized, or diffused, conflict (though not yet violent) if not resolved in a reasonable period of time. There the original roots of the conflict are almost forgotten. Each party considers any success of the other as an unfavorable and intolerable disturbance of equilibrium which, if continued, could disrupt the balance beyond remedy and place one party at the mercy of the other. On that basis, developments are possible which may result in war, just as a chronic disease may erupt into an acute one.

First, a state (A) may declare a "negative interest," or its resolution not to tolerate specified actions on the part of another state (B). The Monroe Doctrine is an example; England's doctrine that the Lowlands could not depend on any great power is another; and Russia's thesis that the Turkish Straits could not be dominated by a great power other than herself is a third. To such constant doctrines temporary ones can be added such as that of the freedom of the seas on which this country insisted in the course of World War I, or the British guaranty to Poland (1939), or the Truman Doctrine (1947), i.e., the declaration on the part of the United States that it would not tolerate an attack on Greece or Turkey by the Soviet Union. Perhaps the whole "policy of containment" —that of the United States and its allies since 1948—belongs in this group. The peculiarity of the situation is this: state A does not want anything for itself; but a movement of state B contrary to a declared negative interest is most likely to become a *casus belli,* partly through the prestige mechanism discussed above.

Second, a state seeing its competitors on the international scene gain strength through the acquisition of territory or political influence or markets may demand that it be granted "compensation" to restore the relationship of strength. When the strength of Prussia increased through her victory over Austria (1866), France unsuccessfully demanded compensation in the form of permission to annex Luxemburg. When France established her dominance over the major part of

Morocco, Germany demanded compensation in the form of the "rectification of boundaries" in Equatorial Africa; this was granted. Unsuccessful claims of this type may sharpen the antagonism and move the nations concerned toward war.

Third, a state may demand "strategic boundaries" to improve its position in the everlasting political game eventually conducive to war. The claims of the Soviet Union as to its western boundaries and the subjugation of the satellites have been often, though hardly validly, explained by the adherence of its government to this principle activated in the climate of a generalized, or diffused, conflict.

The three developments just studied normally emerge in the framework of a generalized conflict. But in the absence of such conflict, they may arise if there is a culture tradition of war and if statesmen are aware that war may come to their country and will come sooner or later. A fourth development is hardly possible outside of the specific situation of a generalized conflict; this is preventive war started by state A because its government has reached the conclusion that state B *will* provoke a conflict, but at a later date, and that time is working in favor of B.

This survey does not pretend to offer an exhaustive list of the inter-state antagonisms conducive to war. But since it is based on a careful examination of the properties of the groups involved and of the properties of antagonistic processes of various intensity, it could be easily expanded to cover additional cases not directly mentioned without disrupting its logical structure. On the other hand, the survey does not pretend to isolate individual developments eventually conducive to war in a manner comparable to the isolation of individual sicknesses. On the contrary, developments of the various types may coalesce, or move from one type to another; such is by necessity the development from a primary, or original antagonism, to a generalized conflict.

The survey does allow us to make these statements: 1) The inter-state antagonisms are not so indetermined in their grounds as the inter-individual antagonisms, because they are related to the specific functions of the state; 2) further, they are not so strictly limited as the conflicts conductive to industrial conflicts; 3) they are best compared with race riots where a primary range of incompatibilities is easily expanded into diversified fields of human interests.

It is noteworthy that the range of possible inter-state antagonisms varies in dependency on the fluctuation of the functions of the state; economic and nationalistic (ethnic) disputes are more easily transformed into inter-state conflicts in our day than they were in the Middle Ages when the state's economic function almost did not exist and national sentiment was vague. On the other hand, inter-state antagonisms on religious background are less likely in our day of separation of state and church than in days when the state was closely aligned with one or another religious body. This is, however, balanced by the easy emergence of conflicts on the background of secular ideologies.

It must be emphasized that numerous inter-state antagonisms are always present in a latent manner but are repressed in the framework of the symbiotic process. There are certain symptoms of the impending breakdown of equilibrium and outbreak of war roughly corresponding to the antagonisms of the various types.

The majority of the antagonisms, namely, those not mentioned in the more specific statements to come, become dangerous if the incompatible goals are lifted to the level of immediate, or short-range, goals which sometimes is done overtly, but sometimes is not. Since the end of the eighteenth century, Russia has contemplated the annexation of the Turkish Straits; however, none of the Russo-Turkish wars (except that of 1792) was provoked by that aspiration. The opening of the Imperial archives has proven that this annexation was relegated to the level of *desiderata* to be fulfilled eventually, under exceptionally favorable circumstances which, it seemed, had materialized with the outbreak of the First World War. In a similar way, since 1866 the newly created Kingdom of Italy coveted the Italian speaking parts of Austria, and since 1871 France dreamed of "revenge" which would allow her to reannex the provinces lost then; but in both cases these aspirations remained for many years on the level of long-range goals, until 1914 when the outbreak of the First World War created a situation allowing them to be lifted to the level of short-range goals. For long periods of time, Latin American republics have made reciprocal claims on territory, but the number of wars provoked by that situation has been small, since these claims commonly remained on the long-range level.

But antagonisms involving prestige are always dangerous, since immediate solution is demanded by the very nature of the situation and no solution can be easily found through conciliatory processes.

Religious and ideological antagonisms become dangerous if the objective situation (e.g., victory in a war of coalition) demands concerted action on the part of states who not only widely differ ideologically, but ascribe universal validity to their ideologies. Such is the case in the great conflict of our day, as we shall see in later discussions.

Generalized or diffused conflicts are intrinsically dangerous. The danger increases if one of the parties formulates negative interests encroaching upon the objectives of the other, or if at least one of them begins contemplating preventive war.

Independently of the type of the antagonisms, there exist a few additional conditions which increase the danger of movement from peace to war. First, if one of the parties is dominated by a militaristic group or if it is permeated as a whole with the spirit of militarism. As such, this does not yet provoke war; but any emerging antagonism may be then rapidly pushed ahead toward war. Second, if the government of one of the parties has come to the nefarious decision to bolster its vanishing domestic prestige by a glorious achievement without. Third, if, between two states, there exists a revenge or inveterate feud situation. The danger of war is created by the fact that many inter-state antagonisms are not so much solved as repressed, becoming components in symbiotic situations. The danger is also increased if many wars were waged between two states in the course of centuries, so that feelings have emerged analogous to those obtaining in a vendetta situation between individuals. Historically such situations have obtained between France and Germany, and Russia and Poland.

Revenge and inveterate feud are hardly sufficient to reanimate a repressed conflict and to lift it up to the war level. But they become operative and sometimes decisive in incipient states of developments characterized by the presence of primary antagonisms.

Normative Inhibitions

The presence of one of the antagonisms described above (especially if one of the incompatible goals is lifted to the short-range level), in combination with one or two of the aggravating circumstances just discussed, makes the situation ominous. This does not yet mean war if other conditions are not present. Let us examine what the other conditions are, using knowledge gained in the course of the inductive study of the development of non-political conflicts.

As we have seen in many cases of non-political violence, fighting is more likely to break out when normative inhibitions are absent or weakened. The existence of the tradition of war makes it evident that, in the situation under study, normative inhibitions must be weak, perhaps contradictory.

Until recently, international lawyers, statesmen, and diplomats did not doubt that war, even aggressive war, was perfectly legal. The leaders of a state were considered entitled to resort to war for achieving the objectives of their nations. War was "another form of politics," supplementing the diplomatic form.[5]

In our day, attempts are made to curb the culture tradition of war by outlawing war of aggression. There is no reason to deny the possibility of the ultimate success of this generous enterprise. But a long time, perhaps many generations, must pass before the culture tradition will really vanish.

Moral inhibitions against war concern unjust war rather than war in general and are weak because it is always possible to interpret a situation so that right seems to be on the side of the interpreter. Note that, when a war begins, prayers are said on both sides of the front, asking the Lord to grant victory "to our just cause."

Customary inhibitions concern themselves mainly with a certain decorum, with the expectation that a state should not attack another without plausible reason, or without previous attempts of solving the conflict in another way, or without declaration of war.

This is a replica of the situation obtaining in societies where race riots and strikes are frequent; in all these cases, the relations between the parties are poorly organized, as they were among individuals before the rise and the strengthening of the political organization.

Therefore, in general, normative inhibitions can be almost neglected when studying war causation. There is one exception. If a nation is already developing an anti-war consciousness it may refrain from war under conditions which, without that conviction, would have caused war. This conviction is, however, a nascent one. As such, it can be rather easily checked and finally destroyed by actions on the part of a potential foe provoking too much moral indignation and/or affecting too many serious interests. Therefore, into the number of the relevant traits of the state of a system prior to the outbreak of a war one must introduce this one: the absence, in the parties to the dispute, of exceptionally strong normative inhibitions against war. This is especially important relative to the party which, under the particular circumstances, is likely to play the role of the aggressor because normative inhibitions cannot work in defense situations: no law, no moral system, no set of international customs could prevent a nation from resisting aggression if the other conditions are present.

The Residual Character of War

While normative inhibitions are so weak as to be almost negligible in the solution of conflicts, vicarious means are abundant. This naturally makes war a residual means for the solution of interstate conflicts just as individual fights or strikes are residual means of solving inter-personal and inter-class conflicts.

More often than not, war is resorted to as an ultimate measure. When an inter-state antagonism breaks out, negotiations are almost always tried. When they fail, other states (or prominent persons) are either asked to act as mediators or they spontaneously offer their services. The existence of the United Nations has significantly improved the chance of a peaceful solution of an inter-state conflict or its reduction to the level of a "local war." The possibility of fulminating against the antagonist before a forum which, in principle, represents world public opinion sometimes exhausts the ebullient energy which otherwise would have been converted into military action. A fine example is the treatment of the Korean action, which could easily have evolved into a Third World War without the presence of the United Nations.

Since the organization of an International Court of Justice, solution by adjudication has become possible, at least in cases when the conflict may be formulated in terms of reciprocal rights and duties, so that only their interpretations would separate the parties. Of course, it is necessary that both parties adhere to the treaty which established the World Court and that they do not deny its competence in the *case at issue*. Unfortunately, these conditions rarely have been met.

Moreover, inter-state antagonisms eventually can be held to the level of non-violent conflict or even lower. The parties to a dispute may try to intimidate one another, to exert indirect pressure by withdrawing certain advantages, deteriorating the other party's chances in competition, etc. Ideological and economic conflicts can be even pressed to the level of *fair competition* for the minds and markets of "the neutralists."

But there are limitations to each of these means. Negotiations fail, or are not resorted to, if at least one of the parties is too rigid (determined to cede nothing), or unreliable (likely to break obligations imposed on it through compromise). Mediation and arbitration fail, or are not resorted to, if really neutral parties cannot be found, or when at least one of the two parties to the conflict does not want to be bound by the verdict of the third and neutral party, or when the verdict would be obviously in favor of party A and against party B. Of course, party B, knowing that the principles commonly used in the solution of similar conflicts would warrant an adverse decision, declines this mode of conflict solution. Adjudication exists more on the level of declaration than in actuality since there is no power superior to that of the parties to the dispute and therefore able to impose the decision on them. Competition in ideological and economic antagonisms can be resorted to only if the two parties agree to choose that form for the solution of their differences. The same is true of holding the dispute to the level of intermediary antagonistic processes, including non-violent conflict. This is commonly the case so long as each party has reason to hope that its objectives could be achieved short of war.

Vicarious means, one sees, are abundant. More often than not, they are tried whenever antagonism of a certain gravity appears on the political horizon. But for various reasons, some of them appear unworkable, other ones are successively tried, but fail. Then the antagonism is maintained on the level of non-violent conflict from which development in both directions is possible: toward peace through negotiation or conciliatory procedures, or toward war. The fateful decision to resort to war is commonly made only if a party to the dispute has lost the hope to achieve its goal by other means, and if the other conditions are present, some already studied, one still to be analyzed.

The Relative Strength of the Parties

In non-political antagonisms, the outbreak of violence has been found to depend on a definite relationship in the strength of the parties: both parties must have reasons to believe that they have a fair chance of victory. In addition, a certain differential between aggressive and defensive situations may be established. Relative to war, the same pattern definitely obtains.

1. As in the other cases, only estimates are possible. The real outcome is usually the defeat of one party; but prior to the event, this outcome cannot be reliably predicted. How the computation of the chances is made, depends on the technique of warfare and on the particularities of the parties involved. A party may rely on the superior prowess of its fighters, or better equipment, or larger financial means, or sheer weight of numbers, or superior organization, or better generalship. Or it may rely on the advantage of taking the initiative and never allowing it to go over to the other party. It may also count on the probable interference of neutrals.[6]

2. In the computation, a general tendency toward exaggerated optimism is normal. The reason is obvious. In every state, the patriotism of the people, the excellency of the military machinery, the superior leadership, etc., are extolled, forming a kind of official truth easily recognized in totalitarian states but also present in democracies. The leaders who are used

to talking in these conventional terms and to being addressed in them, finally are converted to the beliefs they have tried to inculcate in the others; and when the gravest of all possible decisions comes, they choose war, wrongly overestimating the chances of victory. But there is a limit to the possible overestimation, and the penalty of defeat is heavy and well known. When victory is out of the question, nations rarely choose to die with honor. More commonly, they yield to the pressure; thus, war is avoided.

A few cases of this type have been already reported.[7] It is noteworthy that one of the most frequent and disastrous items on the list of possible mistakes is reliance on the help of other nations. In 1870, France chose war against Germany (Prussia) believing that she would be seconded by Austria who was badly beaten four years earlier by France's foe, Prussia. But Austria did not seize the opportunity for revenge. In 1899, the Boer republics wrongly believed that England's European antagonist, Germany, would interfere; this hope was strengthened by foolish speeches of Emperor William II. But at that time Germany did not yet have valid reasons to embark on war against England.

3. The estimate of the chances of victory should be made on a purely rational background; at the present time, the general staff of the armed forces of a nation possesses abundant information necessary to arrive at a sound judgment. But the situation is disturbed and complicated by the possibility of emotional distortion of sheer facts. Here, again, differences in culture, as well as in political organization, are of high importance. If the fateful decision to start a war or refrain from it is to be made by a single man, the probability of emotional miscalculation tremendously increases. In our day, Hitler, a

maniac, could make a choice which almost resulted in an irreparable destruction of his own country. In olden days, autocratic monarchs often chose war for futile reasons, and then lost it, with disastrous consequences for the nations. It is noteworthy that Stalin, no less an autocrat than Hitler, made the corresponding decisions in cold blood—and won.

The virtual superimposition of the emotional element upon the rational makes it extremely difficult for outsiders to predict what decision will be made. But if one can presume rationality, the decision may not be so difficult to guess. Thus, for instance, the prediction that England, France and Israel would not embark on a real conquest of Egypt in the course of the Suez affair (1956) could be made at the moment when it became apparent that they were opposed by both Russia and the United States. The opposition of the United States seems not to have been anticipated—else the three nations would not even have started their ill-fated expedition.

4. One more factor must be considered when contemplating the role of a fair chance of victory: victory may be taken for granted, but this factor of the decision may be balanced by an adverse estimate of cost. In other words, a rational survey of the situation may result in a conclusion like this: state A has a fair chance of victory in a war against state B in a conflict centered around a value C (e.g., the possession of a definite territory, or the establishment of A's supremacy in an important part of the world), but the sacrifices to be brought to conquer C may be evaluated (negatively) higher than the positive value of possessing C. Then, state A, if its government is guided by rational considerations, will refrain from war. The introduction of this factor into the reasoning preceding the decision to make or not to make war does not invalidate

what has been said above. What happens is this: victory is not contemplated *in abstracto,* as the achievement of a particular goal against the opposition of another state; but is evaluated as part of a total situation involving the possession of C minus the probable sacrifices to get it and, as a counterpart, both the non-possession of C plus the value of the probable sacrifices to be brought to the altar of war. In both cases, the two factors are submitted to algebraic addition which may manifest that, after victory in a particular conflict, the state involved would find itself in a poorer condition than the one likely to obtain if the conflict were not pushed to the level of violence.

Of course, the introduction of cost into the estimate of a fair chance of victory is not always made, or, as later developments show, the evaluation of cost might be faulty. In the history of mankind, there have been quite a few "pyrrhic victories."

Reward and Punishment

Three of the conditions making the outbreak of war likely depend on the pattern of reward-and-punishment which is deeply ingrained in the culture tradition of war. The application of this pattern means that the victor in an armed conflict is rewarded by at least a province taken from the defeated. When, in individual cases, this does not take place, the non-occurrence of an expected sequence of events attracts attention and is commonly understood as an exception from a well established rule. The clearest example until recently was Prussia's refraining from the imposition of any territorial punishment, in her favor, on defeated Austria (1866). The great statesman who imposed his will on the Prussian *junkers* in this case cashed the reward for his generosity a few years later when he was able to conclude an advantageous alliance with the defeated enemy.

After the two World Wars the greatest contributor to victory, the United States, did not claim any reward for the glorious deed; incidentally, this happened because in both cases the United States joined the war to preserve its negative interests, which was accomplished by the very fact of the crucial defeat of the enemy who had threatened the interests involved. But in many recent cases, when the application of the pattern was officially denied, it actually played an important role: in dubious situations, provinces were adjudged to the victor. Officially, he acquired them for another reason than victory, but out of the conflicting claims, that one was given dominance which was the victor's claim. This often appeared at the Congress of Vienna (1815) and at the Peace Conference of Paris (1919).

In many recent cases, the pattern has been openly and deliberately applied. The Franco-Prussian war of 1870-1 arose out of a trivial dispute about the virtual election of a Hohenzollern to the Spanish throne eliciting in France the fear of an adverse change of political equilibrium.[8] No territorial claim was involved, but when it resulted in Prussia's victory, France was penalized by the loss of Alsace-Lorraine. Her appeal to the public opinion of the world did not find any response because the demand of the cession of territory was not considered to depart from usage. The First World War emerged from a cluster of suddenly embittered conflicts; no real claim on German territory was made before its start. But at the war's end Germany suffered the loss of one-sixth of her territory and the dismemberment of her allies. After the Second World War, the pattern was applied to Japan, Italy, and Germany; in the case of Germany, it would have been even more burdensome had the so-called Morgenthau plan prevailed.

The pattern of reward and punishment for victory or defeat is amoral. But its presence in the cultural tradition of war threatens not only the defeated state as such, but also the power position of its rulers, and this is what often imposes a salutary restraint on them in choosing war as a means of attaining goals opposed by other states. More than a restraint, it is a mighty brake on war. This brake forces the cool measurement of the relative strength of the parties and the resultant sorting of incompatible goals into those to be realized and those to be reduced to the level of frustrated expectations.

Summary and Conclusion

These considerations warrant the following generalization: Two or more states antagonistic to each other are likely to move from the state of peace to that of war if the following conditions are simultaneously present:

1. The antagonism must have reached the level of danger as specified, and be further reinforced by aggravating circumstances.

2. None of the parties to the conflict, especially the one likely to play the aggressive role, is dominated by exceptionally strong normative inhibitions to war.

3. One of the parties must have lost hope of achieving its goal short of war, after having tried other procedures or rejected them as inadequate.

4. Subjectively, according to the conclusions of responsible

leaders, there is a fair chance of victory for each of the parties, while the problem of cost has not been raised or has resulted in a (subjectively) favorable answer.

These are the relevant traits of the initial state of the system whose movement from peace to war is to be explained. As in cases of non-political conflict studied earlier, the operator or precipitant is interchangeable with one of these traits. In each case the trait which appears last brings the system into movement.

The first trait, i.e., the presence of a serious inter-state antagonism, must be given from the start; in other words, it cannot be the operator, since the other traits, except the second, are meaningfully oriented toward the first. But the particular conditions lifting it above the threshold of immediate danger may be absent at first and then appear and work as an operator. A goal may be moved from the long-range to the short-range perspective, or, in a generalized conflict, military men can come to the conclusion that time is irremediably working against their nation. But such general, aggravating circumstances as the dominance of a nation by militaristic tradition or existence of an inveterate feud hardly could work as operators.

The second trait may become an operator if strong normative inhibitions disappear in a situation otherwise complying with the conditions under which war is likely to break out. (Incidentally, the perfidy Japan displayed at Pearl Harbor almost knocked out the predominantly pacifist attitudes of the American people.)

The loss, by one party, of the hope to resolve the conflict in its favor by means short of war may play the part of an operator. Change in the relationship between the strength of the parties, more exactly, of the subjective appraisal of this relationship, also may function as operator.

Therefore, the operator may receive diversified shapes: in one case, all the relevant traits are present except the third; then something depriving the party of the hope of success short of war seems to launch the war. In another case, change in the relationship in armament, or in the attitudes of other governments, may produce a similar effect. In actuality, no war is caused by the operator alone.

Each of the factors corresponding to the traits of a system necessary to provoke the movement from peace to war may be (although must not necessarily be) governed by "laws" which could be discovered by the social sciences. But the emergence of each factor is governed by "laws" of different content while their concomitance in time and space forms the "conjuncture," the appearance of which is beyond the area covered by the postulate of order. It is therefore out of the question that a "simple" law governing the outbreak of war could ever be discovered. To have war, *all* conditions must accumulate, and when the last one appears, there is war because now *the set* is complete.

The formula above and the explanation following it forms a hypothesis on war causation. As every scientific hypothesis, it must be tested by a confrontation with facts.

6/The Movement from Peace to War: Case Studies

IN THE NATURAL SCIENCES the verification of a hypothesis is most commonly achieved by experimentation, which is impossible in the social sciences, with rare exceptions.[1] In these sciences, a hypothesis can be verified only by its application to relevant events that have occurred. This will be our procedure in testing our notions regarding war and revolution. A case study will be made showing how the hypothesis works relative to a certain number of wars, as well as to a certain number of "negative cases," i.e., situations where war seemed likely, but did not break out. This procedure does not, of course, prove a hypothesis, but it may indicate that it is more or less plausible.

In this case study, we can select a few recent wars as well as a few major wars of the seventeenth and eighteenth centuries; no attempt has been made to dig deeper into the past because of the scarcity of relevant information.[2] The selection has been "random," i.e., the author had no preconceived ideas about the feasibility of applying his theoretical schema to the particular wars. He simply chose those whose backgrounds were more familiar to him. The natural order of presentation in historical studies will be reversed in this discussion, beginning with those wars whose genesis has been best preserved in the memory of the living generations.

The Korean War

The Korean War (1950-53) is a case of war engendered by a diffuse conflict. The conflict was between the Atlantic bloc led by the United States, and the Communist world, including the Soviet Union, its satellites and China. At the outbreak of the Korean War the conflict was already almost four years old. Attempts to solve it by negotiations had failed —by 1950 neither party believed that an acceptable compromise was possible. Solution by arbitration or adjudication was out of the question, since there was no really neutral and, at the same time, authoritative state acceptable to the two parties. Both parties hesitated to resort to solution through the measurement of relative strength, since neither was quite sure of victory. Under these conditions the parties have no choice but to temporize and to resort to "direct action" improving the position of the acting party in the general conflict without eliciting a global war.

In June, 1950, North Korea attacked South Korea, obviously at the instigation of the Soviet Union and (perhaps) Red China, in the hope of moving forward the boundary of the Communist world and thereby eliminating an advanced position of the adversary. The aggressor did not expect to meet serious resistance—especially the interference of the United States and, later on, of the Atlantic bloc under the banner of the UN. To a large extent the aggressor's optimism was based on an unfortunate remark of Secretary of State Acheson indicating that South Korea did not belong to the peripheral zone of American defense. Success would have resulted in the unification of Korea in one Communist state.

But the United States responded to the challenge by a direct, though local, action. One of the most momentous decisions in contemporary history, made by President Truman, ordered the token American force stationed in South Korea to resist; vast American re-enforcements were dispatched to its rescue as fast as possible. The decision was seconded by the UN, and several member states sent their contingents to fight along with the Americans. In principle, the response was to remain on the local level, short of provoking a global war.

It is clear that these events fulfilled the first condition of the outbreak of war—a serious conflict was present. The second condition was also present: the Communist world had no normative inhibition against aggression, since, in fact, that world was still ruled by the maxim that "the good" is anything promoting the Communist cause. As to the United States, there was rather a normative obligation to accept the challenge because South Korea was under the informal protectorate of the United States and was to be expanded, whenever the circumstances would permit, into an all-Korean state under a democratic constitution. The third condition was also

present: the Communist world could not hope to get dominance of South Korea by means of negotiation or arbitration,
nor could the United States and the Atlantic bloc hope that
negotiations after Communist occupation might restore liberty
to South Korea.

As to the fourth condition, both parties to the local conflict
had good reasons to believe that they would win. The aggressor
considered that he would easily overcome the resistance of
the small and poorly equipped South Korean army; the United
States was satisfied that it was strong enough to achieve the
limited goal of repelling the local aggression. Events proved
that the assessment of the situation by the United States was
right. Later on, a tendency developed to exploit the opportunity to reconstruct a unified and democratic Korea; this proved
impossible in the framework of the limited war which the two
parties had tacitly agreed upon.

The Palestinian War

In 1948, war broke out between the newly created state
of Israel and the Arab League. The conflict behind this war
was primarily territorial, Israel asserting her right to exist
in the area assigned her by the United Nations, with eventual
additions, and the Arab League insisting that Palestine belonged entirely to the Arabs, by reason of centuries of uninterrupted occupation. The goals were absolutely incompatible
and were to be attained right away: for Israel, to emerge as
a state and, for the Arab League, to prevent the birth of a
foreign body.

Circumstances assigned the role of eventual aggressor to the
Arab League; they had to expel the Jews from where they

were established. This collective aggressor was not bound by any normative inhibitions. On the contrary, the old tradition of "Sacred War" against the enemies of Islam still survived among the Arab states. Third, all vicarious solutions of the conflict failed: after years of efforts, Great Britain who had held the contested territory under mandate, abandoned the situation, and the decision of the United Nations on the partition of Palestine was a painfully gained compromise which was never accepted by the Arabs. Thus, the Arabs could no longer hope to attain their goal by means short of war. Finally, at the outbreak of the hostilities each party had fair reasons to believe that it would be victorious. The Arabs relied on numbers, being thirty million against a few hundreds of thousands. The Jews relied on modern organization, better military equipment, and help from the outside. Events showed that the Jews were right. But, in the days of decision, nobody could tell with certainty what the outcome would be. Thus, the four conditions for the outbreak of a war, as stated above, are clearly recognizable.

The Second World War

The outbreak of the Second World War and its gradual expansion must be understood in the background of a generalized conflict between Hitler's Germany and the democracies of the West, of which Poland, then a semi-Fascist state, was a dubious ally. In the outbreak of the war, two components must be distinguished: Hitler's invasion of Poland; and France and Britain's entrance on the military scene to protect Poland.

The conflict between Germany and Poland was primarily territorial and rather insoluble. Germany coveted the so-called corridor, a Polish province extending the main area of Poland to the shore of the Baltic Sea. Germany's desire for the area was for the purpose of securing the continuity of her own territory which the corridor cut in two. Her claim was based on more than one hundred years of possession, which she declared was wrongly disrupted at Versailles. Poland needed the corridor for access to the sea and claimed it as part of her historical heritage, grabbed from her in the days of partition (1792) and then restored at Versailles. Both parties also asserted that the population was respectively German, or Polish, at least in its majority. Germany also claimed to act as a protector of the German minority in Poland, which was allegedly badly persecuted. Actually, Poland did not treat her allo-ethnic minorities well and aggravated her case by unilaterally denouncing that part of her treaties with the victors of the First World War which placed her minorities under the protection of the League of Nations. Normative inhibitions were conspicuous by their absence: Germany was swept by the delirium of militarism, and in Poland the government was in the hands of a group called "the Colonels" who succeeded Marshal Pilsudsky, the country's dictator from 1926 until his death in 1935. Of the vicarious means for the solution of conflict, negotiation was tried, but failed; arbitration was difficult because there were no real neutrals. Therefore, for Germany no way existed for solving the conflict in her favor, other than war.

The chances of victory were uncertain. Germany was overwhelmingly stronger than Poland alone, and relied on the reluctance of the Western Powers, especially France, to launch a war for a question which, after all, did not directly concern them. Poland, on the contrary, relied on her French alliance and on the guaranty given her by the British. She expected to win the war as a member of a stronger coalition. Facts proved that she was right, but once again, nobody could be too sure before the military events of 1939-45. Nor could it have been foreseen that, though a member of a victorious coalition, Poland would be enslaved by one of her mighty allies. At the outbreak of the hostilities (Sept. 1, 1939), Russia was not yet an ally of England and France, much less of Poland.

The entrance into the war of France and Great Britain was determined in a similar way. Between them and Germany, the conflict was not territorial, but rather a power conflict about influence in vast areas of East Central Europe. France's influence was paramount there until Hitler's rise to power. But since 1935, the existential equilibrium was rapidly changing in favor of Germany who successfully violated a number of limitations imposed on her by the Versailles Treaty. She annexed Austria, part of Czechoslovakia and the Memelland, and made a dependency of the rest of Czechoslovakia. The conflict was aggravated by a highly explosive prestige situation which emerged as the result of two steps: Hitler's proclamation of the German claim in a form permitting no retreat or long delay; and the British guaranty of Poland's integrity, largely provoked by Neville Chamberlain's bitterness against Hitler's breach of the promise given at Munich a few months earlier. This particular conflict for a while remained on the level of non-violence, but the unleashing of the Poland-Germany war made this no longer possible. For France and Great Britain, the only way to restore their badly shaken prestige was to resort to war. In the particular situation, no normative inhibitions could play a part. Hitler's Germany was explicitly militaristic and aggressive, and the aversion to war, quite strong in France and Britain, was vanishing before successive humiliations imposed on them by Hitler.

For the two parties, hope of victory was fair. Germany, as in the First World War, relied on the dynamism of her armed forces and superior generalship, and on the reluctance of London City and Wall Street to spend too much money on a war involving no major economic problems. Britain and France relied on their naval superiority and on the backing of the New World. The latter proved to be right, but to decide who was stronger, six years of bitter warfare were necessary. Almost to the end the outcome remained uncertain.

One of the most spectacular events of the Second World War was Hitler's attack on the Soviet Union. Prior to the attack, the Soviet Union could be considered as a nonbelligerent partner of the Axis. But, under the disguise of partnership, a formidable power conflict was present: one of rivalry between two pretenders for hegemony in the Old World. Both partners well understood that one would jump on the other at the first opportunity and try to annihilate him. Normative inhibitions were absent. Negotiations failed: Hitler did not want to pay Stalin the price he demanded for remaining faithful to the strange alliance. Mediation or arbitration was out of the question. The conflict could have remained on the level of non-violence, but military considerations induced Hitler not to postpone the decision. Germany was firmly convinced of being stronger than the Soviet Union, and this belief was widely shared throughout the world. The Soviet Union relied on Russia's geopolitical advantages, on the reawakened patriotism of her population, on her rapidly developing industrial system, and on the help of the great powers of the West for whom Germany's conquest of Russia would have made victory almost impossible. In the days of the battles in the suburbs of Moscow and in Stalingrad, the chances of victory or defeat seemed to be even. Once again, the basic conditions under which states resort to war were present when Hitler ordered his armies to march on the Soviets.

The United States formally joined the war after the infamy of Pearl Harbor, but much earlier, ever since the days of the collapse of France, it was a nonbelligerent partner of Britain. This was tantamount to going to war. Why did this happen?

For quite a few years, antagonism between the United States and Germany was evident. This antagonism was ideological, but one important condition of making it dangerous was absent: the objective situation did not require concerted action of the two. However, by lasting, the conflict received the shape of a generalized conflict. In this conflict, the United States evolved a definite and strong, though negative, interest: not to allow Germany to establish herself in a dominant position on the Western shores of the Atlantic, both in Europe and Africa. This was, however, precisely what Germany was trying to achieve after her spectacular victory over France. The United States had to play the role of the aggressor—to push Germany back—and her normative inhibitions vanished through the same mechanism as in France and Britain. Negotiation and arbitration were out of the question since Germany believed that she had already gained victory and therefore was not inclined to make concessions. The computation of the chances of victory gave an indefinite result: the United States relied on her industrial might, her dominance of the sea, and the strength of the democratic ideal. Germany relied on her ability to achieve her goals before the United States would be ready to oppose her on the battlefields.

The last phase of the Second World War began with Pearl Harbor. Japan's decision to resort to war conformed to the requirements of the hypothesis stated in the preceding chapter. There was a generalized conflict between the United States and Japan. Japan coveted and since 1937 was acting toward the acquisition of vast territory and economic dominance in the so-called "Asian co-prosperity area." This conflicted with the negative interest of the United States: not to allow any power to take over China. For long years, the conflict remained on the level of non-violence, Japan resorting to "direct action," and the United States retaliating by the freezing of Japanese assets, etc. The United States possessed normative inhibitions against war, but Japan did not. Negotiations were tried but broke down. Then Japan lost the hope of attaining her objectives by means short of war.

In regard to the relative strength of the parties, Japan counted on her ability to inflict a deadly blow on the enemy's navy which would make Japan invulnerable; she also relied on the fact that not only the United States, but also Britain and France, were involved in a life-and-death struggle in Europe, which seemed strongly to decrease her enemies' war potential in the Far East. The United States relied, as in the previous case, on its enormous superiority in industrial equipment and on the inner cohesion of the nation. History teaches that, in America, solidarity was always achieved in days of crisis. But, prior to the decisive battles, nobody could tell with certainty who would be victorious. The precipitant, as in many other cases, was the breakdown of the negotiations, completing the set of conditions under which wars are likely to start.

The First World War

The outbreak of the First World War was preceded by a serious and generalized, but non-violent, conflict involving two alliances of all the major nations of Europe. Each alliance consisted of three powers. Their conflict was an outgrowth of a cluster of primary conflicts, of which three were most important. Russia and the Central powers coveted Turkey and the Balkans, at least as spheres of influence. Germany sought to extend her economic dominance over these same areas. Between France and Germany, there was an inveterate feud expressed in France's aspiration to reconquer Alsace-Lorraine lost in 1871. Between Germany and England, there was sharp competition for dominance on the world market. Initially, all of these objectives were long-range; they became short-range with the development of the generalized conflict. Russia and England started stressing their respective negative interests in the Straights and in the Lowlands. Every gain by one party was considered ominous by the other; and, in the last few years before the war, gains were made by the Triple Entente: Greece and the small Slavic nations of the Balkans protected by Russia had defeated Turkey, an ally of Germany; Russia's economic and military strength was rapidly increasing. In Germany and Austria, the idea of preventive war was more and more pondered. The murder of Archduke Franz Ferdinand by a Serbian created a prestige situation for Austria-Hungary.

There were aggravating circumstances, besides those already mentioned, i.e., the feud between France and Germany and the prestige situation for Austria. Militarism dominated in Germany. The Austro-Hungarian government thought that the intolerable internal pressure exerted by its various na-

109

tionality groups could be relieved by a short and victorious war. In those days, the idea that a war of aggression was illegal was not yet recognized, so that no normative inhibitions were present. The vicarious means of negotiations were used, but proved futile; many historians agree however that, if the negotiations were better conducted, they could have prevented war; the absence of a forum like the League of Nations or the United Nations made them chaotic and inconclusive. No arbitration was possible. The relative strength of the parties was indeterminate. Russia knew that she could suffer a bad defeat in the beginning, but relied on her historical ability to trade space for time and then use her overwhelming manpower. She also relied on the help of her allies. France relied on her army, supported by that of Russia; Great Britain relied on her navy and her ability to starve Germany. The Germans relied on their dynamism and better generalship which would let them knock out France and then dispose of Russia. She believed that England, after all, would not interfere and hoped that Italy would carry out her treaty obligations and fight on her side. One can see that there were good reasons for each party to believe that victory would be gained.

The generalized conflict was accentuated by the Sarajevo murder creating a prestige situation and compelling the parties to act right away; the breakdown of the negotiations put the system in motion.

The Russo-Japanese War

The Russo-Japanese war (1904-5) started as the result of a territorial conflict with both Russia and Japan coveting Manchuria (a Chinese province), and Korea. Russia wanted the area of Manchuria for her expanding population and as an access to the open sea; she desired Korea to prevent Japan's interference with the area. Japan wanted to create a sphere of economic dominance to take care of her growing population. Normative inhibitions were absent. Negotiations broke down, largely because of Russia's rigidity. Both parties strongly believed that they possessed the superior strength. Russia believed that, being a great power, she was incomparably stronger than the little island state of Japan, with a population about one-third of the Russian; she badly underestimated the progress of the technical and military Westernization of Japan since the 1860's, as well as the people's patriotism and loyalty to the Emperor. Japan gambled on the fact that, 5,000 miles away from her center, Russia was rather weak, especially since there was only one railway uniting that center with Russia's Far Eastern possessions. Moreover, Japan planned to inflict a knockout blow on the Russian Navy in Port Arthur; that dress rehearsal of Pearl Harbor proved to be successful. After 18 months of fighting, Russia was defeated, but not knocked out; in this case, the two parties were wrong. But, prior to actual fighting, each had good reasons to expect victory.

The Franco-Prussian War

Let us now go still deeper into history. The Franco-Prussian war of 1870-1 began as the result of a lasting and generalized conflict between the two nations. France suffered from a setback which had been caused by the increase of Prussia's strength through two successful wars, without "compensation" for France, which, in those days was taken for granted. Prussia wanted to unify Germany around herself, including Alsace, but had not yet openly proclaimed that goal.

Three aggravating circumstances were present: 1) an inveterate feud existed between the two states; 2) a prestige situation was created against France by the nomination of a Prussian prince to the Spanish throne and also by the notorious Ems depeche; 3) the desire of the French government to lift up its inner authority through a victory outside, her prestige having badly declined because the preceding war, the Mexican, ended in the terrible catastrophe of the capture and execution of Emperor Maximilian imposed on Mexico by France. Negotiations were conducted, but resulted only in creating the second and decisive prestige situation.

France attempted mediation after the outbreak of hostilities, but the powers approached declined to interfere. The relative strength of the parties was indeterminate. Both nations seemed to have good armies and good generals. Prussia relied on the better education of her younger generation and on a better system of mobilization. France expected that the South German states would remain neutral and that Austria (defeated by Prussia four years earlier) would join her. Of course, no normative inhibitions were present.

The Wars for the Unification of Italy and Germany

The wars for the unification of Italy (1859) and of Germany (mainly that of 1866) originated on the background of a tension between the rising tide of German and Italian nationalism demanding such unification, and the resistance of "the vested interests," i.e., governments of the fractionary states, whose survival made unification impossible. In both cases, one of the states (Sardinia-Piedmont in Italy, Prussia in Germany), became the champion of the national idea; in this way, an antagonistic situation arose between them and the rest of the fractionary states, especially with Austria. Austria counted among its possessions the Kingdom of Lombardo-Venetia, and, indirectly, the states of Parma, Modena and Tuscany. In Germany, in addition to large German speaking provinces, Austria held chairmanship of the German Union, a loose confederacy created by the Vienna peace treaties (1815). While Austria was German ruled (the dynasty and the court were entirely German), in Italy she was an alien occupant. Consequently, in Italy large portions of the population were soul and heart with the Piedmontese aspirations (as shown by the unsuccessful revolutionary movements of the years 1848-9 aiming at the ouster of the occupants).[3] However, in Germany the aspirations of the nationalists were divided between a small-Germany plan (unification around Prussia with the elimination of Austria despite her German possessions) and the great-Germany plan (unification around Austria).

In both cases the latent antagonism was exacerbated by additional developments. After the failure, in 1848, of the attempt to oust the Austrians from Italy (*Italia fara da se*), the Piedmontese government understood that it had to be assisted by one of the great powers if it hoped to succeed. This could only be France where the regime of Napoleon III was highly nationalistic and, moreover, looked for military glory and expansion in any possible direction. The most desirable acquisitions were French-speaking Savoy and Nice which belonged to Sardinia-Piedmont. But it was impossible for France to make war on the latter. Her national interest could be best satisfied by demanding from Austria the cession of Lombardo-

Venetia to Piedmont and requesting from Piedmont the cession of the two provinces aforementioned (much smaller and poorer than Lombardo-Venetia). Since the latter belonged to Austria, the anticipated exchange of territory between France and Piedmont created an acute conflict between France and Austria, a conflict which may be classified as a specimen of the nationalistic modality of territorial antagonisms.

The Austro-Prussian conflict about the unification of Germany began in the fateful year 1848, the year of a Pan-European revolution.[4] Toward the middle 1860's it was aggravated by a dispute about the administration of the duchies of Schleswig and Holstein which, since 1848, formed a condominium of Austria and Prussia. On the background of the more general and already inveterate conflict about unification, the dispute received an ominous character.

Negotiations were tried, of course, but in both cases rather insincerely: on the part of Austria's antagonists, France and Piedmont in one case, Prussia and the young Kingdom of Italy in the other case which joined Prussia to bring forward the total unification of all Italian lands, and definitely wanted war. The negotiations were hopeless from the very start since, in each case, one of the parties was firmly resolved not to concede anything short of the goal, and the other party, Austria, was obviously unwilling even to discuss concessions.

The appraisal of the relative strength of the parties was, subjectively, one of a fair chance of victory for both sides. The France of Napoleon III remembered that, through the years 1792-1814, she had always beaten Austria, except the last time when Austria was assisted by Russia and Prussia; in 1859, there was no danger of such assistance. The adjunction of small but valiant Sardinia-Piedmont increased the probability of French victory because the armies of that Kingdom had fought well against overwhelming Austrian forces in 1848-49 and proved to be well equipped and led during the Crimean war. Moreover, the Kingdom was now the point of orientation for all the nationalists throughout Italy, especially those living in the provinces which were directly involved.

In 1866, Prussia had good reasons to expect victory despite her smaller population: her army was obviously superior to that of Austria. She discounted the eventual assistance to Austria on the part of the medium and small German states— actually this assistance proved to be negligible. Finally, Prussia was sure that the newly formed Kingdom of Italy would join her and thus retain an appreciable part of the Austrian army in the southwest portion of the Austrian Empire. But, in both cases, Austria did not view herself as in a desperate position. After all, at the outbreak of the war in 1859, she could look back at her victory over Piedmont in 1849. The French were far away behind the Alps and would probably feel it necessary to keep a large army of observation along the Rhine, to prevent an eventual aggression of Prussia whose armaments had been spectacular for several years. In 1866, Austria counted on strong support of the German states who were threatened by a forcible annexation by a too strong Prussia. The interference of Italy was considered unlikely and was not too highly estimated. The latter proved to be true: both on land and the sea the relatively small Southern army of Austria inflicted defeats on the Italians. The rest of the Austrian estimates proved to be wrong. But when the Austro-Prussian war began, common opinion in Europe forecast a protracted war ending in stalemate. Napoleon III already anticipated the role of the arbitrator between the parties to the conflict and hoped to gain some compensation for France (probably the Grand Duchy of Luxemburg, perhaps even more).

Consequently, in both cases, the conditions necessary to elicit war were present. There were serious conflicts of a territorial nature engendered by the discrepancy of existing political boundaries and the demands of ebullient nationalism among the Italians and the Germans (partly, even among the French). No normative inhibitions existed in any of the participant states.[5] Conciliatory procedures were resorted to, mainly to satisfy the etiquette that prevailed in the European "concert of nations." But one could not possibly expect that Austria would voluntarily renounce her dominant position both in Italy and Germany, based on the existential equilibrium as it had been in 1815. In retrospect, the parties to the two conflicts were not fools when they considered that their chances of victory were good.

The Crimean War

The Crimean war (1853-56) started as one of the many Russo-Turkish wars, but developed into a war of a coalition consisting of England, France, Turkey and Sardinia-Piedmont against Russia. On the surface, this war seems to have been engendered by a conflict of claims of Roman Catholics and Greek Orthodox for the possession of the Holy Places in Jerusalem. In actuality, this was one of the most outspoken power conflicts, a conflict between states aiming at the increase of their political influence in a specified area, eventually resisting such an increase to specified opponents. The area was the Near East, approximately in the boundaries of the Turkish Empire.

116

The main contenders were Russia and England. Since the age of Catherine the Great (1762-96), Russia had made successive inroads into the territory of the disintegrating Ottoman Empire and obviously aimed at making it a kind of satellite or annex. England had a strong *negative* interest in not allowing Russia to gain dominance in that region. France had a double interest. Since the restoration of the Empire (1852) she was ostentatiously striving for the restoration of her place among the great powers which she lost with the crushing defeat suffered under Napoleon I (1815). Emperor Napoleon III was backed by the majority of the French elite which, after having overthrown the restored monarchy of the Bourbons (1830), craved for the restoration of the French *gloire*, on par with England and Russia, then obviously occupying the top positions. This elite withdrew their support from the July monarchy of Louis Philippe d'Orléans because that monarchy did little for the fulfillment of these cravings.[6] In addition, since 1850 (when the later Napoleon III still was the Prince-President), the French diplomacy supported by all means the claims of the Catholic Church and ostentatiously protected the Pontifical State from being absorbed by an Italian movement of unification.

For Sardinia, participation in a victorious war of coalition (she joined only when the outcome was almost certain) was an instrument of gaining prestige to facilitate her later successful leadership of the unification movement in Italy (1859-1862 and later). No territorial claims were involved; this is confirmed by the fact that the Paris Peace Treaty (1856) included an almost symbolic cession by Russia of a small part of Bessarabia (conquered from Turkey in 1812) to the principality of Moldavia, then a vassal state of Turkey. But the

117

power conflict was really serious: had Russia been granted the demands she formulated in 1853, the balance of power would have changed significantly in her favor, in the Near and Middle East and indirectly in all continental Europe.

Of course, negotiations were tried. They had been going on for several years prior to the outbreak of a really acute, though still non-violent, conflict. The date of this conflict can be identified with the presentation, in April, 1853, of a Russian note to Turkey demanding that the Greek Orthodox Church in Turkey be placed under the protection of Russia. On the advice of Great Britain, Turkey rejected the note. Both sides then shifted to using the instrument of military intimidation: the Russians occupied the Danubian principalities (Moldavia and Wallachia) and the Western powers responded by sending their fleets to the southern entrance of the Turkish Straits. War actually started in October, 1853, when the Turks crossed over the Danube and several engagements between her army and the Russians took place. In November, 1853, the Russians destroyed the Turkish fleet at Sinope. Still negotiations continued, mainly in London and Vienna. A final note was delivered at St. Petersburg in January, 1854, and only when it was rejected by Russia did the Western powers declare war on her; Turkey had already done so on Sept. 14, 1853.

War broke out in a situation of uncertainty about the outcome; in other words, both parties were considered to have a fair chance of victory. Emperor Nicholas I of Russia acted on the assumption that Turkey was moribund and that resolute action would result in the acquisition of a major part of the heritage (to be partitioned between Russia and the Western Powers). He assumed (and was not far from being right) that the Western Powers would not grant Turkey their all-out support. He overestimated the fighting capacity of his army, basing his judgment on the tremendous successes of the years 1812-1814; it recurs only too often that national leaders estimate the chances of victory in a prospective war on the basis of past achievements without taking into consideration the changes which took place since. Finally, he counted on at least a benevolent neutrality on the part of Austria which he had saved from collapse in the year 1849 by sending his troops to fight the Hungarian rebels who otherwise might have gained independence for their country. In that regard, he was badly frustrated: Austria displayed "black ingratitude" and took a position friendly to the Western Powers which prevented Russia from concentrating sufficient forces in the Crimea where war with the Western Powers was actually being fought.

The Western Powers relied on their superior naval strength, which, they believed, would grant them the possibility to land armies in various parts of Russia and from there advance toward the vital parts of the Russian Empire. However, they underestimated the resistance of the Russian soldiers and could not foresee that a military genius called Todtleben would check, for almost a year, their advance from an insignificant port of the Crimean peninsula. They also did not realize that their generalship had reached one of the lowest levels in military history. But they won, so their total estimate of the situation proved right. However, as testified to by later events, at the time of the outbreak of the war both sides had, subjectively, good reasons to believe in victory.

Once again, the concomitance of conditions making likely the outbreak of a war was present in the situation which preceded the Crimean war.

The European Wars, 1792-1815

The series of wars in Europe which lasted from 1792 to 1815 started as a limited war, quite common in that age. The antagonism which formed the background was primarily ideological, but gradually was reinforced by secondary antagonisms of various types. The original conflict developed between the revolutionary ideas which had gained the upper hand in France since 1789, and the forces of tradition represented by Austria and Prussia. The revolutionary ideas threatened to spread in the western possessions of the two powers and, in the long-range, to undermine the very principle of hereditary and absolute monarchy. Originally, the leaders of revolutionary France had no intention to "export" their ideal to the neighboring countries. But in the confused situation which then prevailed along the boundary of France and the German Empire, some of the German princes (secular and ecclesiastical), had been dispossessed by the revolution since their possessions were simultaneously under France and the Empire. (The Empire's head was simultaneously the monarch of Austria-Hungary-Bohemia and the Southern Netherlands.) On the other hand, the French leaders perceived a direct threat of intervention in the accumulation of French *émigrés,* armed and organized, in the land of the Elector of Trier, across the French boundary. War was desired by those monarchists still within France because they felt that France would be victorious in a limited war and this would restore the prestige of the monarchy not yet abolished; the leftists wanted war because they hoped that precisely the opposite would happen—victory would strengthen the new revolutionary regime. The expectation of favorable developments inside a country as a consequence of victory is one of the circumstances aggravating a conflict—and this existed independently of these contradictory hopes.

There was a long exchange of diplomatic notes in the year preceding the outbreak of the war (April 10, 1792), supplemented by numerous conversations between ministers of foreign affairs and diplomats of the opposite party. But, since the antagonistic situation was primarily ideological and was aggravated because of bright expectations in France, no compromise could be found. Both parties believed that they had good reasons to assume that victory would be theirs. The Austrians and the Prussians believed that the chaotic state of France caused by the revolutionary turmoil would make her an easy prey. The Frenchmen hoped that the war could be limited to the electorate of Trier only partly supported by Austria, but not by Prussia—there was even some foolish hope that Prussia could eventually become an ally. The French relied on the additional strength given to their armed forces by revolutionary enthusiasm.

Events proved that the Austro-Prussians were wrong and the French right, due to the embodiment of revolutionary enthusiasm into an important social invention, "the people's army." This social invention represented a shift from the traditional structure of the army (usually small, consisting of mercenaries recruited among less desirable elements) to a mass army based on conscription and carried by an idea—the revolutionary idea, of course. These were *"les gros bataillons"* that Napoleon later relied on.

There is no need to analyze separately the origin of further wars which entered history under the name of the Wars of the Second to the Sixth Coalition, except the last one which finally brought to an end the period of almost uninterrupted hostilities between the major powers. The Coalitions Nos. Two to Five had basically the same background, though the combination of factors showed a dynamic development. The outcome of the War of the First Coalition (Prussia and Austria vs. France) allowed France to annex territories along her Eastern boundary and widely spread the appeal of the new principles (especially the abolition of feudal rights and of obsolete forms of government). The next Coalition wars were engendered by the revenge attitudes of the Central Powers and the persistent hostility of England (who had joined, though in a limited form only, the First Coalition in 1793). England could not tolerate the expansion of France to the estuaries of the Scheldt and the Maas. (This was one of the most important negative interests of England.) These attitudes were opposed by France's natural desire to preserve her acquisitions, first up to the "natural boundary" of the Rhine (an idea of revolutionary origin), and later on, up to ever-expanding boundaries to the East (in Germany; after the victorious outcome of the Fourth Coalition war, also in Poland) and to the Southeast (in Italy). France vindicated these boundaries for strategic reasons and especially sought them as a decisive weapon against the economic interests of England whose implacable hostility made the new edifice of the French Empire rather precarious.

Most conspicuous was, however, the origin of the war of the Sixth Coalition which started as a war of all the states of Western and Central Europe against Russia, seconded by England. The peace treaty of Tilsit (1807) terminated the war of the Fourth Coalition. It contained the germs of the accentuation of an antagonistic situation which had never passed away since 1792. Russia had been forced to accede to the continental blockade directed against England which deprived Russia of her most important source of import. At that time, Napoleon promised not to foster any further expansion of Poland (partly restored by the same treaty as the Duchy of Warsaw), and to respect the territorial rights of small German princes (some of them were under a kind of informal Russian protectorate). Moreover, the peace treaty tacitly divided the old continent into two spheres of influence: France in Western and Central Europe, and Russia in Eastern Europe including the Balkans and eventually Scandinavia. A situation obtained similar to that now prevailing: two super-powers confronting each other, but both expansionist. Expansionist motivations were evident on France's part, but they were also strong in Russia's war against Turkey (1806-12) from which she acquired the province of Bessarabia, dominating the mouths of the Danube, and against Sweden (1808-9) from which she detached Finland. There were further differences from today's situation: at that time the conflict was no longer primarily ideological, but rather a power conflict. Moreover, there remained a third super-power, England, in the final outcome the strongest of the three.

The antagonistic situation gradually developed into an acute conflict through violation of the treaty of Tilsit by the two major parties. By ingenious devices, Russia circumvented the restrictions imposed on her by the continental blockade. France first enlarged the Duchy of Warsaw by territories ceded by Austria after the disastrous outcome of the Fifth Coalition (1809), then annexed some principalities in northwestern Germany, among them the Duchy of Oldenburg (dynastically tied with the Russian Empire), and did not allow Russia to go as far as she wanted in the conquest of Turkish territories. Both sides knew that the treaty of Tilsit was merely a truce and were arming for another war, which broke out on June 24, 1812.

The event itself was preceded by numerous letters exchanged by Napoleon and Alexander, Emperor of Russia, diplomatic conversations and correspondence aiming principally, on the part of both France and Russia, to impose the role of the aggressor on the other. The negotiations were rather hopeless. The Tilsit treaty had created an unstable equilibrium which could be made durable only by France's or Russia's decisive victory. Naturally, neither was ready to accept a solution making the other the overlord of Europe.

Both sides had reasons to believe that victory would be theirs. Napoleon relied on *les gros bataillons* since he could attack Russia with an army of 500,000 men and be opposed only by 220,000 Russians. For the first time, France was seconded by a coalition embracing all continental Europe, except Spain and Portugal. In these two abstaining countries, French armies fought "rebels" who would not submit to their rule. The coalition also embraced Turkey, then master of the whole Balkan peninsula and currently at war with Russia. Napoleon could even expect that Turkey would join him to avenge four consecutive defeats by Russia in the course of half a century. He could also expect that Sweden would join him, to reconquer at least Finland, and perhaps some of the provinces lost to Russia in the 18th century. The majority of European diplomats and military experts shared Napoleon's assessment of the situation.

Russia counted on the device of trading space for time and Russia's ability to defeat any enemy that advanced too far into her territory (the famous Scythian tactics). This is known from reports of Alexander's talks with the French ambassador Caulaincourt and his letters to his beloved sister Catherine. Alexander knew (Napoleon did not) that Sweden would keep to benevolent neutrality—her acting monarch, the former French General Bernadotte, clandestinely had been promised Norway in case of Napoleon's defeat. Alexander also correctly foresaw that he would terminate the war with Turkey before the start of Napoleon's invasion. He also counted, quite correctly, on the diversion caused by England's help to the Spanish and Portuguese "rebels" and on the heterogeneity of the coalition of France with two recent enemies, Austria and Prussia. Both of these nations preferred Russian victory, allowing them later on to change sides. With Austria, Alexander had conducted a most secret correspondence which allowed him almost to disregard the presence of an auxiliary Austrian corps in the Grand Army. As to Prussia, she had been forced by Napoleon (after the Tilsit treaty) to reduce her army to a minimum.

Events proved that Russia was right and France wrong in the estimate of the chances of victory. But, as has already been stated, early in 1812 the majority of well-informed persons in Europe were almost certain of Napoleon's victory.

The Great European Wars, 1740-48 and 1756-63

From 1740 to 1763, war was waged in Europe and in the European colonies in America and India. All the major and medium size nations were at least temporarily involved—England, France, Spain, Austria, Prussia, Russia, Poland, Saxony, Bavaria, Holland, Sardinia, Naples, and many others. War was interrupted many times by separate peace treaties which were usually broken a few months later. In 1748 a general peace treaty was signed at Aachen, but hostilities between France and England continued on the seas and in the colonies. Then, in 1756, general war flared up again in Europe, with a peculiar "reversion of alliances," partners of the first period of intensive fighting now struggling against each other and former foes becoming allies. Historians distinguish two wars, the war of Austrian succession, 1740-48, and the Seven-Years War, 1756-63. But sociologically one may speak of one multi-phase war which would well deserve to be called the First World War.

For the purposes of this study, it is sufficient to contemplate the original movement from peace to war in 1740 and the second major movement in 1756.

The first movement may be understood as an accentuation of two inveterate conflicts: one between France and England, for the dominance on the open sea and in oversea territories, the other between France and Austria, for hegemony in Continental Europe. These conflicts were aggravated and accentuated by a number of movements on the European chessboard, manifesting the then almost unrestricted tendency of aggrandizement at the expense of vulnerable neighbors.

In 1740, a situation arose which made Austria an easy prey of her neighbors. With the death of Charles VI, the house of the Hapsburgs was actually extinct, for there were no male descendants of former Austrian monarchs affiliated through a line of males. The laws of succession were different in the various parts of the Hapsburg domain. But, according to the desire of Charles VI, the throne passed to his daughter Maria-Theresa. To prevent the dismemberment of the monarchy and to secure the accession of his daughter to all the thrones, Charles VI had first negotiated with the "estates" of his various states, and having received their agreement, issued the Pragmatic Sanction (1724) proclaiming the indivisibility of his domains. Then, he negotiated with all the virtual pretenders and granted them small concessions in exchange for their confirmation of the Pragmatic Sanction. But despite the formal renunciation of their claims, at the death of Charles VI, almost all the pretenders to parts of his heritage (based on marriage of Austrian princesses with foreign monarchs) renewed their claims. They were supported by France from the start, which without being a pretender, looked for an opportunity to take revenge for the humiliating peace treaties which terminated the last wars of Louis XIV.

One of the pretenders, just the one whose interference was least expected, was the first to act. This was King Frederic II of Prussia (whose father owed the title of King to Charles VI). He revived old pretensions of the Hohenzollerns on the duchies forming Silesia, despite formal renunciation by his predecessors. In his memoirs, Frederic explained his decision to grab Silesia as follows: he had a well trained army ready for combat, a well replenished treasury, and the superiority of his own personality (which he never doubted, and perhaps, with good reasons). So, after short and fruitless negotiations, he invaded Silesia and soon occupied it in totality. This encouraged all the enemies of Austria. On May 18, 1741, a treaty was signed at Nymphenburg between France, Spain, and Bavaria (later on joined by Saxony and Sardinia). The treaty aimed at the dismemberment of Austria and was supplemented on June 6 by a treaty of alliance between France and Prussia, thus consolidating the anti-Austrian coalition. Maria-Theresa applied for help to England, who promised a subsidy and limited assistance by an auxiliary army on the continent—she preferred to reserve the bulk of her strength to fight France in the colonies; but indirectly this certainly meant a substantial increase in Austria's chances. Toward the end of the first phase of the war, the Austro-English coalition was joined by Russia.

From the statements above it appears that the outbreak of

the major war provoked by the death of Charles VI was preceded by the maturing of a cluster of antagonisms. The nature of the conflicts was purely territorial, between greedy states desiring the acquisition of additional territories and a state whose territory, because of a particular combination of circumstances, could be claimed by other states with a semblance of justification. The particular claims reinforced the others, because each pretender aspired to acquire a different part of the Austrian heritage. But the Franco-Austrian and the Anglo-French antagonisms were rather power conflicts, the second one being reinforced by economic considerations, namely, command of the oversea trade. The first condition of the outbreak of war was certainly present.

It also appears from the statements above that the outbreak of the conflict was preceded by an unusually long period of negotiations which seemed to have come to a happy conclusion. On paper all the problems were solved. Later events proved that this was not the case. New negotiations began, but the very fact of the wholesale breach of all promises, made them rather futile from the very start.

The last condition, a favorable estimate of the chances of victory by all the parties to the conflict, was also present. Frederic's summary of his estimate has already been reported. Moreover, he and his allies knew that Austria's army had been weakened by several unsuccessful wars with Turkey and that her treasury was empty. Nevertheless, Austria, incomparably larger and more populated than Prussia, had no reason to despair. By the way, that was a period in Austrian history when cohesion between its component parts was stronger than ever before or after, largely because of the attractive personality of Maria-Theresa, well loved by her subjects. This cohesion was one more reason for expecting victory.

Frederic's immediate and easy victory in the first campaign (1740-41) encouraged the other pretenders and France (the force behind them) to evaluate highly the chance of victory. It is obvious that Austria could not stand the combined assault of the coalition formed against her, if its members remained united. But each of them thought only of its own interests and was always ready to sign a separate peace or even to change sides (as did Sweden). This was "the miracle that saved Austria."

The war ended in a stalemate expressed in terms of the peace treaty of Aachen. Frederic got the major part of Silesia but otherwise the *status quo ante* was restored. Nobody was satisfied. Maria-Theresa openly spoke of revenge from the very start. Dissatisfaction was high in France who had fought for several years—to no avail. The boundaries between the English and French colonial empires in America and India remained as uncertain as they had been. Everywhere the feeling prevailed that the peace treaty was only a truce and even an incomplete one. As has already been mentioned, hostilities between France and England did not stop on the sea and overseas.

The outbreak of the second phase of intensive fighting, the Seven Years War, was a consequence of this situation. However, it presented a significant difference as compared with that of 1740: a new and strong military power had emerged, Prussia, menacing all her neighbors. Austria was strongly affected, since her unquestioned primacy in Germany was now challenged. As a consequence, her hostility toward France went down and she soon joined her in an alliance against

Prussia. France did not want Prussia to dominate in the Northern part of Germany, under French influence since the peace treaty of Westphalia (1648). Since France was now with Austria, England, France's arch foe, had to look for an alliance with Austria's bitter enemy, Prussia; Russia stood before the choice of joining the Franco-Austrian coalition, or the new Anglo-Prussian coalition; she decided to choose the former alternative, partly because Empress Elizabeth of Russia coveted East Prussia, the acquisition of which would have encircled Poland. Such was the alignment of the major powers during the second phase of the Great War of the mid-eighteenth century.

The renewal of hostilities was preceded by several years of negotiations which, this time, were conducted by parties aware that war was ahead—the only question being who would fight whom. As has been said already, England for a while was ready to take the side of Austria, her ally of the years 1741-48, but Austria demanded a high subsidy; so England aligned herself with Prussia who requested much less. Russia first signed a treaty of alliance with England, then repudiated it and signed another with Austria; minor powers were anxious to join the camp which seemed to be stronger. When France and Austria signed the Treaty of Versailles (May 1, 1756), war became almost inevitable. Austria started concentrating troops in Bohemia, across the new boundary in Silesia. Frederic requested explanations which he found unsatisfactory and, as in 1740, started the war by a sudden invasion of Saxony, an ally of Austria.

This time the conflict was not primarily territorial, but rather a power conflict, in the meaning of the assertion of the predominance of certain states over the rest. Frederic's reception of information about the Austro-French alliance worked as an operator.

During the years of the truce Austria had worked hard to improve her army and had reasons to believe that this time she would be victorious. Prussia alone could not have stood an assault by three major powers, Austria, France and Russia; but she was not alone; behind her there was England, and this was decisive. With England's subsidy, Frederic could maintain an army of 200,000 in the field. Remember that in those days one could hire subsidiary armies to make up for the insufficiency of one's own population. Frederic's adversaries never had more than 300,000 in the field. Their armies, especially the French one, were inferior to that of Prussia, and the anti-Prussian coalition never was united. By the way, there was never any formal alliance between France and Russia. Each army fought with particularistic interests as background for military decisions, taking little care of the allies. In general, these facts could not escape Frederic II who considered, and not without reason, that his inferiority in numbers would be made up by much better generalship. Finally, England proved to be much stronger than France in the colonies.

Nevertheless, toward the end of 1761 Prussia was in a desperate position. "The miracle that saved Prussia" was the death, on January 5, 1762, of Empress Elizabeth of Russia. She was succeeded by her nephew Peter III, a German prince himself (the Duke of Holstein), and a fervent admirer of Frederic II. He immediately signed a separate peace treaty with Frederic. With Russia's defection, the anti-Prussian coalition no longer had a chance to win. France paid the bill by the loss of almost the totality of her colonial Empire to England. England was the true and only winner of this set of wars in the mid-eighteenth century.

Today we know the outcome. But in 1756, in each country entering the war there were very good reasons to believe that the coalition which it joined would be victorious. In the course of the war, until the end of 1761, the strength of the parties seemed to be almost equal; only then did Russia inflict decisive blows on Prussia and then, a few months later, because of the whim of the new ruler, withdraw. The almost incredible versatility of the military situation during the years of war justifies, *ex post facto,* the optimistic evaluation by both camps of the chance to win. This allows us to say that the third condition of the outbreak of a war was present just as, beyond doubt, the first and second were, too.

The Thirty Years War

Almost forty years of continuous war dominate the history of Europe in the seventeenth century. From 1618 to 1648 there were sequences of interrelated wars in the German Empire; this was the so-called "Thirty Years War." But non-German powers joined it almost from the start. In 1648, peace was restored in Germany, but not between France and Spain, two major non-German participants of the war who fought until 1659. On the other hand, during the first two years of the Thirty Years War, war, in the strict meaning of the term, existed less than rebellion of a state (Bohemia) against its monarch (simultaneously Emperor of the Holy Empire, King of Hungary and Archduke of Austria). Although this monarch was assisted by Duke Maximilian of Bavaria, nevertheless the sociological nature of the conflict in its first phase was revolution, not war. This revolution *led* to a war by a peculiar concatenation of circumstances. The rebellious Czechs elected Count Palatine Frederic V to the throne of Bohemia. Naturally, he started using the forces of his hereditary state to keep his newly acquired domain. So, war broke out between Austria seconded by Bavaria and the Palatinate. This war elicited a chain reaction, the sequence of wars under study here.

As acknowledged by the historians, the original antagonism was rather insignificant; but it worked as an operator which actualized a number of serious, until then latent, antagonisms. First of all, there was the antagonism between Protestants and Catholics which, of course, was not limited to Germany. The Reformation had ended with partial victory by the Protestants, sanctioned by the religious peace treaty of Augsburg (1555); this treaty acknowledged the fact that some of the German principalities had become Protestant and the treaty created a *modus vivendi* between them and the Catholics. But this was a compromise hated by both parties. A new outbreak of hostilities was delayed by several factors: the approximate balance of power of the two parties, the mutual exhaustion caused by forty years of religious troubles, and a number of minor conflicts within the two camps. In 1608 and 1609 a Protestant Union and a Catholic League were formed; but each included only a small part of the states involved and not the most important ones; moreover, the inner cohesion of the two groups was rather weak.

Secondly, there was an established conflict between the Hapsburg powers (Austria and Spain with their numerous dependencies), and France, often joined by other non-Hapsburg powers. The Austro-Spanish combination included a vast colonial Empire and threatened to become a universal state possessing overwhelming power and able to dictate its will to the rest of the world. France was the most threatened nation, since Spain possessed a large part of what is today Eastern France (Burgundy) and the Netherlands,[7] thus encircling her. Spain nurtured a grand style plan to create a territorial link between her Italian possessions, especially Milan, and Burgundy-Netherlands. Obviously, this went against vital interests of France.

Thirdly, there gradually developed an antagonism between the German Emperor (who, with rare interruptions, was also the monarch of Austria—Hungary—Bohemia) and the territorial princes. Since the end of the Hohenstauffen dynasty (thirteenth century) Germany evolved toward the emancipation of the territorial princes from any dependency on the Empire. At the beginning of the seventeenth century, the power of the Emperor as such was almost nil; but the princes feared lest the Emperor, as the territorial prince of a state which by far exceeded the area and population of any other state in the Empire and was moreover seconded by the Spanish branch of the Hapsburgs, should impose his power on them.

Fourthly, there was, in the domain of the Austrian branch of the Hapsburgs, a latent antagonism between the "estates" of the non-Austrian lands (especially Bohemia, Hungary and Transylvania) and their common sovereign who displayed the tendency to centralize the government and to reduce the individual kingdoms to mere provinces.

The four conflicts did not separate seventeenth-century Europe into two clear-cut camps. Powers which belonged to the same camp relative to the first conflict often found themselves in opposite camps relative to the second and third conflicts. It is true that the Austro-Spanish combination was leading the Catholic camp. But France, another great Catholic nation, was the pivot of resistance against the Hapsburgs' pretensions for world rule. In the course of the events of 1618-59, many Catholic powers of Germany joined the opposite camp whenever the "Imperials" seemed to have gained too much strength. This absence of clear-cut separation between the camps explains the delay in the reopening of the conflict created by the Reformation, the length of the struggle, and the tendency of the conflict to flare up again whenever a solution by the measurement of the relative strength seemed to have taken place; new participants joined the war when they perceived that the solution which seemed to have been reached granted too much power to their particular antagonists.

The revolt of Bohemia occurred under circumstances presenting great similarity with the revolt of the Netherlands against Spain:[8] the estates, Protestant in their majority, could not accept the counter-reformation, or the restoration of Catholicism as the only permissible religion, which was imposed by Ferdinand, their new monarch. In addition to religious freedom, they also wanted to maintain the old rights and privileges of medieval origin also threatened by Ferdinand's inclination to absolutism. During the first ten years, war was waged mainly on the background of the first and fourth conflicts, but as unanimously acknowledged by the historians, gradually the center of gravity shifted to the second conflict and, with respect to Germany, also to the third.

The outcome of the forty years of war was this: the conflict between the Austro-Spanish combination (the Hapsburg domain) and their opponents was solved in favor of France which became the leading power on the continent of Europe. The conflict between the Emperor and the territorial princes was solved, due to the interference of France and Sweden, in favor of the princes; the Empire continued to exist, but as a ceremonial institution only. The conflict between Catholics and Protestants was terminated by reciprocal acceptance of the *status quo ante* (with minor exceptions); but this time the adversaries learned the lesson and never again tried (at least in Germany) to impose their religion outside of the states in which it had gained dominance according to the principle *cujus regio, ejus religio*. The fourth conflict, not interstate in its nature, could not be solved by any peace treaty. The Emperor, again King of Bohemia, won there, but had to keep the estates going on in Hungary.

Returning to the outbreak of the war, we may state that the first condition was present. The statements above have aimed at analyzing the total conflict into its constituent parts and giving them precision.

As to the second condition, negotiations did not precede the first stages of the Thirty Years War since in the beginning that was only a local conflict, of an intra-state nature. But, prior to taking to the arms, the parties to the religious conflict in Germany had lived through a long period (60 years) of co-existence similar to the cold war of our day. That co-existence broke down when one of the parties, represented by Ferdinand, Archduke of Austria and King of Bohemia, decided to go ahead and thus destroyed the precarious equilibrium reached at Augsburg. Of course, he had not the slightest idea that a major war would ensue. The major part of the successive entrances into the war of various powers, large and small, were preceded by remonstrations, intimidation, sometimes negotiations, until it became clear that the particular dispute no longer could be solved peacefully.

The third condition was also present. The complexity of

the conflict, the chance that new participants would join the struggle in case of a serious defeat of one or another party, even the chance that some of the participants would change sides (which actually happened several times), allowed each of the parties to entertain the hope that it would be victorious and thus achieve its particular ends. There had been a lot of miscalculations—the acceptance of the Bohemian crown by the Count Palatine, although his adversary, Ferdinand, had a lot of trouble in various parts of his heterogeneous domain; the Count expected to be assisted by his father-in-law, King James I of England (which did not materialize); the interference of King Christian IV of Denmark who was badly beaten by the Imperials; and the very participation of Spain which committed a mistake common to Empires—overextension of aims beyond her real force. But, in those days, Spain's strength was generally overestimated throughout the world. The best assessment of the situation was made by France led by Cardinal Richelieu. In the vast majority of cases, the rulers making the decision to start war had good reasons to believe that it would be crowned by victory.

Two Negative Cases

To conclude, let us analyze a few negative cases. Why did war not break out in 1938? The basic conflict between Germany and the powers of the West was already present, but was not yet so acute as one year later; especially, no prestige situation had obtained. Each party could reasonably hope to achieve its goal without war: Germany could believe that the powers of the West, not having interfered with the remilitarization of the Rhineland and the Anschluss and being ready to grant her the Sudetenland, would acquiesce to further expansion. Britain believed that "peace for our time" was possible through appeasement, and Roosevelt's appeals to the eventual belligerents fortified that belief. The third condition of the origin of war, approximate parity of the strength of the parties to the conflict, and therefore fair reason to hope for the best, was present, but, in the absence of the second, and low intensity of the first, it did not work. Therefore, war did not break out.

Another negative case occurred in 1908. After the annexation of Bosnia-Herzegovina by Austria-Hungary, a serious conflict arose between the latter and Russia whose sphere of interest had been hurt in Serbia. Germany, Austria's ally, submitted a quasi-ultimatum, and Russia desisted from her plans of helping Serbia. In this case, the third condition was conspicuous by its absence: Russia's army was not strong enough to fight against the joint armies of the Central Empires, and she had no hope of being supported by France and Britain.

Throughout the positive and negative cases studied in this chapter, the basic hypothesis proved to work. It could be shown to work in many other instances. Perhaps the peculiarities of some additional cases would require refinements and modifications.

But, could one ask, does the hypothesis "explain" anything? One may assert that it does. It offers a common denominator behind the cases studied, though not of the type which people commonly expect of causal explanations. The common denominator is not an event of a pre-established type, but the gradual accumulation of definite conditions which, when complete, move two or more nations from the state of peace to that of war. A causal explanation of complex events must not and can not do more than that.

7/ The Movement from Order to Revolution

The Pre-Revolutionary Situation

Like the hypothesis on war causation unfolded in the preceding chapters, a hypothesis on the causation of revolution
must take into account: 1) the findings of the inductive study
of the conditions under which men resort to fighting in non-
political disputes; 2) the properties of the social system involved, i.e., the state; and 3) the thought model of social
causation.[1]

Revolution is a political conflict within a nation lifted to
the level of fighting between the government and an opposition party. In war the antagonists are homogeneous: two or

139

more nations represented by their governments and using their armed forces as instruments. In revolution the antagonists are heterogeneous and partly indetermined: the government is opposed by a group (a revolutionary party), or a revolutionary movement (sometimes led by a prophetic leader), or a revolutionary mob, quickly assembling and again dispersing. In the origin of a revolution it is of paramount importance whether the government is isolated, or supported by a minority which may be well or poorly organized, or by large masses, opposed by other, revolutionary masses. Consequently, in revolution, both opposing groups may be small; one may be small and the other large; or both may be large, comprising together almost the totality of the adult population.

The complexity of a revolution as a social phenomenon is not exhausted by these facts. While the government is *one* by necessity, and is more or less united, the revolutionary opposition may be united or divided into two or more factions competing or fighting with one another. Whereas in war there are two clear-cut parties, revolution may receive the shape of *bellum omnium contra omnes.* Each of the revolutionary factions may remain unorganized (a *mass*), or organized, on the lower level of a revolutionary *movement,* or on the higher level of a revolutionary *party* (eventually, a conspiracy).

Between a government and the revolutionary opposition, a sharp incompatibility of goals is necessarily present. The goal of the opposition (eventually, of each of its factions) is change in political leadership and/or change in the government's policy; in more drastic cases, change of the total political and/or social order. The goal of the government is *not* to cede political power and/or *not* to grant the demanded changes. Every revolution is reducible to the political phase of human co-existence. The point at issue is always this: who shall make the political decisions, and what shall these decisions be? But the dissent separating the government from the opposition may be *purely* political, or it may reflect, in political terms and demands, dissent in other phases of social and cultural life, just as war, though always waged on the political level, may reflect economic, nationalistic, religious or secular ideological conflicts.

Purely political antagonisms conducive to revolution may be divided into two levels. On the lower level, the existing organization of the government is not questioned, but, in the opposition's view, the existing government is inefficient, stupid, corrupt, oppressive, or combines two or more of these traits. The goal of the opposition, at least on the verbal level, is to replace inefficient and stupid personalities by efficient and intelligent ones, corrupt functionaries by models of honesty, abject tyrants by men respecting the freedom and dignity of their fellow men.

On the upper level, the very form of the government is questioned. In this case, new political ideals are involved. These new ideals were either generated in the society where the revolutionary movement is going on, or elsewhere, but received through diffusion. An absolute monarchy may be under attack on the part of believers in constitutional monarchy or republic, an aristocratic republic may be denounced in the name of democracy, and so on. But the bearers of "progressive" ideas have no monopoly: those preferring old fashioned monarchy or one of the brands of dictatorship may conspire against democracy and eventually become a revolutionary opposition.

Non-political movements may provoke revolutionary conflicts in the following way. Economic developments create new interests endorsed by new social classes but may remain rather unnoticed or not taken care of by the government. Trade and industry may have been added to traditional agriculture; but the government may remain in the hands of landlords, and it may arbitrarily protect the latter's interests and delay the reforms which would make the law and administrative practice adequate to the new economic structure. The development of industry may result in the formation of a large and self-conscious labor class demanding a higher share of the produce and equal status with management as to industrial relations; but the government may stubbornly refuse to pay attention to these demands and support the traditional structure of industry giving autocratic economic power to the owners of plants and mills. On the other hand, the economic conditions may deteriorate owing to soil erosion, exhaustion of valuable resources, too rapid population growth, loss of foreign markets, and so on; the situation demands resolute and well planned action, but the government remains inert, or acts in the wrong direction, at least in the judgment of many. Under these conditions, the rise of opposition, eventually revolutionary opposition, is likely.

Another important cause of the rise of opposition may be observed in multinational states. In such states, the government often fosters the interests and aspirations of one ethnic group, eventually, of a few ethnic groups, but not of all, and grants privileges at the expense of the residue. The policy may be of the assimilationist type: the ideal of cultural homogeneity is taken for granted by the dominant group, so that the recessive groups are demanded to forfeit their cultural heritage and to merge with the dominant group. So long as the recessive groups are dormant, or do not display interest in preserving their identity, no opposition is present. But a peculiar phenomenon, called national revival, such as the Czech revival of the first half of the nineteenth century, and the Flemish revival of the second half of the same century, sometimes takes place. Then, the assimilationist policies of the government start being opposed; the recessive group demands equality, or autonomy, or even political independence. This has been the case of Austria-Hungary where two groups, the Germans and the Magyars, dominated over nine allo-ethnic groups; and it was also the case, to a lesser extent, in the Russian Empire where, until the First World War, the majority of the non-Russian groups were dormant.

Conflicts of this type may be engendered another way also. In a multinational state, respect of the national cultures was taken for granted but, for one reason or another, the government shifts to the policy of assimilation. Naturally, this results in protest and opposition on the part of the recessive groups. This happened, for instance, in Russia where, until the 1880's very little assimilationism was observable; with the shift to an outspoken assimilationist policy, opposition, though originally rather mild, was awakened in the recessive groups.

Similar are conflicts with a religious, or in our day, also secular, ideological background. In a multi-denominational society, the government may favor one or another group and exert pressure on the other ones. These are likely to resist and to oppose the government.

An important factor in the emergence of revolutionary movements is the spread of education, sometimes even of information. Uneducated masses may remain docile for centuries despite misery and oppression. The situation changes if

143

and when the spread of education opens to many access to information about the possibility of life under conditions involving more satisfaction, more justice, more participation in wealth and culture. Sometimes the rise of class consciousness or national consciousness is caused by a small minority receiving education abroad and then diffusing knowledge around themselves; such had been the case in India, and also in vast areas around her in Asia and in Africa. Sometimes the possibility of a better life is demonstrated by members of an arrogant aristocracy or by functionaries and businessmen of a colonial power among conquered tribes. Such has been the mechanism of the revolt of Asian and African masses against European dominance.

If, in a nation, the soil is well prepared for the rise of a revolutionary opposition, events in other states may act as catalysts. In other words, by means of imitation and contagion, revolutionary movements in state A may suddenly exacerbate similar conflicts in state B. The July, 1830, revolution in France launched the Belgian revolution against the Netherlands, the Polish revolution against Russia, and numerous revolutions in Italy against the Austrian yoke. The February, 1848, revolution in France gave the signal to the outbreak of revolution in Milan, Berlin, Vienna, Prague and Budapest. The Communist revolution in Russia was reflected in similar attempts in Bavaria and Hungary and, many years later, generated the Communist revolution in China; in addition to this, in many countries it provoked the rise of revolutionary opposition against democratic governments. The Fascist revolution in Italy (1922) was reflected in similar revolutions in Spain (1923), Poland and Lithuania (1926) and Germany (1933); the latter provoked a secondary wave of Fascist revolutions in

Estonia, Latvia, Rumania and Bulgaria and Fascist movements elsewhere. Naturally, these revolutions never were caused by imitation only. The elements of a purely political conflict, or of a political conflict derived from economic, nationalistic or ideological conflicts were already present.

Antagonism between the government and movements representing new or newly awakened interests or ideas may remain unsolved for a long time. If this is the case, a development takes place similar to the one observed relative to war. The original roots of the conflict are almost forgotten. Each party to the conflict tries to inflict blame or even harm on the other party whenever the opportunity presents itself. Each success of one party is considered as a defeat of the other. No reform carried out by the government is accepted by the opposition because an appropriate reform changes unfavorably the distribution of influence and allegiance between the government and the opposition. Myths and legends are created and diffused by the two camps. Eventually, in addition to true ones, false atrocity stories are circulated against the government by the revolutionists. False statements about immorality among the members of revolutionary groups are circulated among groups standing behind the government, and so on. The history of Russia during the second half of the nineteenth century and the early twentieth century abounds in telling instances. The most conspicuous of them is probably the unanimous rejection, even denigration of Stolypin's agrarian reform by the opposition (revolutionary and non-revolutionary). *Ex post facto,* it is almost obvious that Stolypin's "middle way" (of which the agrarian reform was the most important item) was the only chance for Russia to escape the abyss of "total revolution."

The roots of conflicts conducive to revolution are as manifold as the roots of conflicts conducive to war. Despite their diversity, they are, by necessity, related to the coordinating function of the state. The state, represented by the government, must perform actions which would integrate into a smoothly working whole—into a going concern—the various groups of which the nation consists, each with a number of specified interests and aspirations. A complete coordination satisfying everybody is quite exceptional. In the majority of cases, the distance of actual coordination from the optimum is rather short, and therefore dissatisfaction is only partial and mild. But, in some cases, the government's coordinating actions are wrong, or insufficient, or at least they are considered to be so by important groups. Then, a revolution becomes possible.

Since the common denominator of revolutionary conflicts is miscarriage (objective or subjective) of the coordinating function of the state, these conflicts, by inner necessity, may be traced back to uneven and disharmonious development of the social system as a whole of which the political system is only a part. Uneven and disharmonious developments produce social tensions.

Social tensions arise from the interplay of two somewhat contradictory properties of social systems. First, every social system tends to be integrated, each part being adjusted to the others and to the whole. Second, individual parts of the whole, or subsystems, may develop semi-autonomously, according to laws particular to each. In other words, they may develop with differential velocity and in divergent directions. If, in a concrete case, two subsystems have developed disharmoniously (e.g., one very fast and the other very slowly, or not at all), there obtain social tensions between them, comparable to the tension of a rubber band attached to two balls pushed in divergent directions. The emergence of social tension contradicts, however, the principle of social integration, or the first of the two basic properties of social systems. If this takes place, certain forces inherent in a social system start working to restore the disturbed equilibrium. Commonly, they succeed; but if the disharmony has become too large, the system might break down; if the system is political, this is revolution.

From this proposition, a corollary may be drawn: revolutions are more likely in dynamic societies than in static societies because in dynamic societies social tensions may accumulate, while they cannot in static societies. This proposition is verified by the observation of the frequency distribution of revolutions such as the one carried out in Sorokin's *Social and Cultural Dynamics.*[2] This conformity of facts with expectations derived deductively from the hypothesis of the engendering of revolutions by social tensions or disharmonious development in the framework of social systems, makes the hypothesis at least plausible.

Social tensions may obtain between the various subsystems of the social system; but they become relevant in the context of this study only when they involve the political system. The government, which is a subsystem in the total social system, is the actor through which the coordinating function of the state is carried out; when a tension obtains, it should act to eliminate or alleviate it. But sometimes it does not act, or acts in the wrong way, or at least is supposed to do so by the opposition. Then, in the minds of the people, the tension turns against the government. A situation obtains which may be interpreted as the lag of the political phase of the social system behind one or more other phases.

To this formula, the majority of the antagonistic antecedents of revolutions conform. A new political idea has arisen, or an old one has been revived, but the government does not adjust its structure or policies to conform with it. New social classes have arisen; the traditional policies are no longer adequate, but the government persists in carrying them on. Or, on the contrary, deterioration of life conditions has become obvious; action on the part of the government is required, but is not carried out. A national revival demands the revision of assimilationist policies or the spread of a new belief makes unacceptable, to many, the privileged position granted to those who adhere to the old one; but no adjustment is made. The spread of education demands the incorporation, into the ruling group, of the rising strata; but the ruling oligarchy does not respond to their claims.

More rarely, it is the government which, by new policies, provokes a tension susceptible of starting a revolution. Such are the cases when national or religious persecution is sharpened or when the government tries to eliminate, by force, some inveterate mores, or even carries out premature reforms.

In all the cases, this essential element is present. There has been change, but the movement in the political sphere has not been in harmony with movement elsewhere: now the government has lagged behind, now—in exceptional cases— it has gone ahead too fast.

The statements above should not be understood as blaming the government for inaction or for wrong action. No objective judgment of this kind is possible or necessary for our purposes. Only this objective fact is important: between the activities of the government and some other development disharmony has obtained eliciting social tension.

The Movement from Order to Revolution

Social tensions reflected in discontent and suffering are probably present in every society. To cause revolution, they must be either serious, or many, or both and, in addition to this, be combined with other relevant traits in the initial stage of a nation likely to undergo a revolution; these traits are to be studied below.

When social tensions are serious and numerous, plans of resolving them are formulated and adopted by various groups and movements. The objective possibility of various solutions of the difficulties is the cause of one of the peculiarities of the revolution mentioned in the beginning of this chapter, namely the heterogeneity of the opposition. Some of the plans for salvation remain unarticulated and do not engender social organization; other ones receive more or less precise formulation and become programs for action. Around these programs, or ideas of tasks to be performed, organization is likely to emerge. Organization is accelerated and strengthened if a truly revolutionary idea is brought into circulation, appealing to the reason of the intellectuals and to the emotions of the masses. Then the intellectuals who, under normal conditions, support, in principle, the government (though not necessarily its personal composition or its particular policies) transfer their allegiance to an organization or organizations opposing it. The government may display lack of resolution, granting and then revoking reforms, or vacillating between contradictory plans. Its inability to cope with the situation may be demonstrated by defeat in war, the deterioration of life conditions, the spread of unrest and unorganized violence. Many members of the ruling group begin to have bad consciences; in other words they start to doubt whether, after all, they are entitled to make the momentous decision, whether it would not be wiser to modify the structure of the power pyramid, or even transfer power to other elements.

When several of these conditions are present, the mentality of the rank-and-file citizens undergoes a symptomatic change reflecting the movement of their society from the state of normalcy or solidarity to that of plasticity. When society is solid, almost everybody is able to foresee what will take place tomorrow. Slight changes are probable, but one knows that, fundamentally, society will continue as it is. On that basis depend such common activities as investing, insuring, and providing for higher education of children. In a plastic society, expectations are quite different: nobody knows what tomorrow will bring; everybody expects, however, that tomorrow will be different from today. Some worry, fearful that the coming change will impair their social status and that of their group, perhaps even of the nation as a whole. Others exult because of bright expectations for themselves, their group, or even the whole nation. If plasticity develops to that degree, a pre-revolutionary situation is present and its background, as we know, is the accumulation of serious social tensions.

Finally, there exists one aggravating circumstance the presence of which, other things equal, lifts the chance of a pre-revolutionary situation to develop into actual revolution. This is the existence, in the culture tradition of a nation, of a specific tradition of revolution. Such was the case, in the nineteenth century, of Russia, Ireland and those parts of Turkey which were inhabited by Christians; in a somewhat different meaning France also had a great revolutionary tradition, and still in another meaning, such a tradition is present in Latin America. Elsewhere, until recently, it was absent, and it is suggestive that where this is absent, revolutionary outbreaks are significantly less frequent.

The discussion above has concentrated on a necessary condition of revolution which has been presented from different points of view; first, as an antagonistic situation involving the government and a unified or divided opposition in a conflict which may be purely political, or reflect, on the political scene, economic, nationalistic or ideological, developments; second, as the presence of a series of numerous and serious tensions caused by the disharmonious dynamism of the social system; third, as the withdrawal of the intellectuals and the loss, by the rank-and-file citizens, of confidence in the stability of the system, then the nation reaches the state of plasticity. These are not three alternative conditions, but just one contemplated from various points of view. The deepest level is that of the social tensions; next comes the particular antagonisms and these are manifested in the attitudes of the people, in the way described.

Normative Inhibitions

The presence of serious social tensions provoking a serious conflict between the government and the opposition is a necessary but insufficient condition of the movement of a political system from order to revolution. To find out the additional conditions which also must be present, let us ask, regarding the causation of revolution, the same questions which proved to be relevant to non-political conflicts and war. First of all, what is the role of normative inhibitions?

Normative inhibitions against the outbreak of revolution seem to be very strong. In every state, the law considers the attempt to overthrow the constitution and/or the government to be a major, sometimes a capital crime; often not only real attempts, but even preparation, conspiracy, propaganda, and incitement are punished. Studying that part of the criminal law and especially the practice, one could build up a yardstick for the measurement of the relative strength of tensions in different societies and at different epochs. The almost absolute freedom of expression which was characteristic of Victorian England and of the United States until quite recently made them a haven of refuge for the proponents of revolutionary violence: Marx could live a free man almost only in the two countries just mentioned, perhaps also in Switzerland. These countries in those days could grant themselves that luxury because social tensions were low, almost nonexistent, or at least, inconspicuous. In our day of high social tension throughout the world, that attitude of complete tolerance would be almost suicidal. Hitler's Germany and Communist Russia, with their hypertrophy of combat against virtual revolution display the existence of strong inner tensions, while Tsarist Russia, compared with them, must be located much lower on the continuum of social tensions and of the repression of political offenses.

But usually, simultaneously with the growth of social tensions which involve the government, respect to the law sharply declines. In general, law is obeyed because of inner acceptance and the fear of sanctions, but in pre-revolutionary situations, the first of these motives shrinks, and almost disappears. Even the second is not so strong as it commonly is. In pre-revolutionary situations, the sympathy of large masses of the population may be shifted from the government to the virtual offenders, especially the political offenders; this sympathy may be expressed in such action as helping the criminals to escape the hand of justice. Denunciation of a conspiracy against a government held oppressive is often considered a highly amoral action.

Moral inhibitions against revolution exist only so far as violence in general is reprehended; but one may distinguish between just and unjust causes of revolution, and not apply the moral disapproval of violence to revolutionary outbreaks labeled just. Great revolutions often aim, among other things, at giving the upper hand to a new moral system.

Revolutions being rather rare, customary norms against them could hardly develop. On the contrary, in nations where revolutions are endemic or a revolutionary movement has been lasting (as in Russia, 1825-1917, and in Ireland) a tradition of revolution easily evolves. It may be expressed in a cult of revolutionary heroes. The vindication of revolutionary deeds may appear as criminal offenses in statute books, but this is one more symptom of high tension and of an approval of revolution in custom.

In consequence, normative inhibitions are often weak just when they would be badly needed, i.e., in situations involving high and dangerous tensions.

The Residual Character of Revolutions

But the residual character of revolution is clear. In situations of high tension, the government has always the choice of accomplishing salutary reforms; or the government, if it feels strong enough, may choose the way of reaction, i.e., of crushing the opposition before it is ready to strike. For instance, the government may curb liberties already granted and thus eliminate tension between actual conditions and openly formulated and widely supported demands. Such efforts may be successful, and then the balance is restored. But they are not always rigorous enough, or carried out in the right direction; sometimes they come too late. If what is done is of a too little and too late type, the social order disintegrates. A revolution breaks out.

The residual character of the revolution is equally clear on the part of the opposition. Depending on the political structure, the opposition may try a petition addressed to the monarch, or an address to the parliament, or consistent propaganda addressed to the people. The margin of these vicarious means is narrower in autocracies (old style monarchies and dictatorships) than in democracies. Hence, the greater probability of revolution in the former than in the latter. Against despotism, political terrorism is sometimes used; though it hardly deters the government, it creates martyrs and this obviously helps spread revolutionary ideas. However, experience has shown that revolution is not impossible in the framework of democracy;[3] obviously this can take place when a revolutionary minority comes to the conclusion that it is and will remain unable to persuade the majority. Then, two decisions are possible: to abandon the purpose, or to carry it out by violence. The danger of revolution in the framework of democracy has been only recently recognized though it was well known to the ancients.

Like war, revolution is a residual phenomenon; it is resorted to when other ways of overcoming tensions have failed. But the process of the gradual elimination of "other ways" assumes another form than the one most commonly materializing in conflict situations between states. There, negotiation is the main instrument; there is a steady mechanism for carrying out these negotiations in the form of diplomacy, the negotiators representing well organized groups which commonly recognize each other's legitimacy. In a pre-revolutionary situation, this is not the case. The opposition against the government may be, and more often than not is, amorphous. It usually has leaders, but in most cases the leaders do not form an organized and integrated system. Moreover, revolutionary opposition is most commonly not recognized by the government as a party equal to itself.[4] Negotiations between the government and some leaders (commonly the moderate ones) may take place, but the leaders thus consulted have no authority to speak for the opposition in its totality or even majority.

Consequently, the process of eliminating or solving the conflict short of revolution is often that of reforms. The reforms may do the job: the tension is overcome, or mitigated, so that the threat of revolution is gone, at least for a while. But they may be of the too little and too late type and therefore unable to appease the opposition; or the government, having granted reforms for one reason or another, withdraws or badly spoils them, which commonly results in a strong intensification of the revolutionary spirit. The majority of the leaders and the politically active members of the mass in turmoil come to the conclusion that no good can be expected from the government. The revolutionary situation is then almost complete and an insignificant episode may play the part of an operator, provided that among the most active members of the opposition the feeling prevails that they have a good chance of victory.

Another way of eliminating a conflict short of revolution is that of reaction. The government comes to the conclusion that the turmoil among the masses has reached a level endangering inner peace and order, especially the continuance of this government in power. It decides to strike against the opposition and suddenly enacts laws curbing the freedom of speech, the press, and assembly, and/or arrests the most vociferous leaders. If it does so, it implicitly displays the certitude that, in an eventual struggle with the opposition, it will gain the upper hand. Sometimes the opposition is so badly hurt that anti-government acts cease, at least for a certain time. But not so rarely, reactionary measures of the type just described provoke an outburst of violence which may, or may not, be arrested by the armed forces and the police loyal to the government. Sometimes, to the consternation of the government, the movement explodes almost spontaneously, without organized leadership, but finds so much support among the amorphous masses that faith in the victory of the "just cause" is tremendously intensified. If, as it has surprisingly often happened, the armed forces and/or the police prove to be less reliable than expected; if they display only sham-resistance, or go even so far as to fraternize with the rebels, a revolution, maybe a successful one, breaks out. In such cases, the non-revolutionary solution of the tension through reaction has been eliminated from the range of possibilities; it is too late for reform; revolution becomes the only outlet available.

The Chance of Victory

Finally, revolution commonly breaks out when both parties have, or seem to have, a fair chance of victory. The government seems always to have that chance since it disposes of the armed forces (army and police) and of the means of communication; technical progress in these two fields has strengthened every government in comparison with days when a revolution could be performed by a small group of men armed with swords and successfully assaulting the seat of the government.

On the part of the revolutionary opposition, an optimistic appraisal of the chances of victory must be present. Because of drastic sanctions, if there is no chance of victory at all, even high tensions and discontent are not conducive to revolutionary outbreaks. Specialists in the art of revolution, the Communists, have worked out a system of propositions concerning situations favorable and unfavorable to revolution. They emphasize division among the ruling group, and defeat by another group (e.g., in the course of a war), as the most favorable conditions for the success of a revolution. Time and again, revolutionary outbreaks take place although these conditions are lacking. Highly dangerous, from the point of view of the maintenance of order, is the spread of subversive movements in the army.

In industrial society, a new instrument of preparing either the capitulation of the government and its resignation to reforms, or a successful revolution, is the general strike; of somewhat weaker potency is a widespread strike in vital fields of the national economy, such as steel, oil, or transportation. In Russia, an almost general strike which took place in Oct., 1905, forced a reluctant government to carry out far-reaching reforms, especially to grant popular representation to a nation which, until that time, had been governed autocratically. But, as shown by the English experience of 1926, a general strike is not invincible; there, the general strike collapsed because of the resolute interference of young men of the middle class and the lack of the support of the strike by public opinion.[5]

Finally, a situation similar to that preceding a race riot sometimes obtains. The revolutionary leadership does not really expect to win this time, but wants to display its strength and its ability to foment trouble and thus to embarrass the ruling group. The aim is that of holding political oppression in tolerable limits. The impossibility to know in advance what will be the outcome, and the presence, in the minds of those responsible for the outbreak, of the idea that there is a fair chance of at least partial success, is therefore a common denominator of revolutionary outbreaks.

Finally, there are cases, and not quite exceptional ones, when revolutionary masses (indoctrinated by subversive ideas or brought to despair) break out of control and start a revolution against the will of the leadership whose estimate of the chance of victory remains low. Such cases cannot be considered as the invalidation of the proposition that, among the conditions of the outbreak of a revolution, there must be a fair chance of victory in the minds of the originators of the outbreak: the masses going out onto the streets, storming armories, prisons, palaces, and so forth, are moved by the hope of victory. And, surprisingly, sometimes the estimates of the masses prove to be right against their pessimistic leaders who then reluctantly join the movement, grant it some organization and direct it toward specified goals.

Reward and Punishment

The reward and punishment pattern is very clear. A miscarried revolution results in drastic sanctions against the leaders and known participants, but a successful revolution often results in mass extermination of the institutional leaders of the fallen order or, in the best case, their relegation to the bottom of the new society. This is why, despite the weakness of normative inhibitions, revolutions are rather rare, the leaders of the opposition thinking it over many times before giving the signal of going ahead. On the other hand, the government, despite the fair chance of victory which it commonly believes to possess, often yields to the demands of the opposition and does at least something to appease it, to avoid the risk of being overthrown by violence.

Conclusion

Summing up, one may say: a revolution is likely to break out in a dynamic society where disharmonious development has created important social tensions which have not been healed by reform or reaction, provided that the government has been weakened by inner divisions or sustained failure, giving a fair chance of victory to a resolute opposition.

It is obvious that the causal background of a revolution is more complicated than that of a war and that, in concrete cases, even *ex post facto* judgments remain more controversial than those regarding the outbreak of particular wars.

As in the case of war, the relevant traits of the political system in its pre-revolutionary phase are interchangeable with the operator. The condition which comes last seems to cause the movement. Very often, but not necessarily, this is the failure (or retraction) of reform or miscarriage of reactionary violence; but a sudden weakening of the government, such as ostentatious division in its midst or its defeat in war, may give the signal to the outbreak of a revolution. But this is just the signal, the precipitant or operator, not the cause. A revolution

cannot break out, still less be successful, if there is no concomitance of the conditions surveyed above.

The final formula of the causation of a revolution is this:
*If, within a state, a tension (or a cluster of tensions) has arisen
between the government and an opposition and has reached
such proportions that the symptoms of plasticity have become
apparent, and if the conflict has not been resolved either by
reform or reaction, a revolution is most likely to follow.*

This formula covers all the four traits characteristic of a
social system on the verge of developing a violent conflict:
tension giving rise to a situation of plasticity stands for the
incompatibility of highly evaluated goals; lack of reform
stands for the breakdown of the vicarious (peaceful) means
of conflict solution since, after all, only the government is able
to resolve such conflicts peacefully—if one discounts the possibility of the withdrawal, by the opposition, of its demands
(which is unlikely in plastic situations); failure of reaction is
tantamount to a situation where both parties have good reasons
to expect victory in the threatening violent conflict (revolution)—the government despite the failure of previous attempts
of solution by reaction, the opposition because of this failure.
Finally, in a situation of plasticity normative inhibitions are
likely to have become negligible.

In the case studies to follow we will often return to this
formula always having in mind that its elements point to the
basic conditions of the outbreak of violence stated in the basic
hypothesis used in this work.

8/The Movement
from Order to Revolution:
Case Studies

THE FORMULA developed in the last chapter offers a hypothesis on the causation of revolution which must now be checked by application to a few major cases.[1] The order of presentation will be the same as in Chapter Six; nevertheless, the first case investigated will be the Great Russian Revolution of 1917 because it is the most important of all recent revolutions. The revolution of 1848 will be studied after that of 1830 since its causal background was the same as of that of 1830, with some accentuation of the individual factors.

The Great Russian Revolution

The Great Russian Revolution may be analyzed in two phases: the collapse of the Imperial government in March, 1917, and the collapse of its successor, the Provisional government, in November, 1917. Only the first phase will be discussed here; the other must be interpreted not as another revolution, but as the outcome of a revolutionary movement begun in March and it will be treated under a different perspective in a later chapter.[2]

A major conflict between the Imperial government and large masses of the Russian population gradually conquered the political scene of Russia. Its beginning may be traced back to 1825, the year of the upheaval of the Decembrists, but it became of real significance since the 1870's. The opposition to the government included the majority of the intellectuals, some of whom were illegally organized into subversive parties; a large section of the labor class which was still small indeed; and, toward the end, indeterminable masses of the peasantry who formed the majority of the total population. Three major tensions formed the background of the conflict.

First, there was tension between the rapid increase of the rural population and the slower increase of the means of subsistence at its disposal. The disproportion was mainly caused by the persistence of an old-fashioned system of land tenure, the so-called *mir* system. Where the system was in force, arable land belonged not to individuals or homesteads, but to agrarian communities which periodically redistributed it among the homesteads, depending on the number of their members or on the number of adult males belonging to them. Each homestead tilled its allotment individually and disposed independ-

162

ently of the produce. But the system inhibited agrotechnical progress since no family was sure that it would retain its present lots after the next land distribution. In general, it was also favorable to the maintenance of routine usages. On the other hand, this system favored rapid population growth; every family knew that its share in the communal land would be proportionate to the number of its members. Many plans were pondered to alleviate the situation, e.g., partitioning the communal land among the homesteads. This plan started being applied in 1906, under Stolypin's leadership (see below). Another was nationalization of the land, including the landed estates (which were outside of the *mirs*) and the prohibition of leasing-renting land and of hired work; this plan allowed a number of variations concerning the organization of work on the nationalized surface. These plans originated with the socialist parties which were plentiful in Russia. One point was certain: government interference was mandatory; but until 1906 nothing but palliative measures were carried out.

Second, there was tension between the rapid economic advance of Russia and political stagnation. The rapid growth had given rise to a business class (the Bourgeoisie in Marxian terminology) and to a turbulent class of industrial workers. Until 1906, Russia remained an autocratic monarchy ruled by a not too efficient and not very farsighted bureaucracy. The new business class, and part of the intelligentsia, professed liberal ideas and wanted Russia to become a parliamentary monarchy (English style) or a parliamentary republic (French style). Another portion of the intelligentsia and rapidly increasing portions of the industrial proletariat were possessed by different socialist doctrines. Toward the end, part of the peasantry was also converted to these doctrines. Again, from the 1870's until 1905-6, nothing happened to reduce the tension between the rigid political structure and the new political ideas. These emerging political ideas were in part concomitant with the incipient process of industrialization but they were also partly anticipating further and deeper changes in the socio-economic structure.

Third, there was a cultural gulf between the top level of Russian society and the masses of the people. The cleavage was deep, for the top level—the court, the bureaucracy, the intellectuals—were well educated and had been thoroughly westernized as the result of the Petrinian reform in the early eighteenth century and its aftermath. At the other extreme were the peasants with almost one-half of their number still illiterate. The remainder had learned the "three R's" in elementary school, but very little else. Arduous efforts were exerted by the agencies of local self-government to educate more and more people. But the rate of population growth was so intense that, without funds from the national treasury, these efforts barely sufficed to keep the number of schools and teachers large enough to take care of the same proportion of the children of school age. Therefore, rather small inroads were made into the ocean of illiteracy.

Around 1900, these three tensions were already matured and had coalesced into a "generalized conflict" (in the same sense as in our discussion of war). However, at that time the tensions began rapidly to lose their intensity because reforms were initiated. In 1906, a grand style agrarian reform, the so-called Stolypin reform, was launched with the objective of granting the Russian peasants the system of land tenure prevailing in the West; but 30 to 35 years were required to accomplish the plan, due to the magnitude of the task. Moreover, this solution was disapproved by the majority of the opposition which favored the other plan: wholesale nationalization and redistribution of the land.

During the same years, a constitutional reform abolished the Emperor's autocracy and created a representation of various groups of the people. Now the concurrence of the Duma was necessary to enact new laws or to change old ones. But the reform was applied in a narrow spirit and did not satisfy the aspirations of the major groups of the opposition which displayed a kind of nefarious extremism.

In 1908, a carefully elaborated plan was put into operation to overcome illiteracy, but more than ten years were necessary to grant access to school to each Russian child. Many more efforts were needed, and partly effected, to improve the level of education received by the masses. In this regard, a bold plan was prepared under the Tsar's last Minister of Education, Count P. Ignatieff. His plan followed American and Scandinavian patterns to a certain extent.

So time was necessary to wipe out the tensions. *But time was not granted.* War came, and with war the social tensions were again accentuated. The second tension became inflamed first: the government used the opportunity of a major war to curb the rights of the people's representatives to participate in political decisions and thus threw back into the ranks of the opposition many persons who had been reconciled. Difficulties concerning food supply, a result of poor management of war economics, but partly related to the first tension, became very serious. The third tension was manifested in the complete lack of understanding, among the masses, of the necessity to fight the enemy to the bitter end. The conflict which had already been generalized in the last decades of the nineteenth century, but had receded in 1906-14, was again exacerbated. The nation was divided into two irreconcilable camps: the government and the revolutionary movement.

As in every pre-revolutionary situation, the government could have prevented revolution by timely reforms. First of all, it could have changed its personal composition and called moderate leaders of the opposition to power who, until the end, preferred reform to revolution.[3] But the government stubbornly refused to do so. It chose *reaction*, but was unable to carry it out vigorously. Individual and unsystematic acts against some of the leaders of the opposition and the abusive manipulation of certain clauses of the constitution embittered the feud and deprived the government of the support of any significant group outside of the small ruling group. And even this group was already shaken in its spirit and weakened by the defection of many prominent persons, including members of the dynasty.

The chance of victory, in the event of a revolutionary outbreak, seemed fair to each party. The government continued to rely on its command of the armed forces and police which had allowed it to crush the so-called abortive revolution of 1905-6. Leaders of the opposition relied on the revolutionary tradition, expressed in the widespread cult of revolutionary heroes. It knew also that the government was weakened by inner division, by indecision and by the almost complete withdrawal of the intellectuals. Normative inhibitions were at least neutralized by the cult of the revolution just mentioned.

The state of Russia early in 1917 was, therefore, an almost perfect case of a pre-revolutionary situation which was not dissipated or even alleviated by vigorous reform or vigorous reaction. Under these conditions, the social process chooses the way of revolution, and this is what happened in Russia.[4]

The Fascist Revolutions

The Fascist revolutions in Italy (1922), Spain (1923), and Germany (1933) can be treated together. They share the peculiarity of having been accomplished not so much by actual violence, as by direct intimidation of the government by revolutionary groups which could display insuperable force. In place of violence, there was extortion. Mussolini gained power through the March on Rome without actual bloodshed. General Primo de Rivera gained power by proclaiming himself a dictator without meeting resistance which would have been hopeless. Hitler was appointed Chancellor by President Hindenburg, after having proven, in innumerable riots and skirmishes, that he had the strength to take power by violence. In other words, in each case conflict was resolved by measuring the relative strength of the parties on a level just below actual violence. This does not preclude the consideration of these events as revolutions.

The Fascist revolutions were preceded by numerous and high tensions. First, there was tension between the official form of the government (democracy) and the political mentality (predominantly anti-democratic or at least lacking in enthusiasm for democracy). However, belief in democracy is a functional requisite of its safe operation. In Germany, democracy was reluctantly accepted after the defeat of the monarchy during the First World War. In Italy and Spain, events proved that democracy existed on the superficial level only; it was reduced to an insipid and rather shameless game among local leaders (caciques) with no actual participation of broad masses.

Second, there was tension between flaming nationalism and national humiliation. Germany was defeated by the Grand Alliance of the First World War; the Germans were almost unable to take it and easily accepted the myth of a *Dolchstooss* carried out by inner enemies. Spain was defeated in the course of a colonial war in Morocco. Italy was badly frustrated when bright expectations about the acquisition of the Eastern shore of the Adriatic and of a large slice of Asia Minor were defeated at the Paris Peace Conference dominated by President Wilson. This frustration was caused by the weakness displayed by Italy during the war; Italy had been badly beaten by the enemy and saved by the allies.

Third, there was tension between economic reality and economic aspirations. This tension was exceptionally strong in Germany who lost her colonies, her foreign investments, and her granary—her Eastern provinces ceded to Poland. After many decades of steady advance, the economic system had to shrink, causing a severe deterioration of the standard of living whose maintenance was naturally the minimum demand of the masses. Economic conditions were also bad in Italy and Spain.

Fourth, there was tension between the natural demand for security so strong among members of the business class and the peasantry and, first, the destructive effects of inflation, second, the threat of communism (in Germany and Italy) and anarchism (in Spain).

In all cases, the government was taken to task by strong and vociferous opposition movements. In no case did the government try to cope with the situation by reform; nor could it think of reaction, i.e., crushing the opposition by force.

Everywhere, the government was exceptionally weak. In Germany,[5] the republican government was rather an impotent arbiter between mighty social forces, organizations of the business class and the labor class. Every cabinet represented nothing but the latest phase in the endless game among the political leaders who led rather small groups indeed. Such governments were firmly resolved upon doing nothing. In addition, the withdrawal of the intellectuals was noticeable; many were contaminated by Communism, others by Fascism. This naturally gave a fair chance to the opposition, or to one of its groups. The governments blindly relied on the inertia of institutions or on some miracle until it was too late. Eventually, surrender to the overwhelming forces of the opposition was the only choice left, except dying for a lost and disreputed cause.

As in the case of the Russian Revolution, the application of the formula offered at the end of the preceding chapter indicates, *ex post facto,* revolution as the most likely outcome.

The European Revolutions of 1830

In 1830, revolutions broke out in France (July), Belgium (August), Poland (November), and in several Italian States (Parma, and Modena, and the Pontifical state). The revolts were evoked by a serious tension created by the Vienna Peace Treaty, a tension between the imposed political organization and the aspirations of the politically active strata of these nations. These aspirations were informed by liberal ideas and nationalistic sentiment. The basis of the tension was twofold: first, large populations were adjudged to states to which they did not want to belong and, in consequence, felt themselves ruled by foreigners. Second, the political institutions imposed on many populations were either an absolute monarchy or something close to it while the people craved for free institutions.

1. In France, the conflict was purely political, without any admixture of nationalistic elements. It was between the government of Charles X which strenuously attempted to restore as much as possible of the *ancien régime* overthrown in 1789, and certain elements of the population of Paris. The people in the "provinces" cared little for political problems; but this was of little matter because of political centralization in the capital, a legacy both of the old monarchy and of Napoleon's time. The opposition was quite inadequately represented in the Parliament (placed there by an incredibly limited electorate), but was *vivid* in the press supported by the professionals, the middle class (the artisans and shopkeepers so numerous and influential in Paris) and also by the "laboring masses" which were then just emerging.

For several years, the opposition tried to persuade and to intimidate those in power. But no reform whatsoever was granted. On the contrary, on July 25, 1830, the government, now exasperated by exceptionally bold attacks of the press, enacted "the three ordinances" curbing the limited freedom of the press granted by the Constitution of 1814. These ordinances functioned as the operator; they intensified the conflict and mobilized the latent forces of the revolution.

The rebellion came as a complete surprise to the King and his ministers who believed themselves safe in Paris, where it seemed sufficient armed forces were concentrated. The people and their leaders obviously relied on the irresistible strength of a popular upheaval in Paris. That strength had been proven on numerous occasions during the years of the Great Revolution. In the course of "the three glorious days" (July 28-30, 1830), the relative strength of the parties was measured. The opposition won the contest; but, up to the last moment, both parties had reasons to believe that victory would be theirs. Thus, the classical situation was given; an important conflict situation, the proven impossibility to solve the antagonism by reform, the impotence of reaction manifested only *ex post facto*, contrary to the estimates of those in power.

2. The Belgian revolution was prepared by gradually accumulating discord which, already in 1828, could be termed acute. There, the main tension was national. The people of the land which was to become Belgium had been placed, by the Vienna treaties, under the rule of the King of the Netherlands. Although a large part of the Belgian population were Flems who spoke a dialect of Dutch, French culture so dominated for centuries that no language but French was spoken among the upper and professional classes. The Flemish played the part of a vernacular. The Belgians outnumbered the Dutch in the proportion of seven to four and were devoted Catholics while the population of Holland was predominantly Calvinist, and the House of Orange ruling there was one of the pillars of Calvinism. The Constitution of the Kingdom granted equality to the two sections of the population, Dutch and Belgian, symbolically expressed in the disposition that the Parliament had to convene alternately in The Hague and Brussels. But the King did not carry out this provision and, in his choices of higher administrative and diplomatic personnel, displayed his preference for the Dutch. The Constitution itself was ultra-conservative and did not appeal to the Belgian intellectuals dominated by the liberal ideas widespread at that time in France.

The Belgians tried for a long time to proceed by legal means, but all kinds of petitions and remonstrations were consistently disregarded by the King. So, to the politically active elements of the Belgian section of the Kingdom, no hope to achieve anything through reform was left. The alternatives were reaction (in this case, tantamount to the maintenance of the *status quo*) or revolution.

The July events in Paris seemed to demonstrate that a hated regime could be overthrown. Thus it happened that, in August, 1830, as the result of a futile incident, an insurrection broke out in Brussels which immediately spread to other cities and towns (in contra-distinction to France where the revolution was confined to Paris).

Of course, insisting on their reactionary course, the King and his ministers relied on the armed forces at their disposal. But it immediately appeared that the army, consisting to a large extent of Belgians and commanded by poor generals, was no bulwark for the waning royal power. The King made some concessions, but it was too late. The revolution won. An independent Belgian state emerged, endowed with a liberal constitution which, for decades, served as a model for nations gaining independence. The results showed that the opposition's estimate of relative strength was correct. But, as is commonly the case, this could not be taken for granted before the event.

3. The Polish Revolution against Russian overlordship was a desperate attempt to overcome a double tension, purely political and national. The tension emerged from the unfortunate idea of Emperor Alexander I of Russia which was sanctioned by the Vienna Congress: to reward Russia for her great contribution to victory in the years 1812-15 by creating a constitu-

tional Kingdom of Poland, with the Russian Emperor as the statutory King. The political tension arose almost immediately because the Emperor-King functioned in two incompatible roles: autocratic monarch in Russia, and a constitutional monarch in Poland (as in another annex of the Russian Empire, the Grand Duchy of Finland). For a while Alexander pondered the idea of resolving the conflict by granting a constitution to Russia proper; but gradually he dropped this plan which corresponded to the advanced ideas of his youth. He remained an autocrat. But the Polish Seim wanted to exert its rights in full measure, rejecting some of the government bills and passing acts unacceptable to the monarch (who, of course, had the right of veto). The Emperor was exasperated; the situation worsened from year to year, but still remained far from becoming pre-revolutionary so long as Alexander was alive. Alexander could wait and procrastinate. But after his death (1825) the dual role passed to Nicholas I whose ascent to the throne had been adumbrated by the rebellion of the Decembrists. For him, the dual position was unbearable. By sharp acts in the style of reaction, he brought his Polish subjects to the awareness that, short of revolution, their limited freedom was doomed. Of course, the political tension between the freedom-loving Polish elite and an autocratic monarch was accentuated by the fact that the King of Poland was a foreigner representing a nation with which Poland had historically maintained a state of hostility. The tensions were there, bitter and hardly solvable.

The Polish leaders obviously knew that Russia was stronger than Poland, but, as compared with other revolutionary situations, they had the tremendous advantage of possessing an army and an administration of their own. This resulted in an additional advantage: the conspiratorial organization which finally launched the revolutionary movement had not been molested.

Moreover, the Poles relied on the support of the population of areas which had formerly belonged to Poland, but since the days of the partitions (1772-95) were incorporated into Russia proper. They had a particular reason to expect support: in that region, the government of Nicholas I proceeded to a forcible conversion of the Uniates to Orthodoxy. Finally, the Poles relied on help from the outside, especially from France. The ease with which the monarchy of the Bourbons in France and the Dutch overlordship in Belgium had been overthrown, led them to believe that in the world of 1830 the idea of liberty was strong enough to perform miracles. It was almost a miracle that they could hold out during several months. Finally, the Russian colossus gained the upper hand. But, in October, 1830, the Polish leaders had plausible reasons to hope that the revolution would be victorious.

Summing up, one may say that at the outbreak of the Polish revolution the three conditions required by the hypothesis offered in this volume were present.

4. The three revolutions surveyed in this section (the Italian ones had been rather insignificant) had much in common. They were provoked by an aggravation of long standing tensions, by a typical mechanism, the government moving in one direction and public opinion in the opposite. The three ordinances of July 25, 1830; several unpopular measures of King William of the Netherlands in Belgium; and the haughty treatment of the Poles by Emperor Nicholas I, played the role of the operator.

The Movement from Order to Revolution: Case Studies

The European Revolution of 1848

In 1848, revolutions broke out in France, several Italian states, the Austrian Empire (independently of each other, in Vienna, Budapest, Prague and Milan), Prussia, and several secondary German states. One may rightly speak of a European Revolution with the shock center located in Paris which was then the informal capital of continental Europe. In Paris, revolutionary events occurred through three days (February 22-24), followed by secondary shocks in June of the same year, and in December, 1851. Chronologically, the earliest revolution of the cycle under study took place in Sicily (January 12, 1848), but that was a peripheral event caused by an inveterate feud between the Sicilians and the Neapolitans. The Neapolitan rule had been imposed on the Sicilians by the Vienna treaties of 1815, while the events in Paris, by a kind of remote detonation, actualized tensions in the countries just enumerated.

What were these tensions? They were almost the same ones which had engendered the revolutions of 1830 which at that time had resulted in some liberalization of the political regime in France and in the independence of Belgium. But elsewhere the situation had remained unchanged. The tensions observable in 1830 grew in intensity and, about 1848, became so acute that Prince Metternich, the most influential of European politicians, acknowledged (in his correspondence) that the danger of the dissolution of the Vienna system was great and imminent. To the two old tensions, i.e., the political (between antiquated political institutions and liberal ideology), and the national (based on the discrepancy of political boundaries and aspirations of large populations), a third had

175

been added in some places, between the capitalists and the workers. This tension was recognized and formulated with unsurpassable strength in the *Communist Manifesto* of Marx and Engels, issued on the very eve of the revolutionary events of 1848.

Most important was the political and the inter-class tension in France where the revolution started. It was manifested in the antagonism (partly already of the type of non-violent conflict) between the government of Louis Philippe which, since 1840, was entrenched in stubborn conservatism, and the libertarian and equalitarian spirit only little satisfied by the July revolution of 1830. As then, the spirit was concentrated in Paris and only slightly supported by the provinces. That this was the case is manifested by the outcome of free and universal elections held a few weeks after the February days; the majority of the French people were still attached to monarch of one or another type, i.e., "legitimist," "Orleanist," or "Bonapartist."

Even the people of Paris were united in one way only; they wanted reform, first of all, of the electoral law, i.e., expansion of the suffrage far beyond the 300,000 persons who possessed it after 1830. And they sought parliamentary reform—to grant more power to the representatives of the people. The upper and the upper middle classes did not want to go farther; but the lower middle class (mainly the artisans and shopkeepers) and the lower class (*la classe inférieure* according to the terminology of the time) were cherishing many of the ideas of their grandfathers, the actors on the political scene in the years 1789-94. They were never satisfied with the modest outcome of the revolution of 1830. The demand of an electoral and parliamentary reform was in full accordance with the rapid economic and cultural growth of the nation since 1815. The artisans and the workers badly suffered from the depression of 1847 and the exceptionally high bread price, bread still being the staple food of the majority of the Frenchmen. But taken alone, the economic difficulties would hardly have resulted in a revolution.

It is noteworthy that the operator behind the movement of the system from order to revolution was an aggravation of the purely political conflict: in February the government prohibited a political banquet scheduled to take place in one of the districts of Paris. Banquets were the main forum in which the demand of reform was brought to the consciousness of the people. The banquets were strictly an upper and middle class affair but unexpectedly the people of Paris took to the arms to obtain the abrogation of the prohibition.

Revolution was chosen only when any hope of peaceful satisfaction of the *desiderata* was gone. The opposition were weakly represented in the Parliament, but they did dominate the Paris press. Further, they enjoyed the support of the large popular masses. They had appealed to the King and Prime Minister Guizot and, also in vain, they had attempted to push reform bills through the Parliament. It is noteworthy that, up to the last moment, a peaceful solution remained possible by moderate reforms in the right direction.

In some states of Germany and in Hungary (then a part of the Austrian Empire) the political tension was generated by the discrepancy between obsolete feudal representation endowed with little power and the demand for democratic elections and for the granting of more power to the representative institutions. Elsewhere, the tension came from the loud cry for far-reaching reforms, e.g., in old-fashioned absolute monarchies which, with rare exceptions (e.g., Tuscany) were not even "enlightened" as had been the case in the second half of the eighteenth century.

The second tension behind the European revolution of 1848 was the national one which appeared in two modalities. The first elicited movements aiming at secession, or at least strong autonomy. The demand of secession was strongest in Lombardo-Venetia, that rich northeastern part of Italy which, according to the Vienna treaty, had become part of the Austrian Empire. Secessionist demands existed in less acute forms in central Italian principalities which, nominally independent, were also ruled by Austria. The demand of autonomy dominated in Hungary and in the land of the Czechs (Bohemia-Moravia). The situation was complicated by the fact that the Kingdom of Hungary which was seeking independence from the Austrian Emperor, was itself subject to demands for political separation on the part of more than half of its population. The population of Hungary consisted mainly of Slovaks, Horvats and Rumanians and they sought autonomy from the Hungarians—but not from the Hapsburg Empire! In the course of the revolutionary events, the original demand of autonomy was replaced by the demand of independence, while part of the population dominated by the Hungarians took side with the Emperor against the Hungarians.

The second modality of the national tension was diametrically opposed to the former: it was expressed in the demand for the unification of historically shaped fractionary states into nation-states. Such was the aspect of the national movement in Italy and Germany. The achievement of the goal was impeded in Germany by the existence of two rivals for hegemony, Austria and Prussia, and in Italy by the existence of the Pontifical state and the Austrian dominance in approximately one-half of the country.

The third tension, the inter-class one, was only in the incipient stage. It was felt more in France and in northwestern Germany where the progress of industrialization was creating a destitute class of industrial workers. In some other parts of Germany, in Austria proper, and in Hungary, it was expressed in the demand for the abolition of the feudal duties and tithes accomplished in France on August 4, 1789, and later on spread through large parts of central Europe as a consequence of the Napoleonic conquest. We should note that *in some places* these reforms were repealed during the period of reaction (1815-48) which naturally created a still stronger dissatisfaction in the social strata involved.

From this short survey, one may conclude that the concrete configuration of the pre-revolutionary tension varied from country to country. The major difference was that in Paris and Vienna no nationality problem was involved; in Berlin and in the secondary German States the national problem was posed in the modality of the strive for unification; while in Prague, Budapest, and the Italian states the problem of liberation from the direct or indirect rule of foreigners was in the forefront.

In many instances, the revolutionary outbreak was preceded by attempts to solve the tensions by peaceful means, i.e., by reform. This was most evident in the Pontifical state after the election, on June 6, 1846, of Pius IX, "the liberal Pope." In the course of two years, he granted an amnesty, a moderate freedom of the press, municipal government to the city of Rome, and modernized the administration in the provinces. He created a Consulta, i.e., a consultative assembly for the whole state, and a Civil Guard, in the image of the French *garde nationale*, thereby arming the middle class whose demand of reform was strongest. His reform fell short of what these elements demanded; moreover, he could not satisfy the popular demand of taking the lead in a war of liberation against Austria because Austria, like Italy, was a Catholic nation. When news of the events in Paris reached Rome, Pius IX was forced to grant a Constitution (March 15, 1848), but a very modest one, indeed. On April 29, he openly declared that he could go no farther. Rebellion started the very next day. Three days later, the papal ministers had to acknowledge that they had no real authority; real power had gone to the *Cicoli* (clubs consisting of liberals and radicals). The situation became intolerable and on November 24, Pius IX, the liberal Pope, left Rome in the garb of an ordinary priest and sought refuge in the Kingdom of Naples. A Roman republic was proclaimed. The revolution was consummated—because the reforms had been of the "too little and too late type" and reaction proved impossible since the Civil Guard was with the revolutionists and the regular army small and poor.

Similar events took place in other Italian states, especially in Tuscany, Parma, and Modena; in Tuscany, despite the rather enlightened character of the rule of Grand duke Leopold III who could not join the movement against Austria because he was, after all, an Austrian Archduke. The rulers had to leave their possessions. Events did not follow the same course in Sardinia-Piedmont whose King, Charles Albert, became the leader of the national movement of liberation and, on March 5, 1848, granted a liberal Constitution.

In Austria and most German states, the governments responded to the plastic situation by reaction, sometimes intermittently with feeble attempts at reform. In Prussia, King

Frederic William IV granted, in 1840, a limited freedom of the press but soon it was repealed. This naturally exasperated the liberals. In February, 1847, he convoked a joint Diet, i.e., a joint gathering of the provincial assemblies still organized according to the pattern of late feudal society (representation of the particular "estates") and endowed only with consultative functions. This satisfied nobody and made revolution probable. In Austria, including Hungary and Bohemia, until the Paris events, the response of the government was unmitigated reaction, i.e., enforcement of the antiquated organization. Under Metternich, reform was unthinkable; so revolution remained the only alternative.

What about the third condition of the outbreak of a revolution—the assumption, on both sides, of a good chance of victory? The situation was as follows. All the governments involved underestimated the strength of the movement, political, national and eventually inter-class, and overestimated its own capacity to crush eventual rebellion. The opposition, though unorganized (with rare exceptions), was penetrated by the feeling that the forces of liberty and nationality were invincible. In the earlier phases of the revolution their estimates proved to be correct. Everywhere the resistance of the government forces proved to be surprisingly weak—in Paris, Vienna, Berlin, Rome, and even Milan, despite the presence there of a 70,000 man army of occupation under one of the best generals of the time, Radetsky. In Paris, the National Guard took sides with the rebels, and the regular army fraternized with them. In Berlin and Vienna, the government procrastinated in striking back, and when vigorous orders were given, it was too late. In Milan and throughout Lombardo-Venetia, the Austrian army was immediately deserted by a large proportion of soldiers of Italian origin, and the rest had to seek cover in the famous Quadrilateral, a group of four fortresses rather impregnable under the mid-nineteenth century conditions of warfare. Outside Paris, the optimistic estimates of the opposition were strengthened by news arriving from that city and telling not only of victory, but also of the ease with which it could be won. The repetition of the Paris events in Vienna granted new vigor to the optimistic estimates of the opposition in the secondary centers of the Austrian Empire, namely Prague, Budapest and Agram (the capital of Croatia), in Italy (which, then, was largely a dependency of Austria) and in Germany (where Austria still played a prominent role in the loose confederacy called *Deutscher Bund*). Therefore, in the initial stages of the revolution, the confidence of the leaders of the opposition and their followers was rather warranted.

Of course, later on, the revolutionary movement was crushed and a period of reaction started almost everywhere. This is, however, a fact no longer belonging to the topic of this chapter. What is important is that the initial phase of the revolutionary movement rather corroborated the optimistic estimates of the opposition. In most cases, it took months before the forces of reaction triumphed. And, after all, only the unforeseeable military intervention of Russia saved the Austrian Empire from dissolution—the Hungarian Revolution was crushed in 1849 by Russian armies, exactly as it happened 107 years later.

The French Revolution

The causal background of the French revolution (1789 ff.) has been studied more frequently and more profoundly than that of any other. Whereas early historians emphasized such factors as the obsolete and vexatious structure of the fiscal system, or the penury of the state treasury, or the misery of large masses, or even the bad harvests of the last few years preceding the revolution, today common opinion is that the real cause was deeper. There was a major social tension between the petrified institutional system taken over from the feudal age and the social, cultural and ideological developments of the nation. Since the middle of the eighteenth century, the educated strata of French society well understood that the institutions which had been justified and functioned smoothly two centuries earlier, became an obstacle to progress. This was critical because faith in progress was one of the keystones of the new ideology.

This fundamental tension was manifested in the fact that the institutional order granted all the privileges, all the positions of honor, and unearned and unwarranted income to the higher nobility. Under Louis XIV (1715) the nobility had been uprooted and concentrated at the Court to render ceremonial service to the King. This was their only function. Actual participation in the administration had been transferred to able persons chosen from the *tiers état,* a term officially covering all the population minus the nobility and clergy. More specifically, the administration devolved to the intellectuals and businessmen from among the commoners. The social *function* which the feudal order had ascribed to the nobility had vanished but the *privileges* remained intact. The nobility was tax exempt and received high monetary awards, partly from the King (i.e., from moneys collected by taxation), and partly through the maintenance of feudal dues. This in spite of the fact that counterparts to those of feudal times no longer existed, e.g., protection of the vassals and participation of the feudal lords in the administrative and judicial activities of the state. The privileged position was shared by the higher clergy, i.e., a small number of magnificently rewarded Church dignitaries chosen not so much on the ground of piety or spiritual gifts, but appointed from among the younger sons of noble families.

The privileged minority was confronted, first, by another minority, the *tiers état* in the narrow meaning of the word which, *culturally,* was on a par with the aristocracy and included a significant number of men of property. Socially, this group was treated as inferior and was taxable. Below the two minorities, there was the "people," consisting of small artisans, shopkeepers, peasants (part of whom were still serfs of the nobles), and workingmen employed in the nascent industry of the modern type. This stratum of the population was working hard, but had to give a large part of their income to the treasury, to the nobility and to the Church, in the form of tithes. In those days of low productivity in industry and agriculture, this condemned them to misery and often left them hungry.

This basic tension permeated the whole social texture and influenced secondary tensions, including some of those mentioned above. To be specific, the penury of the treasury—despite the fact that France was then the richest continental country—was caused by the foolish spending of state revenue by the Kings: on gifts to the courtiers, on incessant building of expensive palaces, and still more, on insipid wars waged under Louis XIV and Louis XV. It is also noteworthy that the existing order of things was no longer believed justified even by many of its beneficiaries, contaminated by the libertarian and equalitarian philosophy of the time.

The first condition of the outbreak of a revolution was clearly present. This did not, however, make the revolution necessary. During the reign of Louis XVI (1774-92) the necessity of drastic reforms was twice grasped by the throne. Outstanding men, first Turgot and then Necker, were entrusted with the task of abolishing the gravest abuses and modernizing the monarchy without depriving the King of absolute power. The reforms naturally were resisted by the beneficiaries of the privileges who had the ear of the King; both times, the reforms were stopped in their initial stage. This was reaction; but there was no force behind it. The revolution broke out by imperceptible steps, without any centralized organization to serve as its promoter. The convocation of the *Etats Généraux* (in 1789, after an interruption of 175 years) was acclaimed by the opposition as a serious beginning of reform which it actually proved to be. But, in the course of the unfolding of the reforms now initiated by the *Etats Généraux* (which soon became the Constituent Assembly), it proved that the government headed by the King had no plan whatsoever and was unreliable, always ready to withdraw what had been granted. This naturally exasperated the reformatory zeal of the members of the Assembly and the outside support to it.

Gradually, the movement shifted from reform to revolution. This could happen because the government was obviously weak. Weak—because of the personality of the King, of his narrow and stupid choice of counsellors, and the almost complete withdrawal of the intellectuals from among the ranks of the supporters of the traditional government. Moreover, the army, composed of mercenaries recruited among the scum of the people and commanded by incapable officers, was unreliable. Finally, there was no organization comparable with the police force of a modern state—such a force had no place in a nominally feudal society.

The weakness of the government was tested by trial and error. The popular masses of Paris grew impatient and carried out several unplanned and unrelated insurrections. The most revealing of them was the assault of the Bastille (July 14, 1789), the day which the French nation considers as the beginning of the glorious revolution. The lack of resistance and retaliation indicated the impotence of the government. After that event, the revolutionary leaders who were selected on the job had very good reasons to believe that they had a fair chance of victory. The government, ill organized and led by nobody, probably relied on the force of social inertia, on the armed forces (which, as has already been mentioned, were unreliable except for a few regiments whose valor was checked by inadequate orders) and on help from the outside. In the last months of the monarchy, the King and the Queen surreptitiously implored the Austrians and, indirectly, the Prussians, to interfere and put an end to the chaos in Paris which threatened to expand throughout Europe. Of these hopes, only the last one proved to have had a more or less solid foundation: the Austrians and Prussians interfered, but weakly, and the result was a new wave of revolutionary energy. The expectations of the opposition which had gradually become a mighty revolutionary force proved to be correct. The French revolution succeeded: since reform was tried but failed, and reaction was hopeless, France had to make the movement from order to revolution.

The American Revolution

The American Revolution can be understood as the joint result of several social tensions, not resolved in due time by reform and not blown out of existence by efficient reaction. The tensions were between the motherland, England, and the American colonies. The background of the tension centers on the fundamental fact that, though still forming one body politic, the motherland and the colonies became two different ethnic groups (nations). Despite this fact, the motherland continued to make all the decisions concerning the whole, while the colonies strongly rejected that pretension. This antagonistic situation was, then, the manifestation of the fact that the two parts had evolved along different lines.

The cause of the divergences of the two lines of evolution is obvious. From the start, the people of the colonies were formed out of elements which held "non-conformist" views on religion and politics. Religiously, they were predominantly Puritans, while in England, despite the Great Revolution of the seventeenth century, dominance had remained with the Established Church; both parties were absolutely intolerant. Politically, the colonists cherished free institutions—local self-government which they significantly developed, while in England, since the time of the physical separation of the two parts, these institutions had been rather curbed. In England, with the exception of the years of Civil War and of the Cromwellian Commonwealth, the King's prerogative was paramount up to 1688 when it was curbed by the Parliament representing, however, only a limited oligarchy. Add to this an entirely new and different environment posing problems unknown to the English people in England, and a progressive accentuation of differences in manners and even language. Finally, English society continued being characterized by extremes of wealth and poverty while in America a much more democratic distribution of wealth and income prevailed. By the last quarter of the eighteenth century, the colonists no longer were Englishmen living on the other side of the ocean, but Americans.

Let us now analyze the individual tensions which obtained between the English motherland and the American colonies.

1) The main tension was purely political. The colonies grew up as almost independent communities, organized (though with some exceptions) along the democratic pattern. Until the middle of the eighteenth century England cared little for the colonies, except perhaps Virginia, as the source of the lucrative import of tobacco. But during the third quarter of the century the interference of London with colonial affairs became more and more ostensible, since George III and his ministers tried to pull together the scattered organs of the British colonial administration. In content, the measures were primarily economic (taxes, custom duties, limitations of commerce). But they were primarily felt by the Americans as curbs of their inalienable rights. The more drastic of these measures were called "The Five Intolerable Acts." The famous phrase "no taxation without representation" was a *pars pro toto:* the Americans could no longer tolerate that a body in which they were not represented would pass acts curbing their old liberties. In general, they objected that a government in London would solve problems concerning them even without consultation with them. Every symbol of English power in America was resented. When, in October, 1768, two British regiments arrived in Boston to enforce acts enacted by the British Parliament, this was felt as "intolerable grievance."

2) The second tension was religious—virtually present since the very start. But it began being felt as a source of trouble when English Anglicans started arriving and openly displaying their faith. How touchy were the colonists about religious problems appears in their reaction to the Quebec Act of 1774. This act granted the freedom of worship to the Catholics in Canada and was treated in the thirteen colonies as a threat of the return to "popery."

3) The third tension was purely social. All the governors sent from England and their aides were of the upper class who had no sympathy with the people and rather openly expressed their contempt. Of course, the people of the colonies hated being treated this way.

4) The fourth tension which arose only in 1774 was territorial. The Quebec Act mentioned above transferred to Canada the northern part of the western territories between the Alleghenies and the Mississippi, acquired from France by the Paris Peace Treaty (1763). However, these territories had been regarded for a long time as annexes to the coastal colonies; some of the colonies had definite claims on specified areas. Many audacious people had already settled there, while other ones indulged in trade with the Indians.

5) The fifth tension which, together with the first, unrolled the subsequent events, was economic. The colonists hated being taxed for Imperial needs, and still more, the arbitrary regulation of foreign trade to the advantage of the motherland, partly also of the sugar planters of British West India, and even of the East India Company. This was aggravated by the creation of agencies more or less efficaciously preventing and repressing smuggling, while, in the mentality of the colonists, smuggling was not considered to be a criminal

offense. On the contrary, it formed one of the most important and lucrative aspects of New England commerce.

Around 1774 all of these tensions coagulated into one conflict, predominantly political. Political because what was demanded by the colonists and denied by the London government was a substantial change of policies. This was a formidable conflict and an inveterate one so that any move of either party was suspected by the other and exaggerated in its meaning and consequences. The first condition of the outbreak of a revolution was certainly present.

For a long time, however, neither party wanted to resolve the conflict by measuring their relative strength by force. They preferred accommodation through direct action, each tending to improve its position. In the process of maneuvering, the American party displayed an exceptional ingenuity. The two boycotts of British trade (of which the second culminated in the Boston Tea Party) have been called by Crane Brinton "quite modern pressure group action." The English usually responded by increasing pressure, sometimes by punitive action —for instance, the notorious Stamp Act. In 1774, the formation of "Committees of Correspondence" gave organization to the movement. Finally, the opening of the Continental Congress (September 17, 1774) manifested the emergence of a "diarchy," i.e., of a new power center opposing the old one. An attempt by a small British detachment to seize arms concentrated by the virtual rebels resulted in the battle of Lexington (April 18, 1775). Each party had lost hope of achieving its goals without violence. The revolution was there.

The consecutive steps mentioned above and many others testify to the fact that both parties firmly believed in their eventual success. The ruling class in England was still under the glow of its complete victory in the Seven Years War (1756-63) which ended, for England, in the annexation of two colonial Empires, the American (Canada and Louisiana) and the East Indian. On the eve of the revolution Londoners said that one British soldier would beat six Yankees. The Ministry could not believe that actual hostilities would break out. Franklin and other prominent Americans in London were warned against the folly of rebellion: the Americans would fail in a contest with the great and powerful England.

But the Americans also had good reasons to believe that victory would be theirs. They understood that the Ocean was a mighty barrier against "despotism," and it really was, as England learned in the years of the American Revolution and again during the Boer War. It is noteworthy that, until 1755, there was no regular mail service between England and the American colonies. Moreover, many episodes of the pre-revolutionary years seemed to demonstrate that the King and his ministers were too weak and preoccupied to impose their will on the colonies by force. The most drastic case was the Boston riot of 1764-65: the leaders of the riot could walk the streets with impunity; nobody dared to prosecute them. The colonial masses could no longer be controlled by respect for the high-born, including the King. Their leaders knew that the British ruling class was far from standing unanimously behind the policies of their government; on the contrary, many outstanding Englishmen (e.g., Edmund Burke) believed that the Americans were right in their demands. It is true that neither did the cause of the revolution find unanimous support in the colonies.

That neither estimate was foolish is proven by the fact that the struggle did last eight years and that, in the final account, the aid of France and Spain substantially contributed to the success of the secession. Of course, both countries had been badly defeated by England only several years earlier, so that an eventual attitude of revenge should have been taken into consideration by the English leaders. But, when movement from order to revolution was in its initial stages, there were no clear symptoms of the actualization of such an attitude. The foreign powers joined the conflict at a later stage, after having been encouraged by the magnificent resistance of the colonials to the armies sent overseas by the British government.

One may assert that the three essential conditions of the outbreak of a revolution stated in the preceding chapter were evident in the American case, and that only their conjunction can be considered to have been the cause of that revolution.

The English Revolution

The two social tensions which engendered the English revolution of 1642-49 are well known. One was political and the other religious. They were closely interrelated because of the existence, in England, of an Established Church, which made Church affairs also state affairs.

The political tension was effected by the diametrically opposed lines of the evolution of the nation and of the government, personified by the King. Despite her omnipotence, Queen Elizabeth never questioned the traditional rights of the Parliament. With the early Stuarts, it was quite different. James I who had been the King of Scotland several years before ascending to the English throne, assessed the English situation according to patterns existing in Scotland (where he had been able to separate the nobility from the clergy) and still more, according to the pattern of absolute monarchy then in full blossom in France and especially in Spain. In the beginning, the main point at issue was taxation; both James I and Charles I were in perpetual conflict with the Parliament just with respect to taxes. On the other hand, the majority of the gentry, the merchants, and the artisans would no longer tolerate the idea of an unlimited prerogative for the King. They called him and his supporters, mainly from among the higher nobility, "Normans, descendants of a group of invaders."

The political tension probably would not have resulted in a revolution—at least not in the first half of the seventeenth century—if it were not accentuated by the religious conflict. The first Stuarts were officially Anglicans, but innerly inclined toward Catholicism. But the vast majority of the population was still under the impact of the Reformation and abhorred anything which could be interpreted as a "return to popery." A very significant portion were Puritans desiring to expurgate from Anglicanism any survival of Catholicism. Neither camp admitted the idea of religious tolerance; each wanted to impose its will on the other. The line of demarcation between the Conformists and the Puritans did not quite coincide with the lines separating the Loyalists from those who wanted change. There were definitely less people who wanted to support the prerogatives of the King than people willing to support the *status quo* in the Church. As in the Dutch Revolution, the non-coincidence of the two lines of demarcation complicated the conflict, retarded its outbreak, and substantially influenced the outcome.

Contrary to an opinion expressed by some historians, there hardly was any particular economic tension (except in the semi-political aspect of taxation). Despite the actual misery of certain groups, early Stuart England was no less prosperous than Tudor England when the monarchy seemed unshakable. But below the overt political and religious tensions, there was a tension which may be called social in the narrow meaning of the term. The social status of the Calvinist gentry and merchants was lower than they thought due them because of their wealth; they were shut out from the higher social positions and from political power.

The antagonistic situation arose already in 1603, the first year of the reign of James I. But at that time nobody thought of revolution. The parties to the non-violent conflict proceeded by using any opportunity to go ahead, each in its own direction, and responded to each step of the opponents by countermoves. Some of the steps were, however, very close to revolution. The earliest of them was the Scottish Covenant (1638) which strongly influenced the situation in England, too. The subscribers swore to resist up to death the recent innovations introduced by the King which they declared to be unwarranted by the word of God, contrary to the Reformation and to acts of Parliament, and tending to restore popery and tyranny. In 1640, at a meeting of the Short Parliament, Pym formulated the grievances as follows: attacks on the members and privileges of the Parliament, religious innovations, the unpopular acts of the past fifteen years. In the opinion of an historian, he did not realize that he virtually proposed a revolution. On his part, the King often acted through the Established Church. Clear examples were the "seventeen new canons" of the year 1640, one of which "sublimated" the King; virtually every clause was offensive to the Puritans. In 1641, acts were passed by the Parliament which abolished all recent measures to raise revenue without Parliament, condemned imprisonment without a cause, and took a large part of the judiciary out of the royal hand. The point of no return was reached on March 17, 1642, when Parliament passed a resolution that the Lords and the Commons possessed the full right to declare what the law of the country was. In September of the same year, Charles I placed himself at the head of an army which soon began fighting the forces representing the Parliament's will. It had taken almost forty years before the parties came to the conclusion that their conflict could not be resolved except by means of the measurement of their relative strength by resorting to violent means.

Both parties had good reasons to expect that victory would be theirs. Charles believed he was a monarch by Divine right; he was fortified by the image of the strength of the monarchy in France and Spain and did not realize the tremendous difference between England (endowed with a Parliament and a well established local self-government) and the two continental nations mentioned, where there was no other power center but the King. But after all, his army, small as it was, was the only army in existence and, during the first years of the Civil War, Charles had, in general, the upper hand.

His opponents, to a large extent, relied on the strength of truth which they believed was absolutely on their side—both politically and religiously. They certainly knew that the ruling class of their time (reduced to a small group around the King) did not display the solidarity and balance necessary for the fulfillment of their function. They were aware of the fact that the King had little power; they well remembered that, in 1637, a riot arose in Edinburgh against which Charles tried in vain to proceed by force. They also knew that the vast majority of

Englishmen were in sympathy with the Scottish rebels. Note that Scotland had been in actual rebellion since 1640 when the army of the Covenant had crossed the Tweed and occupied two of England's counties. However, it took seven years before the victory of the opposition became definitive, which proves that, in the beginning, each party had reasons to believe in its victory.

In summary, there were, around 1640, serious and established tensions between the Crown and the majority of the people. Almost forty years of maneuvering had shown that no peaceful solution was possible. The relative strength of the parties was such that both started the struggle believing victory to be certain or at least probable. The three conditions required by the hypothesis formulated in the preceding chapter were present.

The Dutch Revolution

In the middle of the 1560's, the people of the Lowlands (a term covering approximately what is today Holland and Belgium) revolted against their overlord, King Philip II of Spain. The revolution began by imperceptible steps and gradually acquired the character of civil war. In 1576, a federation of the provinces of Holland and Zeeland was formed, a germ of the later Republic of the United Provinces; later on five other provinces joined them. On July 26, 1582, an Act of Abjuration was signed by representatives of the federated provinces, a preview of the American Declaration of Independence. On that date, the secession of the Netherlands was completed, although the struggle lasted until 1609 and was resumed in 1621 to last until 1648. But these later struggles must be classified as outright war between two states.

The outbreak of the mid-1560's was provoked by at least four social tensions which then existed in the area. The first and fundamental tension arose from the lack of national solidarity between the rulers and the ruled: since the middle of the fifteenth century, the people of the Netherlands were continuously governed by foreigners: first the dukes of Burgundy, then by the Hapsburgs whose major domain was Austria; and then, in 1559, when Charles V transferred power over the Western half of his possessions to his son, Philip, the Lowlands became an annex of Spain. It is noteworthy that the people opposing Philip and his successors were not homogeneous. While the majority spoke Dutch, a language which evolved from one of the German dialects, an important minority, the Walloons, spoke a dialect of French. But the fact that, for several decades, the Lowlands had formed one body politic and that, during that period, Estates General consisting of delegates of the single provinces were time and again convoked, stimulated the emergence of a common national consciousness. It also stimulated an awareness of the opposition between the interests of the emerging nation and the dynastic interests of their foreign rulers, and finally, awareness of differences between them and their neighbors. This antagonism was not evoked until 1559, because the successive monarchs, including Charles V, spoke at least one of the two languages of the country, Dutch or French, the latter being the language of the educated people through the Lowlands (except in the North-East). But Philip II was an outright foreigner who could not speak French or Dutch.

Second, there was a tension between a people firmly attached to ancient liberties and privileges which made each of the provinces a semi-autonomous body politic endowed with the right of self-taxation, and their new ruler, who, being first of all the absolute King of Spain, could not even understand the idea of local freedom which had been respected by his predecessors. This antagonism resulted in the often recurring phenomenon that even reasonable measures taken by the monarch without the concourse of the local authorities were resented and rejected. For instance, when Philip created new bishoprics which adjusted the religious organization of the land to the tremendous growth of the population, the measure was vehemently opposed by the nobility, the lower clergy and the leading elements of the townsfolk.

Third, there was a religious tension. Protestantism (mainly in the form of Calvinism) had begun to penetrate the people, and yet the King wanted by all means to maintain, in all his domain, the absolute rule of Catholicism. It is noteworthy that, contrary to superficial surveys of the Dutch revolution, its outbreak *cannot* be explained in terms of a clash between Protestants and Catholics. All the enlightened people of the Lowlands (then one of the most advanced countries of Europe) firmly stood for religious tolerance, the Catholics and Protestants alike. When Philip (who, after all, only confirmed and sharpened the measures already carried out by his father) issued several edicts ordering a pitiless persecution of the heretics, and when a number of executions ensued, public opinion grew more and more critical toward priests and monks. Lampoons, broadsheets and handbills denouncing the Inquisition were scattered and petitions were submitted to the leaders asking them to intercede before the King. At the outbreak of the revolution, Protestants formed only a small minority even in the North which, later on, for a while, became the stronghold of Calvinism. It is noteworthy that it was not until 1573 that William of Orange, the undisputed leader of the movement of liberation, joined the ranks of the Calvinists. But already in 1564 he openly stated that for him religious persecution was inadmissible. The later concentration of Protestantism in the North and the emergence of Calvinist fanaticism (no less intransigent than that of Philip II) complicated the situation and substantially affected the outcome of the revolution.

Fourth, there was a tension between the great commercial interests of the Lowlands which was then perhaps the richest country in Europe, and a monarch who tried to impose high taxes on them, without their consent, to pay the expenses of his wars, which had nothing to do with Dutch interests. This was also true under Charles V (who, however, never ignored the Estates), but was strongly accentuated under Philip.

The conflict between the King and the Lowlands, which we have analyzed into four specific tensions, was insoluble from the very start. The King was adamant. And William also never would move from these three points: 1) freedom of worship and preaching; 2) restoration and maintenance of all ancient charters; and 3) withdrawal of all Spanish and other foreign troops and functionaries from the Netherlands. Nevertheless, for a long period of time the opposition (which, in the earlier stages of the movement, remained unorganized) proceeded by means of petitions and remonstrations and tried to come to terms with the King who, in the beginning, was forced to yield. Thus, for instance, in 1558, the Estates General granted subsidies required by the King only if they were allowed to raise them by their own means and if the Spanish troops (only 3,000 men!) would leave the country; the hard pressed King was forced to give way. Later on, the restive masses asked the most prominent magnates to negotiate with the King. Egmont went to Madrid, but came back with empty hands. But twice Philip had to remove his Governor-Generals under the pressure of the population, first the Cardinal Granvelle and later on the hated Duke Alva. The second of these concessions was quite important but at the time when it happened (1573) it was already one of "the too little and too late" type. In general, the King treated the situation according to the pattern which, in this volume, is connoted by the term "reaction." In other words, he tried to bring back to unquestionable obedience a people who demanded just the opposite. Events proved that the conflict could not be solved in this way. Since Philip stubbornly denied reforms, and reaction proved to be ineffective, revolution became the only possible outcome. But, from the statements above, one must conclude that the parties resorted to conflict solution by the measurement of their relative strength only after all other solutions proved to be impractical.

The first two conditions for the outbreak of a revolution were present. How about the third?

Philip of Spain obviously did not doubt that victory would be his. Spain was then the strongest power in Europe. Moreover, the King dispatched to the area of the revolt one of his ablest and most reckless generals, Duke Alva. The Dutch leaders relied on the almost unanimous support of the just cause, specially by the population of the Northern provinces. They knew that Spain was far away, communication between Brussels (the see of the Governor-General) and Madrid slow and unreliable, and the zeal of the Spanish mercenaries moderate; in the mid-70's there were mutinies in the Spanish armies in the Netherlands for lack of pay. William of Orange counted also on some assistance from France, then an arch-foe of the Spaniards. However, this did not materialize. But events proved that, contrary to the previsions of the Spanish ruler, the self-confidence of the Dutch people was justified. In 1609, Spain was forced to interrupt attempts to reconquer the provinces in revolt for twelve years, and in 1648, after twenty-seven years of war, she was compelled to recognize the independence of the Republic of the United Provinces; she did so by signing the peace treaty of Westphalia.

Negative Cases

Let us now consider a few negative cases. Around 1860, there was in Russia a great social tension: first, between serfdom and the emerging economic system demanding free labor; second, between the extremely antiquated political and social forms and the cultural level attained by the elite. But the government led by Emperor Alexander II carried out the most needed reforms. The serfs were emancipated, the judicial system completely remodelled, local self government granted. This, for quite a time, absorbed a good deal of revolutionary energy. In consequence, revolution was prevented.

Another negative case can be seen in the avoidance of the repetition of the American revolution in other British dominions. The English colonies in Canada, Australia, and New Zealand have also evolved into ethnic groups different from the original British; but nowhere else was there any revolution against the motherland. In the American colonies, the tensions engendered by this basic fact were never resolved through reform. But reform intervened in the other white dominions before it was too late, for the motherland had learned the unpleasant lesson of the American secession.

A third negative case may be found in the peaceful solution of a most serious inter-ethnic conflict in Belgium, after the end of the First World War. While, originally, Belgian culture was entirely French, there gradually arose an antagonism between the Flems who awakened to national consciousness, and the Walloons whose language, French, was the official language of the country. The seriousness of the threat of a Flemish secession became obvious during the First World War. But it was treated by the Belgian government quite at variance with the policies of the government of the Kingdom of the Netherlands 80 years earlier in a similar situation. The Belgian government embarked on a reform program the aim of which was to make the nation bilingual with absolute equality of the two ethnic groups. As a symbol, the 20th century Kings of Belgium have been bilingual, and the administrative, judiciary, diplomatic, and military personnel are chosen in equal numbers from among the two groups. These officals are also required to speak fluently the two languages. Early symptoms of a pre-revolutionary situation gradually disappeared, and Belgium became a multi-national State of the same type as Switzerland.

In the United States, in 1932, there was a strong tension between the economic potential and the visible collapse of the economic system. The popularity of the political system was rapidly declining. But the government carried out the necessary reforms and restored confidence. A possible revolution, perhaps of a novel technocratic type, was thus averted.

In Communist Russia, there are numerous and strong social tensions; only minor reforms in the right direction are being made; but the government is overwhelmingly strong and does not allow a manifest withdrawal of the intellectuals. So no revolution can take place, until the government is shaken by struggle for power on the top level or by an unsuccessful war. The performance of the Communist leaders seems to prove that a purely autocratic government is stronger than a government making important, but still insufficient concessions to the opposition. The Communists explicitly endorse this proposition.[6]

The negative cases confirm that part of the hypothesis which emphasizes the residual character of revolution and the significance of the relative strength of the parties. The positive cases, on the other hand, demonstrate the significance of social tensions in the genesis of intra-state conflicts conducive to revolutions. Taken together, they make clear that a revolution breaks out not when one condition (e.g., a strong tension) is present, but only when the three conditions concur.

9/The Movement
from War to Peace

The Premises of Victory

War is a means of solving an inter-state conflict by measuring the relative strength of the parties. When war breaks out, the relative strength is ill defined; this is, we know, one of the basic conditions of the movement of political systems from peace to war.

In the course of a war, estimates and expectations of the parties as to their relative strength, including the eventual intervention of neutrals, are gradually replaced by facts. Through fighting it is established beyond reasonable doubt that one party is stronger than the other; in other words, that the anticipation of the former was right, that of the second wrong; or perhaps both estimates were wrong, since, in action, both parties proved to be equally strong. Then, one of the conditions of warfare, uncertainty as to relative strength, is eliminated. The immediate goal of war is attained; continuing it would no longer serve any reasonable purpose. Therefore, the war is over and the system composed of the fighting nations returns to peace.

Therefore, the study of the causal background of the return of political systems from war to peace is tantamount to the study of the premises of victory and of the mechanism converting victory into peace.

1. The premises of victory may be arranged into three levels of depth. Most conspicuous is the military one. Here, men and weapons must be considered, both from the points of view of quantity and quality.

Other things equal, the number of armed men at the disposal of a party as compared with the number of fighters for the other party is of great importance; as stated by Napoleon, *les gros bataillons ont toujours raison.* But other things are rarely equal. An important corrective must be introduced: the *training,* both of rank-and-file soldiers and of the leaders, officers and generals. A smaller army with superior training of soldiers and better generals can inflict a decisive defeat on a larger army consisting of poorly trained soldiers and/or poor generals. Naturally, in the case of the generals, especially those in the highest positions, not only training, but innate abilities are also of great importance. An army commanded by a military genius, of the type of Alexander of Macedonia, Hannibal, Caesar or Napoleon, may gain victory even when all other conditions are adverse. Since a military genius displays his actual stature only during actual warfare, this is just one of the premises of victory about which peacetime conjectures may prove entirely wrong. Early in the twentieth century, Russia was believed to have a great general in the person of Kuropatkin; but his performance in the Japanese war proved to be extremely poor. On the other hand, the anti-Russian coalition of the Crimean war could not have foreseen that the genius of a Todtleben would stop them before the walls of Sebastopol for 11 months.

In any case, relying on the availability of a military genius not yet tested in warfare would be foolish. The Germans who, since the middle of the nineteenth century, developed the best military machine after that of Napoleon, came to the conclusion that, since a military genius may or may not appear, victory should be rather secured by the homogeneity of the training of the military leaders. The aim of this training was that in every particular situation, each general would make approximately the same decision, being guided by a precise military doctrine inculcated in everyone at the military academy. Then, the general commanding detachments operating on a certain front would expect everyone to do what he was really doing; this proved to be one of the decisive factors in the crushing victory of the Prussians over the French in 1870-1.

Thus, a very high level of coordination of decisions and actions could be provided as a good substitute for a military genius.

A larger quantity of decisive weapons is an important premise of victory, other things equal. A numerous and valiant army has to yield to an enemy who can use against it more instruments of death and destruction than it can use for retaliation. The Russians, in the campaign of 1915, had to retreat before the Germans because of a high disparity of the number of shells the parties could fire during a certain period of time. In 1940, the French suffered a crushing defeat at the hands of the Germans because the number of tanks and planes they had was incomparably inferior to that of the foe.

The quality of the weapons is a most significant factor. Two propositions can be stated. First, if one of the parties has arms so superior to those of the other party that the latter is left no chance to use those it has, victory of the former is certain. The victory of Cortez against the Aztecs was gained with 400 men, 16 horses and three guns versus quite a few thousands of men. In recent days, the victory of Italy against Ethiopia (1935) and of Israel against the Arabs (1948) was gained under similar circumstances.

Second, if one of the parties has an absolute weapon (i.e., a weapon against which there exists no adequate defense) and the other one has not, victory of the former is certain. An absolute weapon, the A-bomb, knocked out Japan who did not have it. For the first few years after the end of the Second World War, the Soviet Union was contained by the A-bombs stockpiled in the United States while the former had none. Today the parties probably differ as to the quantity and quality of A-bombs and perhaps also H-bombs: therefore, the second of the propositions just enounced is no longer applicable.

2. The second level corresponds to the general background of the nation which has to supply armed men and weapons. Here one may distinguish three major components. First comes the demographic component, i.e., the size of the population and its sex and age distribution. Not the total figures,

but the numbers of young adult males (age group 18 to 35, perhaps 40) is decisive. The Soviet Union was at great advantage during the Second World War since its population was larger and better provided with young adult males than that of any other belligerent. After the end of the war, its position deteriorated because of heavy losses in that group. Now, more than twenty years after the outbreak of the war, the balance as to the population of military age has been restored; but at the same time the effect of the birth deficit during the war and the first postwar years is strongly felt. This deficit was generally overlooked in the estimates of the Soviet population, except by Prof. S. N. Prokopovich and this author[1] whose "predictions" have been almost completely verified by the census of 1959: the age group 10-19 (born 1939-48) was much smaller than the preceding and the following ones: 31.7 million in the age group 10-19 vs. 48.4 million in the age group 0-9 (born 1949-58) and 38.7 million in the age group 20-29 (born 1929-38).

The second component is technological and economic: how much militarily relevant raw material is available? This includes coal, iron, oil, and now also uranium. What is the industrial equipment allocated for manufacturing the weapons? How much skilled labor is available to operate the equipment? What is the food supply? And what is the level achieved by the transportation system necessary to deliver raw material to the places of manufacturing, food to the places of demographic concentration (commonly coinciding with the former), and men and ready arms to the battlefields? Russia's underdeveloped industrial and transportation systems were mainly responsible for her defeats in World War One, while America's technological superiority was one of the decisive factors of the victory of the democratic coalition in both World Wars.

The third component is political—the quality of general leadership. War is not only the supreme test of military leadership, but of political leadership also. A nation may rely either on the appearance of a superior leader of highest ability, perhaps "by God's will" (e.g., by being granted a hereditary monarch possessing the properties of superior leadership), or by the self-assertion of a "great man" avid for power (such was the case of Napoleon), or by the play of institutions provided that the people freely elevate to supreme leadership men deserving that position. In the course of the First World War, the American, British and French democracies had the advantage of being led (at least toward the end of the war) by men deserving that position (Wilson, Lloyd George, Poincaré, Clémenceau) while Germany and Russia were led by narrow-minded monarchs. During the Second World War, America and England had still better leaders (Roosevelt and Churchill) while France had the ill luck of being led by Daladier and Pétain. In the Soviet Union, the great leadership ability of Stalin, a man who imposed himself on the oligarchy which had seized power in 1917, is beyond doubt, despite adverse moral judgments concerning his policies.

In the course of a war, one of the most salient traits of good leadership receives the greatest importance: this is the ability to concentrate on one purpose, that is, winning the war. Diversion of attention to other purposes, particularly preoccupation with the problem of what will happen when war is over, is often conducive to defeat. This proposition was tested many times in the course of the Napoleonic wars by the

Austrians, who suffered many crushing defeats because their military plans were always subordinate to political considerations.

Many contemporary authors in their *ex post facto* discussions often disregard this proposition and blame the supreme leaders of the West for militarily correct though politically disadvantageous decisions. Of course, many mistakes were made also from the purely military point of view, often due to misinformation about the strength of the enemy. The most disastrous was the decision of the United States to pay a high price for the Soviet Union's help against Japan while that country was already defeated.

3. The third and deepest level is morale, or the will of a nation to gain victory; more exactly, its readiness to accept all the sacrifices necessary to achieve that purpose. Morale is comparable with motive power in a machine. A perfect machine does not accomplish anything if not supplied with motive power. A nation at war (as well as at peace) does not accomplish anything if there is no identification of the individuals (at least their vast majority) with the collectivity, no internalization of the national goal which is to gain victory. Morale is one of the intangibles in the prewar estimates of the chance of victory, a big X hardly calculable in the complicated system of equations in which these estimates could be expressed. It is commonly higher in defensive than in aggressive situations. It is also higher in conflicts of the nationalistic or ideological types than in conflicts about territory or economic advantages. It fluctuates depending on partial victories and defeats, and this again depends on specified culture traits of the combatting nations. There are nations which can be demoralized by initial defeat; there are nations

in which defeat rather strengthens morale, so long as hope of victory is not gone. Such was, in the last war, the case of England in the days when she had to fight alone, of the Soviet Union in the days after Hitler's spectacular successes in the summer of 1941, of the United States after Pearl Harbor.

Moreover, morale can be manipulated. It is a rather recent discovery that public opinion and morale can be influenced by propaganda which, during the war, strives for the strengthening of the morale of the nation where it originates and for the undermining of the morale of the foe. Today propaganda is the subject matter of a special branch of sociology. Naturally, we will not discuss these sociological findings here. It suffices to say that after a period of exaggeration of the virtual effects of propaganda, more moderate views have prevailed. We know that propaganda can only re-enforce and crystallize existing attitudes, perhaps help select some of the existing attitudes and eliminate or at least weaken the opposite ones; but it never can create a system of attitudes out of nothing. A nation which does not want to fight will not fight despite skillful propaganda, e.g., Italy in the Second World War. But in a nation where opinion about the validity of the arguments in favor or against war has been divided up to the day of decision, skillful propaganda can re-enforce the former and press down the latter. In a nation losing hope of victory, skillful and efficient propaganda by the enemy may hasten the crystallization of attitudes conducive to surrender. We know also that, other things equal, propaganda achieves most when its objectives coincide with the natural, though often vague, aspirations of the addressees; that it is more successful the more it is adapted to their cultural level; that its success depends on frequent and systematic repetition and, if possible, demonstration on the level of action.

These rules are now known everywhere. But their application by the two parties may be differential. Then, at least one of the parties succeeds, at least partly, in undermining the morale of the foe without losing anything of its force of cohesion. This, eventually, may change the relationship of the strength of the parties.

The Interrelation of the Premises.

The premises of victory and defeat are many and diversified. Some can be measured exactly, such as the size of the population, or the number of men with military training, or the productive capacity of the relevant branches of industry. Some can be measured only approximately. Thus, for instance, attempts to measure morale have been made, directed however toward the establishment of trends—whether it is going up or down, not towards establishing absolute magnitudes which could be compared. Some cannot be measured at all; for instance, the quality of military training, or the ability of military or political leadership. This is one of the major reasons why estimates of a nation's relative strength are so problematic, so long as the nation has not come under the test of war. Another reason is that the individual premises of victory are interrelated in a complicated manner. Therefore the magnitude of each item may play a larger or smaller part (to be expressed by applying to them coefficients above or below one).

1. In an imaginary system of equations corresponding to the particular factors (or premises) changing coefficients must be applied to some of them depending on the general

level of culture and the mode of warfare conditioned by it. In the early Middle Ages, the demographic and the technological components were quite insignificant while the valor and the training of the individual fighters was decisive. In the age of the mercenary armies, the decisive factor was economic: the country with more gold could pay larger armies, and for a longer time and, in this manner, win war. This explains the very important role of the Netherlands in the military affairs of the sixteenth to the eighteenth centuries. Then there came an age when the number of fighters, as determined largely by the size of the population, was paramount; this period lasted from the Revolutionary and Napoleonic wars until the First World War. Beginning with the latter, technological superiority has received the highest importance; naturally, to work, a nation's industry must be sufficiently manned and the nation's morale be high.

2. As in every social system, in states at war the principle of minimum efficiency is in force. In other words, the military potential of a nation is determined by the weakest link in the chain. Lack of trained manpower destroys the significance of a vast industrial establishment; poor generalship condemns to defeat large and valiant armies; insufficiency of weapons, insufficiency of transportation, lack of food, miserable leadership on the political level, poor morale, may become decisive factors of defeat. If political leadership is good, the weakest link in the chain is recognized at due time, and all efforts are concentrated on strengthening it. In this way, defeat may be averted. But if political leadership is poor, the weakest link will remain undetected, or efforts to improve the situation will be inadequate.

On the other hand, correct recognition of the weakest link

in the system of the enemy may result in victory. During the First World War, Germany's enemies correctly recognized that her weakest point was food supply and the supply of some strategic materials so they successfully used blockade to defeat her. The reminiscence of that success deceived, however, Germany's foes in the Second World War; they also heavily relied on blockade, but this time the device did not work since Germany was able to get food from the nations conquered by her during the first phase of the war and to replace crucial material by substitutes.

3. While the potential premises of victory or defeat are given from the very start, their actualization (or mobilization) takes some time because no nation can live in the state of perpetual and complete preparedness for war. The differential ability of mobilization, or of the velocity of efforts to achieve maximum strength may be decisive. Germany launched the two world wars in the belief that she would be ready much earlier than her foes and knock them out before they would have actualized their potential strength. As a counterpart of the device of rapid mobilization, nations may use the device of trading space for time, in other words, retreating so long and so far as possible to achieve maximum strength and then to strike back. Naturally, this device can be used only by nations disposing of vast space. In this regard Russia with her gigantic territory is the most favored nation. The advantage of trading space for time was recognized already by the Scythians, the predecessors of the Russians on their present day territory. Many times in Russian history, victory was won deep in the country, after the foe's initial momentum had slowed down, and the Russians had gained strength. This happened under Peter the Great in his war against Sweden

won at Poltava (1709) deep in the Ukraine, in the war against Napoleon (1812) in the south and west of Moscow and in the Second World War, most conspicuously at Stalingrad (1943). Great Britain was well protected by water which always gave her time to gather strength against a dynamic enemy who attained maximum strength in the beginning, but then was exhausted by the war effort. On the contrary, France is handicapped by the short distance of her capital from the most vulnerable of her boundaries. In our days of tanks, airplanes and A- and H-bombs, the device of trading space for time has lost a good deal of significance. This increases the importance of rapid and well planned mobilization. Efforts of the too little and too late type may easily result in irreparable catastrophe.

4. The intensity of mobilization, in other words, the percentage of manpower to be induced into the army and the percentage of the amount of basic commodities to be spent to produce munitions is determined by military and political considerations. Too many men inducted into the armed forces may mean not enough men left over to operate industry or produce food; this was one of Russia's chief mistakes in the First World War. Too much iron, coal and oil diverted to produce munitions may mean not enough for transportation or for essential civilian consumption. The latter may lower the morale, especially if morale is not very high. Correct decisions in this regard sometimes transcend the wisdom of very able statesmen, not to speak of leaders of average ability. But victory or defeat may depend on them.

5. In wars of coalition, the elements of strength and weakness must be calculated not only relative to the individual participants, but also to the coalition as a whole. Members

rich in industrial equipment may provide the poorer ones with munitions; nations rich in population may provide the other ones with additional fighters which in turn depends on the availability of adequate means of transportation. Lend-lease, convoys to Murmansk and delivery of war goods through Iran to the Soviet Union are instances from the last war.

An additional element enters into the equation. This is the degree of cohesion in the system formed by the coalition. From this point of view two types of coalitions may be distinguished, coalitions in which one of the states plays the role of the hegemon, and coalitions of the co-equal partnership type. Coalitions of the first type offer better chances of cohesion; this was the case of coalitions led by France under Napoleon, by Germany under William II and Hitler. But even these coalitions broke down when the specter of defeat clearly appeared on the wall of destiny.

Coalitions of the second type are difficult to manage. Many coalition wars against revolutionary France and Napoleon have been lost because of reciprocal suspicion and lack of coordination. The First World War was almost lost by the allies because of poor coordination; only facing defeat did France and England agree to have a supreme commander of their armies. In the Second World War, this lesson from history was well remembered and the principle of unified command was adhered to from the very start. In the latter part of the war, the United States tacitly and tactfully played the part of the hegemon which allowed the allies to maintain cohesion on the highest level; this was, of course, an important factor of victory.

Summing up, one may say that the integration of the numerous factors of victory or defeat into the real outcome of the war (actual victory or defeat), resembles the solution of a system of indetermined equations, i.e., of equations whose number is smaller than the number of the unknown variables so that the magnitude of the other ones can be calculated only on the foundations of choices relative to some of the unknown variables. This complexity is still increased if a war of coalition is waged, or if neutrals are likely to join one or another party. For a particular member of the coalition the chance of victory depends mainly on having chosen the right side, and then on the effort contributed by that member itself. But the total effort to be contributed by the coalition must be higher than that of the foe.

One could not insist enough on the fact that, though the determinants of victory are objective facts, their assessment by the leaders of the parties to the conflict is a mental process which may lag behind the unfolding of the objective process. For quite a time, initial defeats may be considered as temporary setbacks only, and they may prove to be so. In any case, hope may persist that a reversal of the trend will occur, owing to more complete, though delayed mobilization, or the deterioration of the morale of the enemy, or the interference of neutrals. But a moment comes when hope is lost. Then, one more of the conditions of warfare is gone, more exactly, is replaced by its opposite. To go to war, at least one of the parties must have lost the hope of achieving its objective by means short of war. Now, at least for one of the parties, there is no longer hope to impose a favorable solution of the conflict through war. The impact of the change on the state of the political system at war depends on the answer now supplied by objective facts to the question of the relative strength of the parties.

War and Revolution

The Mechanism of the Return to Peace

If this relative strength proves to be approximately equal, so that the estimates of the two parties are shown to have been wrong, negotiations commonly start, sometimes induced by "good services" of a third and neutral party. The outcome of these negotiations can be foreseen in advance. This is, in principle, return to the *status quo ante*, sometimes with mutual and slight adjustments correcting some defects in the prewar situation. A typical example would be the peace treaty of Ghent (1814) which terminated the Anglo-American war that started in 1812. The Korean war was terminated in a similar way, by replacing a conventional boundary corresponding to a geographical notion (the 38th parallel) by one based on topographical conditions; the new boundary intersects the old line, but is more appropriate for defense.

Usually, the differential strength of the parties is established. Then, it is for the weaker party to ask for the termination of hostilities and thus to induce negotiations. Very much depends on the magnitude of the differential. If one of the parties proves to be overwhelmingly superior, negotiations may be replaced by a "dictat" on the part of the victor, or even by outright annexation; or, if negotiations take place, only minor points are subject to debate while, in general, the will of the victor is decisive. After some of his campaigns, Napoleon unilaterally annexed small states which chose the wrong side. In 1866, Prussia annexed four minor German states which sided against her with Austria. The South African War resulted in the annexation of the Boer republics (1902). The first phase of the Second World War resulted in the partition of Poland between Germany and her non-belligerent ally, the

Soviet Union. Typical instances of "dictat" include the peace treaty of Pressburg (1805) imposed by Napoleon on Austria (after a few hours of negotiations) or the treaty of Brest-Litovsk (1918), after Trotsky's tactics of "no war no peace" proved not to impress the Germans, and the conditions of the armistice of 1918 imposed on Germany by the allies. The Second World War was terminated by a series of "unconditional surrenders," but the appearance on the horizon of a new conflict between victorious allies resulted in making rather mild the peace terms imposed on Italy and Japan. The same is true with respect to the agreement of the Western powers with the German Federal Republic signed in 1952 which is a peace treaty in all but the name.

If the difference between the strength of the parties proves not to be high, actual negotiations are entered by the belligerents. They may break down; then war is resumed, and the relative strength of the parties is tested again. The result of this test is then reflected in negotiations whenever they are resumed. If the stronger party gains new successes, its demands may harden; on the contrary, if no further successes are forthcoming, they may be pressed down. Finally, by gradual approximations, a compromise solution is found based on the principle of the lesser evil. The weaker party accepts the terms because the demanded concessions mean the cessation of war which, by this time, has been recognized as an aimless waste of manpower and national goods with no hope of achieving favorable results. Accepting the terms may mean avoiding still greater concessions which could be demanded by the enemy after further warfare resulted in additional beating for the weaker party. The stronger party may accept to make peace on conditions somewhat milder than the demands made at the beginning of the negotiations because the advantages of the return to peace plus those stipulated in the peace treaty overbalance additional expectations which might be realized by continuing hostilities. Thus, when signing the peace treaty of Frankfurt (1871), Prussia renounced her claim on Belfort which was stubbornly denied by France. When signing the peace treaty of Portsmouth (1906), Japan was satisfied with the annexation of Southern Sakhalin and the acquisition of Russia's rights in Manchuria, but dropped her demands for military indemnity and surrender of Russian warships interned in neutral ports.

Such is the mechanism through which a political system consisting of two or more belligerent states returns to peace. The conditions of peace are determined partly by the immutable nature of the states as territorial power structures, partly by the views on the subject ingrained in the culture of the nations involved, more especially in the victorious nations.

The Territorial Conditions of Peace

Since the states are territorial groups, and since a vast number of interstate conflicts are directly or indirectly territorial, the most basic feature of a peace treaty is territorial. The victor is rewarded by a province taken from the defeated party, or even by the latter's total territory. This is, as we know, the manifestation of the principle of reward and punishment playing the part of a mighty brake against war. When war is over, its application is tantamount to the adjustment of the normative equilibrium in the framework of a family of nations to the existential equilibrium found by the measurement of the relative strength of the parties. The equilibrium thus found becomes normative since every peace treaty is part of international law; this new state of normative equilibrium is to last until another major crisis in the area is resolved by another war, that is, a new test of real equilibrium.

The pattern of reward and punishment may be further analyzed, and then the following elements appear.

1) The pattern corresponds to a *de facto* situation: the victor occupies the contested territory, perhaps some additional territory, and the enemy has lost the hope of expelling him by the force of arms. Since, according to international law, the relationship between the belligerents is a pure power relationship, the difficulty can be solved only on the basis of the *do ut des* or the reciprocity principle, redeeming of the losses and eliminating the prospect of further disadvantages by abandoning still more territory. Therefore, the frontier thus traced may be considered as the objectivization of the existential equilibrium of the states involved. Since the boundaries persist for a long time, the political map roughly corresponds to power equilibria which were given at the time of the preceding crises in relations between the states involved.

2) There is, however, in the pattern of the transfer of territory from the defeated to the victorious party more than a sheer expression of the differential strength; very often the acquisition of territory is interpreted as the exertion of a right. This point of view is closely connected with another element of the war-and-peace culture tradition, namely, with the interpretation of war in terms of judicial combat, or God's judgment. Then, success in arms is claimed by the victor to be tantamount to the judgment that his cause was just; time and again, the defeated agrees. Thus, for instance, the Japanese war (1904-5) was considered by many Russians as

unjust; the defeat was accepted without bitterness, and cordial Russo-Japanese relations could be established a few years later. Similar was the attitude of many Englishmen toward the war with the American colonies. Many transfers of territory after the First World War have been interpreted in the same way.

It is noteworthy that such an interpretation survived long after the elimination of the judical combat from the means of solving conflicts within the states, because the constitution of international society of our day is the exact counterpart of the constitution of tribal society which acknowledged the ordeal. So long as a development parallel to the elimination of the latter does not take place in international society, thinking of war in terms of judicial combat cannot be entirely eliminated anymore than the justification of territorial acquisition by the very fact of military success.

3) The possibility of acquiring territory after victory and the interpretation of such acquisitions in terms of right does not suffice to explain the facts: not every possibility is used, not every right is exerted. An additional element must enter into the total configuration; the leaders of the victorious state must believe that a territorial aggrandizement is an asset. This is an idea which emerges naturally: the greater the territory ruled, the greater the social prestige of the rulers, the greater the possibilities as to taxes, natural resources and recruits. In certain historical periods, for instance, during the age of mercantilism, the advantage of acquiring territory was considered a self-evident truth. In the beginning of the French Revolution other justifications for the acquisition of territory were substituted (see below); but it is an interesting example of social inertia that, very soon, the old pattern reappeared on the scene. Beginning with the treaty of Campo-Formio

(1797), revolutionary France started acquiring every territory which could be annexed as the result of victory.

In this regard, a certain change of culture tradition is undeniable. In our day, in certain cases, the possession of a particular territory is considered a liability rather than an asset. The corollary is eventual abandonment of territory. One of the earliest cases is the gift of the Ionian Islands, on the part of Great Britain, to Greece (1863). Another is the emancipation of the Philippines by the United States. On a gigantic scale, the pattern of the abandonment of a territory has been expressed in the emancipation of India, Pakistan, Burma and Indonesia; later on, in the precipitous dissolution of the French and the Belgian colonial empires and the emancipation of most English colonies in Africa. But the old pattern has survived in the minds of the men in the Kremlin who, in general, live in the mid-nineteenth century atmosphere in which Marxism was born. They did not doubt that, as victors in a global war, the Soviet Union was to be royally rewarded and they embodied their faith in the notorious annexations along their Western border and in the Far East.

In territorial peace settlements, the principle of reward and punishment is partly supplemented, partly reenforced by four more principles.

Among the justifications of territorial claims (or of objections to such claims) reference to past facts plays an important part. A state claims a territory because it had possessed it a few years, or a few centuries, ago. In consequence, later change of possessors is denied validity, is declared to have established merely precarious possession on the part of the acquiring power, and not that legitimate dominion which in public affairs corresponds to property in private affairs. Sometimes, this type of claim is given the particular aspect of "legitimacy"; then, the claim means that, in international law, no change of dominion has taken place and the claimant aims at the restoration of the order which was violated by another state's interference. Logically, this particular justification could be used only against the beneficiary of the last treaty who is now declared to be a trespasser. One of the most important cases when this justification was applied—this was at the Vienna Congress (1814)—the principle was used to revive territorial rights abandoned through freely signed treaties. Austria, Prussia and other states claimed and, in general, received territories which were lost by treaties framed according to the pattern of reward and punishment.

The principle of historical rights was often used by the French kings in the seventeenth and eighteenth centuries to justify the eastbound expansion of France. In many cases the principle of legitimacy was manipulated in such a manner that not the formerly possessed territory, but an equivalent one was adjusted to the claimant. This introduces a modification of the pattern, "compensation."

Once more, the principle of historical rights played a large part in the peace settlement of 1919. The return of Alsace-Lorraine to France without plebiscite was justified by the allegedly unjust (though legal) character of their acquisition by Germany in 1871. Part of the boundaries of Czechoslovakia was traced according to this principle. The memoranda submitted by the Czechs as well as the Germans to the peace conference are very illuminating. The Czechs claimed the totality of the "historical lands" (with about 30% of German population), firstly, because they were the authochtons and the Germans but late immigrants and, secondly, because the Czech kings had for centuries ruled the area in question. The Germans could not deny the latter fact; in consequence, they partly rejected the principle in favor of the self-determination then in vogue among the victors, and in addition to this, introduced historical counter-claims maintaining that the Germans had inhabited the territory long before the first Czechs arrived.

Reference to historical rights has been often made in the course of the interallied feud between the Soviet Union and Poland. For a while, this feud was revived in the exchange of angry notes and declarations which took place in 1943-45. The facts are these: large provinces East and West of the so called Curzon line[2] have alternately belonged to the two parties; there was a time when the Poles possessed not only Vilna and Lvov, but also Kiev, Poltava and Smolensk, and there was a time when the Russians possessed Warsaw. The Poles rejected with indignation any reference to the latter fact in which the outright injustice of Poland's partitions was manifested. The Russians answered that the partitions came as a kind of retaliation for the injustice committed by Poland and her predecessor in the area, Lithuania, when conquering Russian principalities in the course of centuries during which Russia was weakened by the Tartar invasion. They added that, at the third partition (1795), Russia merely acquired territories which had belonged to her before the conquest just mentioned. This contention, by the way, is expressed in the manifesto of Catherine II which emphasized the historical aspect of the annexation: "I have taken back what had been torn away." They said, furthermore, that in 1815 purely Polish territories were not incorporated in Russia, but given autonomous existence, as Czardom Poland which the Poles forfeited because of their revolution of 1830-31. The Poles replied that this revolution was caused by the intolerable inter-ference of the Russians in Polish affairs, contrary to the liberal Constitution of 1815;[3] they added that in any case, Eastern Galicia had never belonged to the Russian Empire, so that the Soviet state could not have any claim on it even if it had inherited the historical rights of the Russian Empire. To this, however, the Russians could object that, up to the 14th cen-tury, Eastern Galicia had belonged to the Russian system of principalities and had been ruled by princes of the house of Rurik; only then was it annexed by Poland.

It is obvious that, commonly, the reference to "historical rights" leads nowhere because many territories changed hands many times so that two or more nations can claim them on the basis of such rights—by choosing different periods of the past.

As to compensation, this type of territorial settlement has reappeared on the scene in the famous offer of the Soviet government to Poland (not to the Polish government in exile!) on January 11, 1944, that Poland be made "strong and in-dependent" by the reannexation of territories grabbed from her by the Germans through the centuries. Here, once more, the principle of historical rights, and rights of venerable antiq-uity, was used. Moreover, the reannexation of these provinces was offered as a compensation for the loss of the eastern provinces to the USSR. Thus, denying the legitimacy of the Polish claims on the contested territory in the East, the Soviet government still thought it necessary to compensate Poland for its loss. Compensation was offered at the expense of the loser, Germany, in partial fulfillment of the pattern of reward of the victor.

A further principle of postwar redistribution of territory is that of strategic boundaries. The victorious state demands a territory because it makes this state militarily invulnerable or weakens another state which is considered as a virtual aggressor. Though this principle was often used since the Middle Ages, it received full recognition during the earlier part of the French revolution when France officially claimed her "natural frontiers": the Rhine, the Alps, the Pyrenées. Later Napoleonic conquests often secured for the French armies favorable jumping boards for starting further campaigns. The principle was not officially used at the Vienna Congress, but the change of boundary between France and the Netherlands effected in 1815[4] aimed at increasing the security of the latter against the former: France had to cede a line of fortresses along the boundary traced in 1814. The annexation of Metz by Germany in 1871 was justified by military considerations. At the Paris Conference, 1919, strategic considerations prevailed in granting Southern Tyrol to Italy and tracing the Czech border along the crest of the Bohemian framework of mountains. In 1943-46, the territorial claims of the Soviets have been interpreted by many in terms of military security. Therefore, the Western democracies have made quite a few unsuccessful efforts to guarantee that security to the Soviets, offering, for instance, a formal treaty of military alliance for long years. The rejection of these efforts has proven, beyond doubt, that the desire of security had not been the mainspring of the annexations.

Still another principle influencing the postwar redistribution of territory is that of economic and administrative expediency. This reason for territorial settlement has appeared on the historical scene rather late, simultaneously with the increase of the role of economics in national life and the expansion of the state's functions and, therefore, administrative activities. Today such claims as "access to the sea" and "continuity of territory" seem to be almost self-evident, but in the eighteenth century many European states had neither access to the sea, nor continuous territory.

When one studies the results of the Vienna Congress (not the declarations of the participants), he is struck by the consistent though implicit or tacit application of the principle of economic and administrative expediency to the settlement of territorial problems. Compare the Hapsburg monarchy in 1789 and 1815: the territory and population were approximately the same, as the result of the application of the principle of legitimacy, with its corollary, compensation, but in 1815 the state was made definitely stronger than it had been in 1789. At Vienna, a natural economic unit, the Danubian basin which offered all facilities for efficient administration, was made a state. The application of this principle explains the relative stability of the Vienna order much more than the principle of legitimacy; where the Vienna statesmen were unable to create states adjusted to economic and administrative exigencies, their work proved to be less durable. In the later unification of Germany and Italy, the principle of economic and administrative expediency has played a role, along with that of nationality; one of the particular phases was the annexation, by Prussia, of those German states which separated her into an eastern and a western half.

In the operation of the principles thus far studied the states appeared as actors and claimants. With the rise of democracy, another set of actors appeared on the historical scene, the populations involved. Reference to the will of the people as

228

a factor in territorial settlement may be objective or subjective. In the former case, the claimant asserts that the population of the contested area forms part of a definite ethnic group and therefore ought to belong to a state best representing that group. In the latter case, the population is permitted to express its desires by means of a plebiscite which is then used as the basis of territorial delimitation. Only in the latter case is there a genuine "self-determination of nations," a term which is often improperly applied to designate also the other case.

Historically, the principle of nationality has first appeared in the subjective variety: the famous plebiscite held in the Comtat Venaissain[5] in 1791 was used to certify the will of its population to join the French state. Some later conquests of the French republic, e.g., Belgium, were vindicated on the ground that the inhabitants of the conquered areas were French and therefore had to belong to France. At the Vienna Congress, the principle was frowned upon as one of revolutionary origin. But in the nineteenth century it became paramount. Greeks, Serbians, Bulgarians, and Rumanians, gained national independence after having asserted their will to separate from Turkey through the strongest of all arguments, armed insurrection. The Polish revolution (1830) and the Hungarian secession from Austria (1848) were defeated, but in 1830 the Belgians gained independence from the Netherlands in the same way as the Balkan nationalities. Plebiscites ratified the unification of the Italian nation and the transfer of Nice and Savoy to France (1860-2); this was in the subjective style of the early French revolution. In the unification of Germany the will of the people was not checked; there is, however, no doubt as to its endorsement of unification, except in the case of Alsace-Lorraine where the objective modality of the principle was used; people inhabiting the Alsace and the major part of the Lorraine spoke a German dialect and therefore ought to belong to Germany. The history of these provinces under German rule shows, however, that the inhabitants would have chosen France if asked the question in the form of a plebiscite.[6]

At the Paris Conference (1919), the principle was used mainly in its objective variety. New states were created and boundaries rectified with the view of making states coincide with ethnic groups as described by their spokesmen. Once more, the principle was applied to Alsace-Lorraine; people living there were declared to be French in their hearts (if not in tongue) and consequently were attributed to France. When the principle of objective nationality did not yield a clear cut solution, the pattern of the reward of the victor came to the rescue: mixed populations were adjudged to the members of the victorious coalition and their newly born allies. In a few cases only (Schleswig, Upper Silesia, Allenstein, Carinthia) the subjective form of decision through plebiscite was used. In Eastern Europe, things still were in flux, and only tentative solutions could be reached.

In the preceding survey of principles which are used by nations partly to formulate, partly to justify their territorial claims to be embodied in peace treaties or their substitutes, a remarkable tendency to persist has appeared. Even in such a recent settlement as the creation of Czechoslovakia, the following elements were present: historical rights, strategic boundaries, economic and administrative expediency and objective nationality, in dubious cases supplemented and integrated by the pattern of the reward of the victor to whose number the Czechoslovak nation was considered to belong.

The recent Russo-Polish dispute has been characterized by insistence on the relatively older elements of the culture pattern. Historical rights and objective nationality have been in the forefront, and it is only in the denial of real-determination that the two parties agreed. As has already been stated, the Russians have rediscovered the Vienna principle of compensation for frustrated expectations based on legitimacy.

The culture pattern here considered, as every culture pattern, is subject to change. One of the obvious tendencies of the development is the gradual withering away of the principle of the reward of the victor corroborated by its disappearance from the verbal expressions of the participants. But it has not yet disappeared, and in any case the men in the Kremlin have continued to hold to it in their actions.

Other Conditions of Peace

The territorial aspect of peace treaties is the most basic and important, but it is not the only one. Peace treaties may include military and economic clauses, obligations concerning ethnic and religious minorities, and declarations on the moral level.

Military clauses commonly mean the restriction of the sovereignty of the defeated state in the matter of armament. The pattern was invented by Napoleon when, in 1807, he imposed on defeated Prussia the obligation not to raise an army above 43,000 men. This was repeated by the victorious allies in 1919 when they prohibited Germany to have an army based on conscription and the system of trained reserves. In addition, they limited her standing army to 100,000 men. After the Second World War similar clauses have reappeared in the peace treaties with Italy and Germany's satellites. The peace treaty of 1814 imposed on France the obligation to tolerate allied garrisons in several frontier cities. The Paris peace treaty of 1856 prohibited Russia from having a navy in the Black Seas. The Versailles Peace Treaty (1919) demilitarized the Rhineland. It is noteworthy that none of the limitations has proven to be durable. Through circumvention or explicit repudiation, the military sovereignty of the states in question was restored.

Economic clauses of a peace treaty impose on the defeated nation the duty to compensate the victor for his military expenses; this is another expression of the pattern of reward-and-punishment. In recent peace treaties, disadvantageous commercial agreements have been imposed on the defeated parties, even economic servitude. For instance, according to the Portsmouth treaty (1905), Russia granted Japan fishery rights in her territorial waters.

In peace treaties which concluded the many Russo-Turkish wars, Russia was granted the right to protect specified Christian and/or Slavic subjects of the Sultan. In the only war in which Turkey, helped by France and Great Britain, was victorious (the Crimean War, 1853-56), these privileges were abolished. But analogous clauses appeared in peace treaties with nations defeated during the First World War: their minorities were granted the protection of the League of Nations. The recent peace treaties with Germany's satellites impose on them the obligation not to discriminate against their minorities. Like the military clauses mentioned above, these also commonly prove to be ineffective.

Finally, peace treaties may include moral clauses such as the recognition of the defeated nation's guilt in the causation of war, the obligation to punish war criminals or to deliver them to the victors, or the obligation to follow strictly the precepts of international law. So far as the latter tends to assert the prohibition of war of aggression, the emergence of such clauses may serve as a brake against unwarranted resort to war as a means of conflict solution.

Does a Peace Treaty Solve a Conflict?

In a peace treaty, the solution of an inter-state conflict through the measurement of the relative strength of the parties receives finality. It is worthwhile to compare the content of peace treaties with the points which were at issue during the conflict that preceded the war.

Through the application of the principle of reward and punishment, the conflict is often solved in a manner which could not obtain if the parties had resorted to adjudication. One of the parties receives more, sometimes much more than it claimed when resorting to war, while the other party loses more than it was not willing to cede them. However, it is not always so. If a war makes manifest the approximate equality of the two parties, or at least the lack of overwhelming superiority, the winner must be satisfied with less than he demanded; in case of a stalemate (equal strength), the party on the defensive wins, and the aggressive party has to quit fighting with no increment of possessions or rights.

What happens however with the antagonism itself? Is it actually terminated, or only relegated from the surface to deeper levels of social interaction?

The two outcomes are possible. Sometimes the defeated party changes its goal orientation by dropping the goals which proved to be unattainable. After her defeat in the One Hundred

Years War, England no longer claimed the French crown or parts of French territory. After her defeat in the American War of Independence, England no longer aspired to restore her sovereignty over the thirteen colonies. After her defeat by Japan (1905), Russia renounced the idea of overlordship in Manchuria and Korea and maintained rather friendly relations with the former foe. There are good reasons to believe that after 1945 Japan has dropped her imperialistic dreams and that this time the Germans will forget their dream of world dominance. In such cases, a war produces salutary effects: the road for international cooperation is opened.

In other cases, the aspirations of the defeated nations are only repressed. This is especially the case if, through the play of the principle of reward and punishment, a nation has been deprived of what it holds essential for her survival. France never was resigned to accept the loss of Alsace-Lorraine. Germany never accepted the limitations imposed by the Versailles Treaty. Russia never accepted the cession of territory to Poland after her defeat in 1921. Of similar cases, there have been thousands. Then, a peace treaty replaces conflict by a neutral process in which the antagonistic component remains strong and is easily brought back to dominance. The peace treaty proves to be a mere truce.

Which of the two possibilities will materialize in a concrete case? The first is probable if the war was considered unjust by a large part of the population of the defeated nation (the American War of Liberation, the Russo-Japanese War) or if the peace treaty has been surprisingly mild (the Austro-Prussian War of 1866). The second is probable if the peace treaty has been especially hard, or if between the nations there already existed an inveterate feud. Sometimes, however, ex-

234

treme hardship makes the resurgence of the conflict improbable: this is the case when, as the result of defeat, a state is annexed by the victor.

Let us now summarize the findings of this chapter. A political system consisting of several nations is likely to return from war to peace if, through fighting and victory of one of the parties (or stalemate), one of the conditions of fighting, uncertainty as to relative strength, has been eliminated and another, hope to achieve the objective by means short of war, has been replaced by its opposite, that is, the loss by at least one of the parties of the hope to achieve the goal through fighting. Since the factors determining victory receive their definitive shape only gradually, the initial state of a system on the eve of moving from war to peace may be described as the emergence of certainty about the relative strength of the parties with respect to all factors but one. The appearance of the last acts as the precipitant or operator. More often than not, the symptom of its appearance is the breakdown of morale, of the will to resist on the part of the weaker party. Through peace, the conflict is either entirely terminated, or replaced by a neutral process of the symbiotic type as it was before the war.

10/The Movement
from Revolution to Order

The Premises of Victory

Revolution is a means of resolving an acute political conflict between a government and its opposition by measuring the relative strength of the parties. Before the outbreak of the revolution, one could only conjecture which of the two parties was stronger. In the course of the revolution, estimates become certainties as one party proves to be stronger than the other: the weaker party has to give up.[1] The revolution is over, the political system returns to the phase of order.

This process is, in many regards, analogous to the return of a political system from war to peace. But in other regards it is more complicated and also less definite. First, the revolutionary measurement of the relative strength may take place not through actual fighting, but through the deployment of force. It is true that a similar situation may obtain with regard to war. One state may intimidate another by a display of overwhelming power; then, the other one yields. If the state which played the role of the aggressor proves to be stronger, it gets what it coveted. If the state on the defensive proves to be stronger, no change occurs. In both cases, no war has taken place.

The same is true of revolution if, by a display of strength, the government frightens the revolutionary forces and order has thereby been preserved. But if the opposition is able to display such strength that the government has to yield (abdicating, fleeing, or transferring power to the opposition), a revolution has vicariously taken place. The very deployment of formidable anti-government forces may be a decisive test of strength. The government ceases to be the "overwhelming power" which it must be in every state. Such a deployment is therefore already a most serious disorder, a movement from "order" to revolution. For instance, this was the case in the Fascist revolution in Italy and in the National Socialist revolution in Germany. The King of Italy made Mussolini Prime Minister after Mussolini had launched the march on Rome which could not be resisted. The appointment was contrary to the constitutional practice and was followed by the complete transfer of power to the Duce. President Hindenburg appointed Hitler Reichschancellor after having despaired of preserving order against the rising tide of National Socialism. Soon after, rather in violation of the constitution, he transferred supreme power to the Führer. In both cases, the program of the revolutionary party, respectively Fascist or National Socialist, became the moving spring of a far-reaching transformation of the two societies which the preceding governments did not want to perform.

Second, while war is ostentatiously terminated by a peace treaty, the victory or defeat of a revolutionary movement may not be so clear-cut. A defeated opposition may go underground and soon try again. More important is the fact that, in case of the victory of the opposition, the revolutionary energy may not be exhausted, and therefore the revolutionary phase in the life of the political society may not be terminated. This is closely connected with the fact that the revolutionary opposition may not be a unified and well-defined organization, while, in war, the two opponents are thoroughly organized. The revolutionary movement may consist of a number of currents. Uniting their strength, they might have been strong enough to overthrow the government. But, after having gained victory, they might start quarreling for the spoils, just as might happen with a victorious coalition of states. The new, that is, post-revolutionary government rarely is strong since it is not backed by the mighty force of tradition and since its members rarely possess the skills necessary to govern men efficiently.

Consequently, the former allies may fall apart and resume struggle for power. This may go on indefinitely, at least for long periods. The French historians agree that the Great French Revolution which broke out in the form of the successful attack on the Bastille (July 14, 1789) ended only ten years later, after Napoleon's "18th of brumaire" (1799). The Russian revolution started by mob action in Petrograd early in March, 1917, and in certain aspects ended when civil war was over, at least in her European part (November, 1920). Much longer has been the Chinese revolution; actually it started with the deposition of the Manchu dynasty in 1911 and after having gone through many phases ended only late in 1949, when the Communists succeeded in conquering all of China, short of Tibet and Formosa. A clear-cut symptom of the termination of a revolution may be, however, derived from earlier statements. So long as the people are dominated by the feeling of plasticity—nothing is certain, everything could change overnight—the political system is in the revolutionary phase. When the feeling of stability comes back, when everybody plans his life on the basis of the expectation that tomorrow will be approximately as is today—at least in the political phase—the political system has returned to order.

These complications make the study of the return of a political system from revolution to order difficult, but not impossible. Since the return depends on the solution of the problem of relative strength, it is tantamount to victory in struggle (or intimidation), and the relevant traits to be observed in a society going back to order are tantamount to the factors of victory. Since there exists no science of revolution comparable to the science of war, the factors are less known than those of military victory, but still can be derived from historical observation guided by the knowledge of the properties of political systems and of the nature of conflict.

1. The strength of the government is determined by a) certain properties of the government, and b) the size of the sector of the population on which it may rely as well as the maximum effort which this sector would be willing to exert in favor of the government.

a) In the ideal, every government should contain, at least

on the top level, a number of persons of high leadership ability. These men should be able to judge about the situation realistically, to visualize the best means to combat an eventual revolutionary opposition, to persist in plans once chosen, but to change them when events would prove that necessary, to apply force (eventually conducive to the curb of the opponents) whenever necessary and, last but not least, be united. The outbreak of a revolution, just as the outbreak of a war, is the supreme test of a government. Large numbers of revolutionary outbreaks have failed because the government possessed the traits just described; in historical annals, these outbreaks are mentioned only *in passim*. Better remembered are the cases when the government did not fulfill the requirements and therefore succumbed. The weakness of the government of Louis XVI in France is proverbial. The Russian government, at the outbreak of the revolution of 1917, was headed by an Emperor who had very little understanding of political realities and, in actuality, had transferred supreme power to his wife, an hysterical woman dominated by the pseudo-monk Rasputin, and a Prime Minister appointed a few months earlier despite his sincere declaration to the monarch that he was unfit. The Provisional Government which took over was weak *ab ovo,* because political power was divided between it and the executive committee of the Congress of the Soviets. The Italian and the Spanish governments at the outbreak of the Fascist revolutions were headed by men brought to the summit of power by the accident of the pseudo-democratic game which characterized the political scene of the two nations. The Spanish government defeated by General Franco in 1936 consisted of heterogeneous elements which never could agree on consistent policies. In the majority of the cases these facts were well known;

this knowledge was one of the factors in the outbreak of the revolutionary upheavals since it gave the opposition a fair chance of victory. But only in action did these defects prove to be true and fatal; change of personnel or change of policies could have prevented the collapse.

b) To win, the government needs at least the resolute support of the army and of the police which, normally, must be considered inherent parts of the government machine but, in the course of a revolution, may join the opposition or actually refuse to fight. This support is, however, almost always taken for granted: monarchs, heads of states, generals commonly are sure that their orders will be obeyed. There are good reasons for thinking so. In the framework of organizations, especially organizations emphasizing discipline, men act predominantly on the level of institutional motivation; orders coming from above have become, in the rank-and-file members, strongly embodied stimuli automatically eliciting the expected response. Still, personal motivation plays a part. Soldiers and policemen are members of the nation, and violent opposition to the government, dominating the strata from which they are recruited, may undermine their learned response of subordination. Consequently, the army and the police may become unreliable; this is what happened during the March, 1917, revolution in Russia. This was not so likely in days of mercenary armies when no motivational links existed between the people and the army who were often recruited abroad. On the other hand, the army is never quite reliable in countries where the revolutionary tradition is strong and has received the shape of *pronunciamento*.

An important part of the government's strength is support by public opinion. Strong and united public opinion in the

North helped Lincoln's government to win the Civil War. But during the American revolution, public opinion in America was divided; this largely explains the early reverses and the very duration of the struggle. It is noteworthy that, on the other side of the Ocean, public opinion was rather indifferent. It strongly supported the revolutionary movement during the early phases of the French revolution and the Russian revolution of March, 1917; but it was rather indifferent on the eve of the Communist revolution of November, 1917, and the Fascist revolution of 1922; it was badly divided at the time of the National Socialist revolution in Germany.

Whether the armed forces are reliable or not; whether the public opinion is for the government, or neutral, or hostile— is never definitely known prior to the revolution. The unfolding of the revolution replaces question marks by certainties and thus prepares the final solution of the revolutionary equation.

2. The strength of the opposition is determined by a) certain traits of the revolutionary leadership, b) the size of the forces following them, and c) certain traits characterizing these forces.

a) The revolutionary leaders must possess the general traits of leadership plus specific traits demanded by the revolutionary situation. First, to inspire the followers, they must have a clear vision of the goal and have the ability to convey this goal to the followers. Second, they must be able realistically to define the situation, and, on that background, make correct predictions, especially if the views about the outcome of specified plans of action are controversial. Lenin gained final ascendancy after having correctly predicted that the upheaval against the Provisional Government would be successful. This had been denied by the majority of the "inner circle." The effect of this correct prediction was enhanced when he proved to be right in asserting that the Brest Litovsk Peace Treaty with Germany would not remain in force for more than one year. Stalin gained final ascendancy over the Communist party after having correctly predicted that the peasants' resistance against collectivization could be broken. Hitler gained final ascendancy over Germany after having correctly predicted, contrary to the opinion of the experts, that the restoration of compulsory military service, the remilitarization of the Rhineland and the annexation of Austria would not involve Germany in war. It is very probable that a sequence of correct predictions is the very basis for the establishment of the so-called charismatic leadership:[2] the ascendancy of a successful prophet is a primary fact so easy to understand that it does not need further explanation.

Third, there must be ability to create and manage the appropriate organization, so-to-speak, the general staff of the revolution, by placing the right men in the right jobs. Fourth, and this is a peculiarity of success in revolutionary leadership, there must be an indomitable will to break resistance and achieve the goal at any price, such as shedding blood, accepting dirty compromises, breaking promises, and so on; revolutions are not made in white gloves.

Revolutionary leaders are commonly many. It is obviously an asset for the revolution if the leaders form a pyramid consisting of men whose loyalty to the supreme leader is beyond question. If the revolutionary movement lacks one commonly recognized leader, because of rivalry between the heads of the factions forming the revolutionary coalition, this rivalry must be temporarily repressed so that an attack by united forces can be launched.

Before the outbreak of the revolution, nobody is able to

judge reliably about this factor. Eloquence, which may be of paramount importance in pre-revolutionary situations, does not always coincide with the most essential traits of revolutionary leadership; such was the case of Kerensky, a fiery speaker, but a poor organizer lacking the ability of realistically appraising the situation. On the other hand, pre-revolutionary quarrels between leaders and factions do not always preclude unity of action at the time of the revolution, to last as long as the government is not yet down. Only in the unfolding of revolutionary events does the caliber and unity of the revolutionary leadership become conspicuous. A commonly held view makes strong leaders a necessary condition of the outbreak, still more of the success of the revolution.[3] However, in the initial stages both of the French and Russian (March) revolutions, revolutionary leadership was weak and divided; in both cases this weakness was balanced by the extraordinary weakness of the government and the high tension of revolutionary energy in the masses. Leadership was, however, exceptionally strong in the Communist revolutions in Russia and China and in the Fascist revolutions. Moreover, weak leaders showing up in the beginning may be replaced by other, more energetic ones, by a process of natural selection (see below).

b) Revolutionary leaders can achieve success only if they are followed by a number of people sufficient to break the resistance of the government. Depending on the phase of the pre-revolutionary disintegration, "the revolutionary forces" (let us apply this term to designate the followers or the revolutionary leaders) appear in different forms.

If the process of disintegration is in the initial stage, the ascendancy of the sociocultural elite is not yet shaken; the nation continues to follow the leadership of those who form its upper level, by reason of birth, wealth, education, personal achievement and the like. The disintegration then consists in tensions within the sociocultural elite itself, especially between those in power and those out of power. If a revolution takes place under these conditions, the crisis is solved within the elite. The rest of the nation obediently follows suit. The most typical example is probably the French Revolution of July, 1830.

If the process of disintegration has advanced beyond the initial stage, the exclusive authority of the sociocultural elite to make decisions for the nation is no longer recognized by those who do not belong to the elite. However, that elite is not yet excluded from the number of the determinants of the social process. This is a situation where the decisive role belongs to the nation, perhaps minus the former government. It is a rather exceptional situation to which superficial enthusiasts of democracy wrongly ascribe universal validity. One of the clearest cases was that of Russia under the Provisional Government. Some of its members believed that democracy, once established, never could be overthrown by violence" because the whole people would rise in its defense." Consequently, they resisted and even sabotaged efforts to curb the anti-democratic propaganda of the Bolsheviks.[4]

In later stages of disintegration, the decisive role belongs to the "people," that is, to the nation minus the sociocultural elite. This situation obtains in "great" revolutions of the French and Russian type. Its symptom is commonly the loss of self-confidence among the sociocultural elite, especially the loss of the belief, so firm in times of "normalcy," that the role of leadership naturally belongs to it.[5] One of the conspicuous cases is that of Weimar Germany: no spectacular success could be credited to the leadership of that period, and the grasp of this fact by the masses produced a situation in which, when the revolution came, the "people" became the determinant of the social process. This case indicates, by the way, that it is immaterial whether an adequate response could or could not be found by the elite; perhaps in the particular case of Weimar Germany, the challenge of history embodied in the policy of the victors of 1918 was too strong to be adequately dealt with. Decisive was this fact: no response was found, and the right of the sociocultural elite to exert its function of leadership was challenged by the masses.

Within the case mentioned, specification is sometimes possible. In some cases, the army officers (a part of the sociocultural elite) assume the role of the elite in its totality and determine the outcome of a revolutionary situation. Examples are frequent in the Iberian and Latin American provinces of Western civilization. But similar developments have taken place in Poland (1926), Bulgaria (1934), Greece (1936), and recently, in several Arab and African countries.

In other cases, the army minus the officers, that is, the armed mob, becomes the determinant of the social process.[6] In still other cases, the situation is complicated by the fact that the delimitation between the sociocultural elite and the masses is rather vague. Intermediary levels always exist, such as the lowest stratum of the middle class, or the group called, in Russia, "semi-intellectuals," consisting of persons with limited education and occupying minor positions in the administration, local government, and the professions. This intermediary level, repressed in its aspirations by the sociocultural elite, may join the "people" in times of advanced pre-revolutionary disintegration. Such was the case in the Russia of 1917. In Germany, elementary school teachers, a depressed social stratum, belonged to the number of the most enthusiastic followers of Hitler.

The foregoing statements should not be understood as assigning providential, and consequently, immutable roles to particular categories of persons in specified societies disintegrated by coming revolution. More often than not, in the process of disintegration, the decisive role is shifted from group to group. Thus, in Russia, in 1916, a revolution seemed possible in which the sociocultural elite would have played the decisive role. In March, 1917, this role was ascribed to the "nation." In November, 1917, it quite obviously belonged to "the people," that is, to the nation minus the sociocultural elite, the Bolsheviks being repudiated and even ostracized by the vast majority of the intellectuals. With respect to Germany, the contention of the National Socialists was that, if they had not seized power, later developments would have shifted the decisive role to the masses supporting the Communist revolution. There is obviously no means to verify this assertion.

Naturally, the success of a revolution is most probable if the revolutionary mass coincides with the nation. But minority revolutions carried out by factions of the elite or by the army may be successful, if the majority does not care enough to fight. On the contrary, a "people's" revolution could be checked by a resolute minority led by a strong government and disposing of reliable armed forces.

c) The size of the "revolutionary forces" is, as we see, not decisive. Two additional traits are of high importance. First, whether the revolutionary forces have, or have not, access to the arms. The government led forces always have. In this regard, technological advance has, in general, strengthened the chances of the government and curbed those of the revolutionary opposition. In olden days, the revolutions were decided by fighting with clubs, swords, or old style pistols; these weapons were eventually available to everybody. Now the government fights a revolutionary outbreak by machine guns, hand grenades, even artillery and airplanes. These weapons are not at the disposal of the revolutionary forces, except in two cases: when the army, or part of the army, is with the revolution, or when a daring stroke has provided the revolutionary forces with weapons stored in an armory, an arsenal, etc.

But, as a counterpart, at the present day the revolutionary forces dispose of a weapon which was unavailable before the so-called industrial revolution. This is the general strike. It proved decisive in the so-called abortive revolution which took place in Russia in 1904-5. The general strike, supported by mutinies in some military detachments, forced the government to grant the opposition some of its demands. In this way, the social process chose, at a late stage, the modality of reform, and the revolutionary movement rapidly disintegrated. In an eventual Communist revolution in Western Europe, this weapon would play an important part.

This points to another property of the revolutionary forces. Cohesion in its midst is of differential intensity and subject to fluctuation. More often than not, there is a nucleus, around the leader or the leaders; sometimes those who belong to it are actually ready "to die for the cause." The rest of the revolutionary forces is usually not ready to go beyond participation in protests or demonstrations. The intensity of the revolutionary energy is lifted if the revolution is animated by a grand style revolutionary idea, the promise of a millenium in case of success. If the initial stages of the revolution have been crowned by success, the mechanism of the bandwagon plays its usual role.

As in discussions above, the statement must be made that the existence and intensity of those properties of the revolutionary energy which is propitious for victory can be ascertained only in action. The unfolding of the revolution shows whose estimates were closer to reality, that of the government or that of the opposition.

The substitution of certainties for estimates takes place gradually. Something like an algebraic summation of the inner strength of the government and of its support by the armed forces and the people at large, of the ability and unity of the revolutionary leaders, and of the favorable and unfavorable properties of the revolutionary forces, takes place. This summation does not follow any predetermined order; on the contrary, each of the items to be summed up may receive a definite magnitude before or after any other one receives it. Moreover, these magnitudes are susceptible of change. An irresolute government leader may be replaced by a strong man; poor revolutionary leaders may be ousted by more efficient ones or, on the contrary, an able leader may be killed or captured by the government. Initial support of the government by public opinion may be reversed, or, *vice-versa,* revolutionary forces may capture an armory, or a military detachment may change sides; a general strike may be proclaimed and succeed, or fail to materialize.

A time comes, however, when all the unknown factors of the revolutionary equation have received definite magnitudes. The relative strength of the parties is now established. As has already been said, the revolution is over, at least for the time being, since one of the necessary conditions of revolutionary fighting is no longer present. Another condition, the hope, by one of the participants, to win by means of fighting, is also gone; now at least one of the parties knows that it cannot win by fighting. As to the primary condition entering into the revolutionary equation, the existence of a serious and acute conflict derived from the accumulation of social tensions, the discussion of its persistence must be postponed until the end of this chapter.

The relevant state of a political system causing its movement from revolution to order is, as we see, confined to the ascertainment of the relative strength of the parties. Since this strength is an algebraic sum of many factors, the appearance of each of these factors in a certain form may be considered as a relevant trait of the system under observation prior to the movement. Since there is no predetermined sequence of the appearance of the single factors, the last to show up and to make the series complete may be considered as the operator. This is why the termination of a revolution, just as the end of a war, may be said to be caused both in a very simple way, by victory, or in a very complicated way, by the gradual accumulation of the factors of victory.

The Outcome of a Revolution

Just as in war, the return of a political system from revolution to order is not confined to the cessation of fighting and disorder. The question must be asked, what order will there be, just as in the case of war, not only the end of hostilities, but also the terms of the peace treaty are relevant. The additional problem now to be investigated is that of the final outcome of a revolution.

The answer is rather simple, if the *government* is victorious. Through victory, it is usually strengthened; it now emphasizes "order." "Order reigns in Prague," is the term of the famous proclamation of General Windischgrätz after he had crushed, in June, 1848, a revolutionary outbreak in the capital of Bohemia. Often relying on increased strength and additional prestige, the government embarks on reaction. In other words, it curbs those liberties and takes care of those weaknesses in its own structure which made the revolution possible (by giving fair chance of victory to the opposition). Such a policy is often called counter-revolution. A good example is the "reaction" in the major part of Europe in 1815-30, after the final victory of the traditional governments against the forces brought to the forefront by the French Revolution. And this happened again in many parts of Europe after the defeat of the revolution of 1848. Sometimes the government is intelligent enough to seize the opportunity to carry out delayed reforms, to alleviate social tensions and thereby make less probable another revolutionary outbreak. This was the case in Russia in 1905-11, under Count Witte and Stolypin who, after the defeat of the abortive revolution of 1904-5, granted Russia a moderate Constitution, carried out a judicial reform amplifying that of 1864 and a sweeping agrarian reform aiming at the abolition of the *mir,* or agrarian community.[7] The struggle between reaction or reform in the American South has been the main theme of American politics after the defeat of Secession.

Much more complicated is the situation if the revolutionary forces win. Usually, a new government is formed from the ranks of the revolutionary leaders. According to contemporary usage, it is called a "provisional government." It is almost an empiric law that the leader of the victorious group becomes the head of the new government. But, victorious dictators in Latin America *pronunciamentos* often begin by ascribing power to "revolutionary juntas." On the other hand, the defeated government abdicates, or is declared deposed. This is a counterpart of a peace treaty terminating a war.

Then, if the revolutionary movement aimed at something more ambitious than change in the personal composition of the political leadership, a dynamic period of revolutionary reforms begins. This is no longer actually an unfolding of the revolution, but the fulfillment of its purpose. It is commonly accepted, among others by Sorokin and Brinton,[8] that by inner necessity, the fulfillment consists of two phases, the ascending and the descending. During the former, destruction of the old regime is in the forefront, while reforms are nebulous and convulsive. Then, there comes a turning point (of which Thermidor, an episode of the French Revolution, is best known), after which construction of a new order prevails according to more moderate plans. Events in Russia after the Communist revolution invalidate this hypothesis; there, at least four phases must be distinguished, the first and third ascending, the second and the fourth descending. It is even possible that, after the relative stability of the years of 1936-53 (secured by terrorism without a counterpart), a new period has begun, especially marked after Khrushchev's ascent to full power. The Chinese revolution has perhaps consisted of even more phases than the Russian. On the other hand, in palace revolutions and *coups d'état*,[9] the dynamic period may be short and consist of one phase only; such has also been the

July, 1830, revolution in France. In consequence, no "natural history of a revolution" can be constructed, applicable to all cases.

But, in all cases, after a while, the revolutionary energy is exhausted. Society is again stabilized and may even become stagnant.

During the revolutionary period and immediately after, a cult of the revolution may emerge. The revolution is treated in a stereotyped way. It is called glorious, great, etc. The post-revolutionary government protects itself against further revolutionary outbreaks. This can be done by police measure, but also by more or less energetic effort to usurp tradition and to receive its mighty support. Napoleon has shown the way to post-revolutionary governments, by restoring the brilliancy of the pre-revolutionary court, by opening the doors to emigrés willing to accept the new regime, by merging pre-revolutionary and revolutionary institutions. Since the mid-thirties, this process has been most conspicuous in the Soviet Union. There, a number of symbolic items (traits) of the pre-revolutionary days such as ranks, uniforms, insignia, have been restored; the revolution of 1917 is no longer treated as a break of continuity. On the contrary, the new order is explained to be the natural outcome of Russia's millenial history.

These are the general traits of a society having passed through a victorious revolution. But, as has already been said, a more specific problem is involved. What will be the final outcome of a revolution as compared with the objective possibilities of the pre-revolutionary period embodied in competing groups and their leaders? In other words, what solutions will be given to the problem posed by the social tensions of the pre-revolutionary period? This is a problem analogous to that of the content of a peace treaty terminating a war.

Which of the objective possibilities will be embodied in post-revolutionary society is decided by a process of natural selection among the leaders and their programs. What are the conditions of success in this highly antagonistic process, often involving fighting among those who defeated the previous government?

Let us begin by contemplating the revolutionary forces brought into motion by the pre-revolutionary or early revolutionary events. These forces are not simply there; at any time, they are imbued with more or less specific ideas concerning the adequacy or inadequacy, justice or injustice, of the existing social institutions and the desirability of changing them. The range of such ideas depends partly on objective interests, both material and non-material, of the members of these forces, but mainly on culture tradition.

In times of crisis, frustrations which perhaps existed already in days of normalcy are accentuated, and dominance is easily gained by systems of ideas focused on the basic frustrations. On the other hand, the conditions of plasticity, characteristic of the pre-revolutionary situation, are caused sometimes not so much by actual frustrations as by the conversion of large masses to a new creed—religious, political or social; the range of ideas to be embodied is then based on these new creeds. The revolutionary masses are highly responsive to programs reflecting such ideas, whereas no great man is able simply to impose his program on them. To designate a set of ideas to which the revolutionary force is readily responsive, the term "natural program" will be used.

To restrict examples to recent events, it may be said that

in Russia in 1917, the natural program of the revolutionary forces was "land, peace, and bread" and the withdrawal of the *chinovniki,* that is, of the bureaucrats who imposed taxes and drafted young people to military service. Similarly, in Italy, in 1922, and in Germany, in 1933, the natural program was the combination of emphatic nationalism and social reform of an anti-capitalist, more exactly, anti-big-business, trend.

Both the objective situation and the ideas circulating in the revolutionary forces are reflected in the minds of the competitors for power and give rise to their individual programs, expressing their views of the situation, possible outcomes and the desirable solutions of the crises. In each program, first of all, the actor's definition of the situation is expressed, especially the diagnosis of the human mass to play the decisive role in the midst of the revolutionary force. The correctness of this diagnosis is highly important for victory. Both Lenin and Hitler won because they correctly defined the situation as a revolt of the "people" against the sociocultural elites, whereas their opponents wrongly addressed the nation and particularly the sociocultural elite, or specified elements in this elite.

On the other hand, the program of each potential leader, in its original form, not yet accommodated to the competitive situation, reflects the life history of the actors and the culture history of the groups to which they belong. Lenin's program was determined by his early conversion to Marxism in its revolutionary interpretation with an admixture of extreme radicalism. This easily gained the upper hand among the Russian *intelligentsia.* In Mussolini's original program, the school of George Sorel was conspicuous. In Hitler's program, the drill of the Germany army, the fantasy of Georg Feder, the anti-semitic climate of Vienna—reenforced by some ideas imported by Alfred Rosenberg from Russia—were easily recognizable.

Almost necessarily, each competitor compares his original program with the natural program of the revolutionary forces as defined by him. This comparison yields either conformity, or discrepancy. If there is conformity, the situation is judged favorable for the competitor. Through the mechanism of wishful thinking, many competitors for power have wrongly assumed conformity when, in actuality, substantial difference was present. This is one of the most frequently recurring mistakes of the actors on the historical scene. In any case, if conformity is supposed to exist, the natural course is to organize propaganda according to the competitor's original program.

If discrepancy is established, a problem both technical and ethical is posed. The potential leader has to decide whether he is willing and able to conceal the discrepancy and to pretend having a program that conforms with the expectations of the revolutionary forces. In revolutionary situations, sensible men cannot promise much more than "sweat and tears." On the other hand, the masses are inclined to accept optimistic interpretations of the situation and to welcome superficial views about remedies. This explains why rarely truly decent men gain power in great revolutions.

Very good instances of the accommodation of the original program of the finally victorious competitors to the demand of the revolutionary forces can be found in recent Russian and Italian events. In his younger years, Mussolini was a violent revolutionist, atheist, anti-monarchist, and an internationalist. To gain and maintain power, he had to accommodate his original program to the expectations and ideals of social groups whose members were predominantly religious-minded, monarchists, and nationalists. Lenin's agrarian program was based on Marxian theorems which could not appeal to the peasants who formed the bulk of the eventual revolutionary forces of the time. To gain their support—or even neutrality— he temporarily adopted the program of his chief adversaries, the Socialist-Revolutionists, and gave it the force of law through the first decree issued by the government headed by him.

An additional condition of the success of a competitor's program is its adjustment to the level of intelligence and knowledge of the addressees; the lower the level, the simpler the offer must be. Since the level of the "people" is lower than the level of the sociocultural elite, situations where the decisive role belongs to the people are favorable to the victory of maximalists, right or left, for their plans are naturally of the simplest kind, as "expropriate the expropriators," or "kill the Jews."

It may be taken for granted that, except in the case when the Army becomes the revolutionary force, a human mass playing the decisive role in the contest for power is shapeless. Gradually the particular dominance-submission relationship is established between it and one of the competitors for power. The initial relationship is, however, precarious. Cases are known when an incipient power structure soon broke down. To make final the crystallization around a specified competitor, the incipient relationship must be reenforced by adequate action. Since the simplest aspect of social power is physical dominance of man by man, the demonstration of the ability to break resistance is one of the most important requirements. Let us not forget that we are discussing situations in which institutional rules about the distribution of power have broken down, so that only acts decide. This ability must be demonstrated in many face-to-face situations and finally integrated into a new social structure transcending such situations. This is why, among the factors of victory, a certain amount of recklessness among the leaders must be mentioned. In general, all the specific traits of leadership discussed above reappear when the problem of victory in the natural selection of leaders is posed: those traits which are likely to grant victory against the government are also likely to grant victory against competitors for post-revolutionary leadership.

Summing up, it may be said that (1), other things equal among the competitors for dominance in post-revolutionary society, those possess a greater chance of victory who offer a program best adapted to the natural program of the revolutionary force, and that (2) other things equal, out of the competitors for dominance in post-revolutionary society, those have a greater chance of victory who are endowed with the highest capacity for revolutionary leadership, especially the ability to define correctly the social situation, and the willingness to adapt their initial program to that definition.

When in regard of a certain consequence (in our case, the outcome of the competition for power in a revolutionary situation), two propositions are formulated, both containing the "other-things-equal" clause, it is clear that the solution of the problem resembles that of a system of simultaneous equations: neither the differential ability for leadership, nor the differential appeal of the programs decide. Both are decisive taken together, but exact quantitative statements are obviously impossible.

It is by no means predetermined that the same competitor for power would be simultaneously endowed with all the properties suitable for victory. If, in a concrete case, one group has a more appealing program to offer, but another has better leadership, a long and complicated struggle ensues. If the two sets of advantages are present in the same group, its victory is easy.

Unfortunately, the two sets are often combined in groups consisting of fanatics. Of course, this does not imply that this advantageous situation is possible only in groups consisting of fanatics, nor that every group of fanatics would possess those advantages. The frequent occurrence of the combination under study among groups of fanatics can be easily explained. Fanatics are characterized by subnormal inhibitions: they do not see anything but their own ideas and their projection into reality, and are blind to other ideas and expectations. The lack of inhibitions permits them, on the one hand, to offer the people the most radical, that is, the simplest program, and, on the other hand, to break resistance by brute force. They are designated for victory when competing for power in conditions of high disintegration, but only in such conditions. Had Russia and Germany not been submitted to the process of disintegration and transformed into highly plastic societies, Lenin would have died as an obscure commentator on Marx, and Hitler as an obscure painter.

The possibility of an opportunist accomodation of the competitors for power to the natural program of the revolutionary mass is full of important implications for the final outcome of the revolutionary crises. It is obvious that the original program of a competitor is only temporarily repressed in favor of the opportunist accomodation. If, as the result of accomodation, the competitor wins, the repression gradually ceases to operate when the new order is consolidated, especially in the political phase. Under such conditions, the new leaders are able to realize not only those elements of the program which gave them power, but also part, at least, of the residue, i.e., the points which were not at issue during the period of competition.

This mechanism has been conspicuous in the Communist revolution in Russia. The people never endorsed the antireligious crusade of the Communist leaders which, previous to the revolution, was not included in the Communist offer to the people. But after power had been acquired and consolidated, a violent attack on religion could be launched. The temporary repression of the agrarian program of the Communists could be dropped only twelve years after the seizure of power. In Italy and Germany, the majority of the people who helped Mussolini and Hitler to power never imagined nor endorsed the criminal excesses of the victors which were implicit in their original programs.

This phase of the process cannot be overemphasized. It introduces into the problem of the final outcome of a revolution a personal coefficient which is so evident in the works of the historians, but tends to disappear in sociological treatises. The task of sociology is, however, not to eliminate the personal coefficient, but to understand the mode of its operation. In the particular process studied here, it operates as follows: accomodation of the virtual leadership to the natural program of the revolutionary mass; acceptance, by this mass, of the offer thus formulated; delegation, to the successful competitor, of the authority to proceed to reconstruction on the basis of this program; gradual withdrawal of the repression and return to the original program; exertion of power according to this program, and no longer to the natural program of the revolutionary mass. And since the revolutionary situation is no longer present—in other words, since society has returned to normalcy—the propositions concerning revolutionary situations no longer obtain. Whether it likes it or not, society has to endure the power structure formed in the course of a revolutionary competition for power. Whether the nation continues to accept this leadership will be decided during the next revolutionary crisis when society once more will have become plastic. Obviously, the test of a nation's attitude towards its government receives quite another form, if the revolution results in establishing a true democracy. Unfortunately, this is rather exceptionally the case.

It is also obvious that the departure from the official program of a revolution on the basis of opportunist accomodation is lacking in cases when there is actual conformity between the original program of the victorious competitor and the natural program of the revolutionary forces. It is also obvious that the possibility of concealing the discrepancy between the two programs varies in inverse ratio with the level of the general, and especially political, education of the nation. Moreover, even the opportunists are not omnipotent. When returning to the original program, they may commit actions creating new tensions and provoking new revolutionary shocks. To prevent these, they are often compelled to proceed to further accomodation, once again giving up part of the original program. This was the case of Stalin who, in the middle and the late thirties, was forced to carry out what, in another work, the present author has called "The Great Retreat"—from doctrinal Communism to opportunistic Communism. This allowed the regime to survive. This movement formed the fourth (the second descending) phase of the Communist Revolution in Russia.

Post-revolutionary Society

In one way or another, a post-revolutionary society is formed. Such a society is characterized by the merger of some institutions of pre-revolutionary origin, in particular those the destruction of which was not part of the natural program of the revolutionary forces; of some institutions derived from the original program of the victorious leaders; and of some inventions eventually made in the course of the revolution. This may be well perceived in the outcome of the English, American, French, and Russian revolutions, while the Fascist revolutions in Germany, Italy and their satellites were not given the opportunity to run through the complete cycles.

Now we can return to a problem reserved in the previous discussion: what happens to the social tensions which preceded the revolutionary outbreak? Obviously, no general answer is possible. If the government is victorious and resorts to re-action, the tensions and their reflection in attitudes of the citizens are repressed to the level of underground currents, but may reappear on the surface when another opportunity presents itself. If the government is victorious, but proceeds to reform in the right direction, they disappear. If the revo-lution is victorious, and the dynamic reforms following it are conceived and executed in the right direction, along the line of those natural aspirations of the revolutionary forces which are in conformity with objective conditions, the tensions are alleviated. The system is thereby relieved of tensions and a long period of normalcy, allowing evolutionary development, becomes most probable. If the revolution is victorious, but the revolutionary leaders go far in the direction of their original program, initially repressed because of its incompatibility with the natural program of the revolutionary forces, new tensions are created which may be treated by reaction (or curb of freedom). But some time in the future these new tensions will require cure by reform. Otherwise, they engender a state of plasticity forecasting another revolution.

11/A Theoretical Restatement. Comparative Evaluation of Other Theories

Restatement

A comparative case study of conditions where men attempt to solve their differences by testing their relative physical strength has so far seemed to yield two sets of propositions. One has been formulated for war, the other for revolution. But for both, the following judgments have been found relevant to every case:

1. Serious conflicts must be present involving essential elements in the power systems of the parties to the conflict.

2. All peaceful means to the solution of the conflict must be considered utterly inadequate by at least one of the parties.

3. Relative strength of each party must be perceived by the other in such a way that each judges that he has at least an equal chance of victory.

Our cases indicate that normative inhibitions to war have been relevant only exceptionally. We have not been able to identify any particular operators or precipitants. So-called "conditions" for war seem to be the *last* phenomena to appear before open conflict, though there are identifiable conditions which make war more or less intense.

Logically less precise are the findings concerning the return of the political system (or systems) from war to peace and from revolution to order. The difficulty here seems to rest on the fact that the return to peace is conditioned by victory, but these conditions in turn can be stated only tentatively. These propositions all center around one proposition: With the victory of one of the parties, the certainty of the other party's victory is eliminated and the hope of achieving objectives through tests of relative strength is replaced by its negation (i.e., despair of achievement through test of relative strength).

Since the factors determining victory can be observed only gradually taking a specific form, the initial state of the system (i.e., its readiness to return from conflict to peace) can be observed only in the *accumulation* of all the factors involved. If we think of the *last* of these as a precipitant, it more often than not appears as a breakdown of the will to resist on the part of the weaker party, its government, or ruling elite.

The propositions in the processual relationship of peace to war, and from established social order to revolution, or from war to peace and from revolution to established order, form a logically integrated system, symbolically represented in Figure 1. In preceding chapters, we have demonstrated in our

Figure 1: Logical Relations in the Process Relations

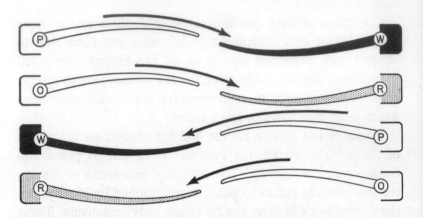

cases how these movements are analogous to those observable in outbreaks of fighting not defined as war or revolution. It will be readily and simply noted that all the propositions in the reversal processes, from war to peace and from revolution to established order, are the logical converse of the propositions in the original statements of the processual relationships. The step from the logical integration of this processual model to the meaningful or ontological aspect is dependent upon basic properties existent in the actual political system(s) and the conflict(s) emergent or going on between them.

Symbolic or logical relationships do not of course come packaged with guaranteed conformity to the ontological or real relations. But in examining the movements from peace to war, and from established order to revolution, we have presented cases to validate the propositions. If cases can be found to invalidate the propositions, they, of course, must yield. We do not believe this is possible in this framework. The propositions for the movements from war to peace, and revolution to established order have all been related to concrete cases.[1]

In one sense this theory can be interpreted as very disappointing. This is the level of common sense, and at this level, it is almost trite. What the theory says in commonsense terms is that a political system will move from peace to war or from order to revolution when there exists a serious interstate or intrastate conflict. This is just about like saying that a horse is a horse and not a cow; or that a thing is equal to itself. Is this all theory can say? Reduced to this simplest, common-sense view, this is all the theory or any theory can say!

The key concept here is the one signified by the term "reduced." It might be suggested that we deepen our theory, or make it a bit more sophisticated. More specifically, we might ask: "Under what *conditions* do such conflicts arise?" In our analysis only major areas of friction have been outlined, and those conditions under which frictions are "likely" to evolve into serious conflicts. Should not a theory on causation of war and revolution go deeper and anchor its propositions in the roots of *virtual* conflict?

On the assumptions we are making in this study the answer must be in the negative. The reasoning behind this answer can be made explicit in several directions. We are choosing two: one by way of a more or less concrete example, the other by way of a more abstractly logical discussion.

We stated previously that virtual conflict is analogous to collision. If an observer knows the positions and movements (direction and velocity) of two automobiles, and if he projects the movement onto coordinates of time and space, he will be able to predict that they will or will not collide. Something like this is true of antagonistic processes in human affairs. If we can ascertain the goals toward which two states, or two groups within a state, are moving, and project a kind of path according to which they are moving, we can assess with more or less accuracy whether or not these paths will cross in concrete time and space, and whether or not there will be a collision!

What logical implications are involved in this analogy of war and collision for our theory of causation? Simply these. If the scientists, as they do, reduced the observable elements of their phenomena into other causal relations, e.g., time, space, coordinations, projections, automobiles, and were simply satisfied with the process, they might go on being *infinitely* satisfied. But by the same processes they would infinitely never reach a theory of why automobiles collide; but only infinitely explain the causes within the factors to which automobile accidents were reduced in the first place. This isn't wrong. And, as we suggest, it can be much fun and very enlightening. But it doesn't really give us the cause of the phenomenon we started out with in the first place.[2]

This fallacy of reducing a phenomenon to its component phenomena *ad infinitum* in an attempt to explain it causally is very common in scientific analysis. It is sometimes called "argument in a circle" since sooner or later the person analyzing comes to the phenomenon he started out with in the first place. Take the meteorologist, the weatherman, making a forecast. He derives his data about tomorrow's thunderstorm from concrete knowledge about the presence of currents of hot and cold air masses moving with specified velocities in given directions, or the absence of these. He explains rain or fair weather by calculating the chances of all these (factors) meeting at the point where he is interested in knowing tomorrow's weather.

But if, instead of making this calculation he simply began to tell his listeners what causes hot and cold air currents, the velocity of winds, the humidity in the atmosphere, the makeup of the atmosphere itself, the weatherman would never get to making the prediction about the weather here tomorrow. What is more, to explain the "other" phenomena to which he is reducing the possibility of tomorrow's weather, he would sooner or later (and rather sooner than later) begin making references to weather (the very thing he is attempting to predict here) in another place. This is necessary because that weather is setting up the conditions of the atmosphere, the currents of air, velocity of winds, etc., which cause the weather here tomorrow. Simply speaking again, we are at the principle of identity: weather is weather, not simply the factors to which it may be reduced.

Our major point now is this: to arrive at a logically integrated theory through the use of analogical cases assumes this principle of identity. We said that at first blush our theory would seem disappointing; it *is*, if it is no more than this explaining of a thing by itself. But it is more, too. For now in explaining war as it is in itself we are sure that we are not merely reducing it to its factors or conditions, but that we are *causally* relating it to these by analogy. And since analogy assumes identity, our causal chain now logically links with causal chains in other orders of natural phenomena,[3] including physical nature. War, like collisions or the weather, is analogously predictable.

This is not possible in a reductionist theory where one set of phenomena is reduced to another. Our theory does not rest upon the processes of analyzing or describing war in terms of demographic, economic, political, cultural, or other factors.

A theory or theories of war and revolution using this process of analysis can go on *ad infinitum* with each factor in the series having some weight. Experimentation in this tradition has found it hopeless, ultimately, to express relatively or absolutely all the weights in order to predict war. A summary of this and allied types of theory will perhaps reflect greater clarity on our own.

Three Classes of Theory

We have stated our theory not as just one more of a rather lengthy (and still growing) list, but as an integrated one. This is to say that its intention is realized in a set of logically related propositions which integrate the majority of conjectures about the processes involved, and assigns to each a place in a comprehensive thought system, thereby explaining why some factors which seem to be causally relevant in some cases do not in others.

There are, may it be noted, abundant theories about the processes in the peace to war, and the order to revolution, movements. Studies of movements in the opposite directions are scarce.

Furthermore, existing theories have been formulated on two levels:

A. *Causal time sequences.* At this level a particular war is understood as caused through references to events: a...bc....d.. e...fghi, occurring simultaneously or in discrete time. The last "event" in the sequence is the war. Similarly with events leading to, and therefore "causing," revolution. This is the usual logical sequence given in historical accounts of war and revolution, where historians rarely confront their explanations of particular wars or revolutions with analogous explanations in analogous situations. Of course, the logical sequence of any one war can be used equivocally to destroy the same explanation when applied to another particular war or revolution.

B. *Causal references abstracting from time,* but reducing the event of war to one, some, or all factors: A, B, C, D, or their combination. These theories similarly reduce revolutions to all, some, or one, factor, A_1, B_1, C_1, D_1, or their combinations. Factors in this level are usually defined in group concepts or concepts which have logical group referents. This is the level at which sociologists, cultural anthropologists, and social psychologists commonly offer causal theories.

This latter type of causal theory may be further typed as monistic, pluralist, or integralist, depending simply upon whether or not the theory reduces to one, many, or all (or combinations of) factors. There are cases where theories of causation of war and revolution written without names and dates are referred to as "natural history" of war and/or revolution. But even without the names and dates it should be evident that these are simple historical sequences and should be classified at the first level (above).[4]

Monistic Theories

Monistic theories of war and revolution depend upon one determined factor to which is ascribed the causal power of the phenomena of war and revolution. Some species of what we are calling monistic theory really are not scientific theory at all.

a. *Fatalist approach.* In this view, wars are manifestations of destiny. They take place because they have to. Perhaps no one has expressed this view as clearly as Leo Tolstoy in the relevant sections of *War and Peace*. Nobody, he says, was responsible for the Franco-Russian War of 1812. Tolstoy poses the explanations given by the contemporaries of the war, and his own contemporaries (he wrote fifty years after the event), and attempts to show their inanity. It simply had to be, he concludes, that the peoples of the West, led by Napoleon, would move East; and it had to be that the movement would be checked and followed by an opposite movement of the peoples of the East towards the West. Really, as we have already suggested, this is no scientific theory at all, but a statement of a kind of philosophy or belief capable neither of proof nor disproof, but highly interpretative of experience.[5]

b. *The Great Men Theory*. Logically, this is a kind of opposite of the fatalist approach, and still really not a scientific theory. As *no* one causes war in fatalism, a kind of "infinite" causation is now attributed to one man. Carlyle must be considered as the most brilliant exponent of one man theory in historical accounts. Some revival of this reasoning is involved in the thinking of those who attribute wars and revolutions to men like Hitler, Mussolini, Lenin, etc.

The basis of this *attitude* (rather than theory) is again a highly personal and interpretative one rather than an empirically justified, logical system. Men like Lenin, Hitler and Mussolini *became* great in popular estimation; they were equally unpopular and impotent in others. The *processes* whereby they became great personal influences in producing wars and revolutions are the very processes in whose logical integration we are interested. Hence, from our viewpoint, the "Great Men Theories" beg the question.

c. *The Decision Theory*. This position is vigorously expounded in an article published some time ago by Professor

Theodore Abel.[6] He begins his thesis by stating that war is a phenomenon of growth and development and not an invariable effect of some cause or causes. Among the elements in the pattern of war development is the last and fateful one—the decision. It is taken when those in power face the alternative either of resigning from their position or employing violence.[7] The decision is commonly made on the background of a careful study of chances and an anticipation of consequences. According to Abel, the decision to fight precedes by one to five years the outbreak of hostilities.

This is precisely the weak point of the theory. A decision made one to five years in advance cannot but be a *condition* (certainly not *a* or *the* cause) of an event. The decision to be *realized* evidently awaits the realization of *other* conditions. The decision element, at best, is a precipitant of the movement from peace to war within the total political system where other factors are already present.

d. *Biological Theories.* Theories of war in this category point not so much to individual persons, but to processes or factors rooted in the biological nature of men. Among the variety of this kind of monistic theory is that of the Social Darwinists who pointed to war as a necessary instrument for keeping men and nations strong, hard and progressive. War is a species of natural selection, securing the survival of the best in mankind and doing away with the weaker.[8] Others emphasized the idea that war is linked with the pugnacious instinct in man and animals and therefore is something quite congenial and necessary to him as a biological organism.

e. *Psychological Theories.* Like biological monisms the psychological forms appear in multiple expressions. The most frequent descriptions of war in psychological terms refer to war as repressed hatred and hostility. More recent psychologists are inclined to ascribe an important role to mechanisms of frustration and aggression. Hostility, they say, once provoked, tends to feed itself; habitual stereotypes of the enemy emerge and influence public opinion. Finally tension rises so high that war (one could also say revolution) becomes inevitable. "We have war because we develop war fever," says Waller.[9]

Very similar is the view of M. May.[10] To him war is a learned habit, viz., to love, to hate, to fight. One learns to love and to defend one's country and to follow leaders to this end. One learns to hate to fight and to destroy what stands opposed. E. Walsh[11] attributes revolution to a deterioration either of the responsibility or of vigilance in social, economic or political trusteeship. He describes a kind of cycle in the processes of deterioration, defining stages and ultimately pinpointing revolution as its end product. Walsh's work comes to be a rather colorful descriptive model of a revolution, but hardly a causal explanation of the movement involved.

Psychoanalytical modes of explanation appear to be but species of psychological theory. To explain the National Socialist revolution in Germany, for example, F. Schuman[12] identifies the feelings of the Germans about the loss of Alsace-Lorraine after the First World War with the castration complex. This is, by the way, a magnificent example of the psychoanalytical approach's tendency to explain unknown things by the still less known and to resort to startling terminologies surreptitiously ascribed the value of scientific explanations.[13]

f. *Demographic Theory.* War and revolution are explained as effects of population pressure, as the result of disproportions in the ratio of people to resources. In a more sophisticated form war is viewed as linked with migration which is linked with "too many people" for "too little subsistence."[14] Logically, of course, these links can be joined *ad infinitum* with other links and the theory ends up nowhere, except in infinity.

g. *Economic Theories.* There is great variety in this category of theory and it is not to our purpose to attempt a logically systematic classification. In fact, on the surface at least, it seems impossible to classify economic theories logically, for variations seem almost endless.

The Marxian theory has been a most influential one, and it has gone through a kind of continuous speciation. Marx originally pointed to classes gaining power through economic concentration. War and revolution evolved from the class struggle. Lenin's version (endorsed by Stalin) centered economic power struggles in the great national powers searching for markets which under the spread of capitalism have become scarce. The rise of the Russian proletariat has lifted class struggle to the international level. On the basis of this theory Stalin predicted (in 1946 and again in 1952) war between the United States and Great Britain as the two central competitors for the world markets.

This doctrine has been emphatically repudiated by Khrushchev who believes that World Communism can be achieved by peaceful means. By establishing in Communist states a model society so perfect and attractive that all nations will accept it, the original Marxian theory has led to almost its theoretical opposite: peace through economic establishment.

h. *Morbid National Culture Theory.* War here is thought of as a phenomenon provoked by high bellicosity in the national character. Some nations, some cultures are just predominantly militaristic.

Wars of the Roman Empire have been frequently explained

this way. So have the wars of France under Napoleon. Berdya-yev points to a cry for social justice as the central theme of Russian philosophy and literature, and infers that the Russian revolution was at least a partial answer to this demand of the national Russian culture.[15]

Perhaps the most extensive literature in this vein is that developed to show that the German national character is the source of authoritarianism and militarism which was part of important war situations in the last two centuries. The proof for the existence of such a character is often traced back to the writings of German philosophers and political thinkers. J. H. Herder (1744-1803) wrote that Germany was the bulwark of Western Culture. J. Fichte in his *Addresses to the German Nation* (1807-8) gives a glamorous picture of Germany's achievements.[16] Some trace the origin of this character to Luther's theology and to Hegel's famous contention that the Prussian state is the highest embodiment of Absolute Spirit.

The analysis of the processes leading to war and back again to peace are quite evidently incapable of valid proof or valid disproof at this level. Literatures apotheosizing national character are common to almost every rising national state, and there is no reason to assume that this German literature grew with the growth of German nationalism but not as its cause.[17]

Pluralistic Theories

The mark of these theories is an attempt to combine many kinds of evidence, many kinds of data, and therefore speak of many kinds of antecedents or "causes" of war and revolution. Most frequently, too, the authors of this type of theory point to the fact that in their theory no one or even combination of antecedents necessarily predicts or forecasts war, though they may attach some kind of relative weight or degree of probability to one factor rather than another.

Our discussion here must be very selective for reasons of expediency, if no other. And for the sake of making our general point and no more we have selected two theorists, and no more, as "typical."

The most elaborated specimen of a pluralistic theory is that developed by L. L. Bernard.[18] He arranges the causes of war into seven classes, each in turn with many subdivisions. The major classifications are:

a. psychological (including the fighting instinct, tribal jealousy, fear, anger, greed, feelings of superiority, tradition and propaganda)
b. demographic
c. economic
d. imperialistic (including predatory, dynastic, commercial, strategic, administrative or power)
e. political (including nationalism, irredentism, international intrigue, personal diplomacy, secret diplomacy, political propaganda, disturbance of the balance of power)
f. geographic
g. cultural and miscellaneous (including the rivalry of nations, clash of ideologies, political, moral and religious)

A theory such as this is impressive as a catalogue. Logically, however, it can yield only one conclusion: anything *might* lead to war, but nothing will *certainly* lead to war.

The second pluralistic theory selected for purposes of discussion here is that of Pitirim Sorokin. It must be noted that

"Sorokin's theory" is in a way misleading. Actually, in the course of his lifetime Sorokin has changed his theory, and even when viewed at any one period of his own theoretical change, he is not always consistent. His various theoretical positions are reflected in several major works.[19] In the first version of his sociology of war and revolution which appeared in Volume III of the *Social and Cultural Dynamics*,[20] he suggests an approach logically following from the definition of war as breakdown of the organized relationships between states. If this were his only position Sorokin might better be placed among the *monists* above.

But one year after the publication of this position Sorokin modified his position in this way:

> As sociologists we know that the state is a network of relationships and a system of cultural values. We can deduct that each time when relationships between two or more states and the pertinent values become shattered, or muddled, or indefinite, such a change favors the chance of war.[21]

Still further modification becomes evident some six years later when Sorokin adapts his theory of causation of war and revolution to fit a redevelopment in his general systematic theory.[22]

> The main cause of international peace is the presence in each of the interacting societies of a well integrated system of ultimate values and the corresponding norms of conduct.

This is somewhat surprising. Two well integrated societies may be bearers of two incompatible value systems which would make war between them likely. Sorokin is obviously aware of the problem in his proposition for he continues:

When within a given universe of societies the integration of values declines, especially suddenly and sharply, the chances for international war increase.

Then discussing evidence to validate this proposition Sorokin confronts the value systems of two or more societies and naturally comes to the conclusion that war or peace depends largely on the compatibility of value systems.

Throughout this phase of his development Sorokin is still basically monistic. Then in 1947 he published a monumental volume entitled *Society, Culture, Personality*.[23] In this version of his theory he indicates his belief that the more fruitful way of discovering the main, the necessary cause, is to distinguish it from supplementary factors that only facilitate or inhibit the action of the main cause. At the same time Sorokin maintains that he rejects any multiple or pluralistic theory of causation.

In support of his view Sorokin states that in the history of a nation wars tend to multiply during periods of political, economic and social growth and expansion, as well as during those periods of decline and decay. Both growth and decline are tantamount to clashes between the bearers of old and new values. In the history of wars between coalitions of nations wars tend to increase during periods of acute transition and change occuring "out of time" within and between the nations involved. Periods of transition from one fundamental type of culture to another are those in which wars attain their maximum probability. Revolutions occur similarly. All major revolutions[24] arose from a rapid and fundamental change in the basic values of one part of a given society while the other part did not undergo it or moved in the opposite direction.

Finally, in a short article published in 1949,[25] Sorokin repeated the judgment that wars are more frequent during periods of the disintegration of the dominant system of culture but, contrary to what he said in the previous works and especially in the *Social and Cultural Dynamics,* he declares that sensate, rather than idealist or ideational culture, is especially vicious. In this final view he also denies that differences between the basic values of particular nations provoke wars and demonstrates his thesis through many examples of peaceful coexistence of nations of quite different cultures.

Sorokin's discussion of wars and revolutions is always most stimulating. Most of his writing is. But at best his theory revolves, has many faces, and is sometimes logically inconsistent.

To gain a logically integrated theory one must judge quite opposite of Sorokin very frequently. Correlations of the frequency of wars and revolutions with the fluctuations of culture from one style to another can at best point only to remote, not to immediate causes. Further, these fluctuations contribute to what Sorokin calls the positive supplementary factors and to the exacerbation of the negative factors. But for reasons made explicit above, the derivation of long chains of causes behind specific events is not a scientifically fruitful pastime.

Others have worked out logically similar theories which suffer similar logical ills. Among these should be mentioned: L. P. Edwards,[26] Crane Brinton,[27] Q. Wright.[28] Of these theories let us choose for presentation that of Edwards which is frequently quoted up to the present time.

In his presentation of "the natural history of a revolution," L. P. Edwards is handicapped by the duality of his concept of revolution. For him, real revolution is tantamount to the commonly slow, essentially peaceful and largely unnoticed process of change in the distribution of power in a society. The violent outbreaks commonly called revolutions simply make evident that such a passage has taken place. These violent outbreaks are due to conservatism which makes the economically favored classes unwilling to recognize the fact that a real and peaceful revolution has already been accomplished.

In the final account, Edwards is forced to examine just these outbreaks (revolutions approximately in the meaning ascribed to this term in the present volume). For him, revolution is the slowest forming of all social processes; it requires the lifetime of at least three generations. The earliest symptom is the increase of general restlessness, chiefly among the upper and middle classes. The members of the lower classes feel that their legitimate expectations and ideals are repressed; but objectively their wealth, intelligence and power are increasing. The allegiance of the intellectuals is transferred from the existing government to something else, while the system of repression rapidly loses the respect of the public. But so long as the body of repression believe firmly in themselves and in the rightness of their actions, they cannot be overthrown by a revolution. The outbreak of revolution is commonly signaled by some act insignificant in itself which precipitates the separation of the repressors from the repressed. Commonly, a revolutionary mob is formed, but it is important only in some revolutions. The mob is always raised and organized by a small group of revolutionary leaders.

This is obviously a predominantly psychological theory; but some of the factors mentioned (such as mob formation, revolutionary leadership, the occurrence of an incident) cannot be so classified; therefore, the theory might be called integrative.

Logically Integrated Theory

The theory we are presenting in this monograph is certainly not of the monistic variety. It is much more pluralistic. But even this is not accurate. Logical integration implies that our theory of causation subsumes other theories yet focuses each into a total, logical view. How does this happen?

While our theory does not offer simply another modality of the natural history variety, it states that the movement from peace to war and from order to revolution requires the concomitance of definite conditions; it states that none of them predetermines the appearance of the others. While the concomitant conditions are real, their operation in a dynamic system is in part also the operation of the perceiving subject.[29] In other words, the *fact* that different conditions at different times effect war is in part the product of the perceiver.

In the logical model upon which our theory rests most of the factors mentioned by the monistic and pluralistic theorists reappear. The fatalistic notions of Leo Tolstoy and the too sociologistic theory of Pitirim Sorokin point to the general background of war: anarchy in international relations, the inevitable clash of interests and values both within the individual states and among them, the traditions and precedents for war and revolution, etc. The inherent tendency of many states to aggrandize, population pressure, struggle for markets, the prestige and national pride issue, the balance of power, national, religious and secular crusades and perhaps many more such items, appear as potential causes of inter- and intra-state conflict, related as they are to the very nature of the state. In modified form, the great man theory is reflected in the decisions which must be made by political leaders of nations as to the chances of achieving the goals by peaceful means, or through war and/or revolution.

Obviously the meaning of many generalizations asserted by other theories and models must lose their character of uniqueness. They may not logically pretend to express the "sufficient" character of the factor treated as the cause of conflict. What for economic, demographic, or psychological thinkers appear as unique causes of war and revolution, both necessary and sufficient, appear now as shaping causal tendencies in some social system toward conflict. These *can* become causes only if *unchecked* by other causal tendencies operative in the same society in the same time and space.

Similarly, judgments like those of Sorokin, e.g., "the absolute cause of war and revolution is value conflict," can be understood only as expressions of causal tendencies pointing toward conflict, but causing war and revolution only when supplemented by other causal tendencies operative in the same direction.

The best and simplest way we can finally put the conclusion is: war and revolution in the concrete are always the result of the concomitance of several conditions, always the same, but appearing in different forms and in a variety of sequences.

12/ A Scientific View of the Future

Diagnosis

A scientific theory is expected to yield clearer understanding of complex phenomena. It is also expected to work as a predictive instrument. And when the events predicted are harmful, the theory should indicate the possibility of preventive controls.

It is our intent in this chapter to apply the theory developed and extended throughout this work to diagnose the present day international situation and derive a prognosis regarding the crucial question: "Shall there be war or peace in our day?" We must emphasize, however, that our prognosis is intended to be no more and no less than that of a doctor, a weatherman, or even of an engineer about to push the button on his first experimental spaceship. Scientific forecast, it will readily be admitted, never achieves more than greater or lesser degrees of probability. There are always failures, but this is no deterrent to the prediction. Indeed, perhaps even the failure of the theory to predict or forecast a particular phenomenon may help enforce and correct the theory.

Conflict between the United States and the Soviet Union is the great mark of our twentieth century. The conflict is not territorial. Neither power is seeking to establish new boundaries at the other's expense. The conflict is not economic. Balances of trade and commerce do not appear as issues. Yet, in a sense, it is all of this, and more. The struggle *does* appear as a struggle of ideologies, even more dangerous because both parties ascribe a universal validity to their ideals and aspirations. Each considers its territorial policies inviolable, each looks upon its own economic system as the absolute best achievable, each considers its political mechanisms the "freest."

At the same time, certain objective situations develop not only in these two countries, but in a variety of ways all over the rest of the world. Populations expand rapidly; new technologies appear giving other nations new and undreamed of capacities; and perhaps above all, atomic fission makes it possible for any one or all to destroy all others. The roots of the conflict centered in two powers have developed enough to become the branches of conflict in others. What was once concentrated conflict has become generalized conflict, so that the success of one party can now be appraised throughout the world as the failure of the other. In the earlier part of the period of "cold war," the Soviet Union brought forward the argument of strategic boundaries. But this was never empha-sized.[1] With the Truman Doctrine, the United States began formulating negative interests—all of them diametrically op-posed to some positive interest of the Soviets. For a while the notion of preventive war was pondered in the United States as it was in the Soviet Union.

It is noteworthy that there was a comparatively long period when the particular aggravating circumstances which make an international conflict especially dangerous were conspicuous by their absence. This period lasted from the end of the de-clared war and open hostilities of the Second World War until November 27, 1958, the fateful day when Khrushchev posed the Berlin problem almost in the form of an ultimatum. On that day the Soviet Union pledged to the rest of the Com-munist World the abolition of the exceptional status of Berlin, while the leaders of the Western bloc have pledged its main-tenance. A tremendous problem of prestige is at issue here.

Ideologically, the roots of the problem were established after the cessation of hostilities of World War II. At that time it became clear that the government of the Soviet Union had no intention to allow the countries occupied by her armies to choose the form of government or the social order they wished, while the United States proclaimed many times that it would recognize any regime in the liberated areas so long as that regime was chosen by the people as representative of their in-terests. Expressed simply, the United States has no formal intent to dominate the entire world, whereas the real government of the Soviet Union—its strongly centralized Communist Party —makes no attempt to conceal its policy aimed at world domination.[2]

A Scientific View of the Future

Is War Probable?

All negotiations have utterly failed. Since the breakdown of talks at the Geneva Conference "on the summit" (1955), and the spectacular disruption of plans to elicit a *détente* by another summit conference (1960), no one really believes that the differences can be solved on a give-and-take basis. Arbitration is impossible: there is no third and really neutral party available. Further, between the parties there is no common definition to serve as the basis of the adjudgment of particular interests.

Some other means still remain open—means of "indirect action." The Soviet Union may continue hoping to advance its interests by stirring up trouble through Communist Party activities in many places. Still better, the Soviets will probably continue, and expand, a policy of economic aid to under-developed nations in competition with similar policies of the United States. More directly, the Soviet Union may also advance itself by "hot action" of the type fostered in Korea and Indo-China. Limited war in limited areas does not bring about final success, but neither does it provoke global war. As a result, Russia can ponder and develop other trials for other parts of the world. The recent events in Cuba, Laos, the Congo, and Zanzibar are telling instances. Success of these and perhaps more such enterprises will not, of course, be the equivalent of world domination. But the Communist ideology as professed today does not demand that all be accomplished all at once and everywhere. In fact, this ideology at the moment prohibits the use of violence unless the chances of immediate success are very high.[3]

It is remarkable that the recently unseated Soviet ruler, Premier Khrushchev, not too long ago stated a view expressed by Marx in 1872 in a speech delivered in Amsterdam. Contrary to his earlier statements on the subject, Marx here acknowledged the possibility of a peaceful evolution from capitalism to socialist-communism, particularly in England, the United States, and Holland. This is the only point in the Marxian doctrine on which Lenin allowed himself to disagree with the founding father. In his *State and Revolution,* written shortly before the seizure of power in Russia by the Bolsheviks, he stated that developments in capitalist societies after 1872 left no chance whatsoever for peaceful evolution.

But Khrushchev explicitly acknowledged the possibility, and even the necessity of change in parts of the doctrine inherited from Marx and Lenin in August, 1960, in a speech delivered at Bucharest. The leaders of 81 Communist parties issued a statement after their lengthy meeting in Moscow, November, 1960,[4] a statement which one could well call "The New Communist Manifesto." It is noteworthy that this statement makes ample use of the possibilities opened by Khrushchev's "permission" to deviate from Marxian orthodoxy. The central theme of this Manifesto is the possibility of peaceful coexistence of the Capitalist and the Communist worlds, based on the principle that peaceful transition from capitalist to communist society may take place.

The argument of the new Manifesto runs further

. . . the instability of capitalist economy is growing. Although production in some capitalist countries is increasing, the contradictions of capitalism are becoming more acute on a national as well as international scale. Some capitalist countries are threatened by new economic upheavals while still grappling with the consequences of the recent economic crisis.

On the other hand,

. . . in developing industrial and agricultural production in their countries at a high rate . . . the Communist and workers parties of the socialist countries consider it their international duty to make full use of all the advantages of the socialist system . . . to carry out, by joint effort and as speedily as possible, the historic task of surpassing the world capitalist system in overall industrial and agricultural production and then outstrip the economically most developed capitalist countries in per capital output and in the standard of living.

Consequently,

. . . the foreign policy of the socialist countries rests on the firm foundation of the Leninist principle of peaceful coexistence[5] and economic competition between the socialist and capitalist countries. In conditions of peace the socialist system increasingly reveals its advantages over the capitalist system in all fields of economy, culture, science and technology.

The policy of peaceful coexistence meets the basic interests of all peoples, of all who want no new cruel wars and seek durable peace. This policy strengthens the position of socialism, enhances the prestige and the international influence of the Communist parties in the capitalist countries. Peace is a loyal ally of socialism for time is working for socialism against capitalism.

All of which adds up to this: the Communist side of this most serious of world conflicts has not lost the hope of achieving its goal—world Communism—without resorting to war!

On the other side of the conflict, the Atlantic nations cannot *immediately* make the world democratic except through war. But the proximate goal of containing Communism—of limiting its expansion—may be attained relatively peacefully. Without open warfare with Soviet Russia the West has contained Communism in Iran (1946, and again in 1953), Greece, Turkey, Berlin (1949), Korea, Indo-China. Why should the Western nations despair of the possibility of further containment? And there is always the vague hope that at some time in the near future changes in the inner workings of Russia might make global agreement realistically possible.

Therefore, we can say that none of the parties has a cogent reason to abandon all hope, and the second condition for the outbreak of war is not fulfilled.

But there is yet a third condition, the relative strength of the parties in conflict, that must be weighed in this prediction. Good estimates are possible.

Among political experts and leaders in the United States, opinion ranges between two poles that we may simply designate as optimist and pessimist. A similar situation probably exists in the Soviet Union, but one commonly hears in America the opinions of the optimists rather than the pessimists. But in both countries neither the one nor the other ever brings forward one hundred percent convincing arguments for their view.

Prior to the Second World War this expert opinion knew the number of divisions, guns, and airplanes available to both sides of the conflict, plus the tempo and limits of possible expansion of forces. But even the experts of that time were often mistaken in predicting the course of events that finally led to war, and the particular course of events that the war entailed. At the present time, however, "absolute weapons," H-bombs, and guided missiles, are known to be available to both sides in quantities more than sufficient to annihilate the other. The Soviet insistence on the abolition of American bases around the world points to the fact that the Communists are by no means sure of victory while the insistence of the West on real disarmament with rigid control indicates that neither is the West so sure of its superiority. For the first time in history a state of saturation obtains with respect to the means of aggression. How much armament does exist on either side above the level of saturation is rather irrelevant. Since each side could annihilate the other in a short time the strength of the two is in reality equal. Each has more than a fair chance to win but by the same token, and in the same proportions, must consider the probability of complete annihilation.

The cost factor enters here as a modifier of the third condition for the outbreak of war. Each party may consider that it has a fair chance to win, but each party also knows that the cost of victory would be prohibitive; physical destruction of 90-95% of the total population, almost complete destruction of industrial equipment, transformation of almost the total territory into an uninhabitable area because of radiation, contamination of air, water, plants and animals and other natural resources. Under these circumstances victory can be worse than the most crucial defeat before this atomic age. Each of the parties to the possible conflict has full reason to refrain from attack.

Someone might, however, object along these lines. The leaders of the U.S.S.R. know very well that the leaders of the

Atlantic bloc will not give the signal to an almost complete destruction of civilization, perhaps of the entire human race. Regardless of their propaganda the Communist leaders know that in the West normative inhibitions against war are stronger than ever and are reinforced by the knowledge of the Soviet's strength. They also know that in America the days are gone forever when men like the late John Foster Dulles could assert that the Soviets acted "from a position of weakness." Therefore, the Communist leaders might decide to take a chance, destroy all the major centers of the Western hemisphere by a surprise attack by H-bombs and missiles and then occupy, without meeting much resistance, the periphery of the Old Continent.

But, and this is the plain answer to the objection, the Communists also know that the dangers expressed in the objection, and validly, are well realized by the leaders of the West and at the first signal of an all-out attack from the East the tremendous forces of the West dispersed throughout the world would be put in motion to annihilate the aggressor as well. The "hot line" between Washington and Moscow symbolizes this answer.

The impossibility of resorting to war in our day was recognized two months before the appearance of the "New Communist Manifesto" in an influential Soviet journal *Mezhdunarodnaya Zhisn,* which, in free translation, means "Foreign Affairs."[6] The article is signed by Major-General Nikolai A. Talensky, a prominent military theoretician active in the U.S.S.R. He says:

The idea of winning a war with the help of an unexpected blow as well as with the help of preventive war in conditions of atomic saturation is erroneous. A surprise attack might gain a momentary advantage to the aggressor but with the present level of nuclear stockpiles the conflict would eventually culminate in the destruction of the aggressor as well as of the victims of the attack.

In the concluding part of his article the Soviet expert says further:

. . . in the modern development of military technique, any further increase in the destructive power of weapons will not produce serious strategic advantages.

Consequently, the development of the technique of

. . . the destruction of the people makes it impossible now to use weapons for the solution of political problems, as has been the case in the course of thousands of years.

One might suspiciously hazard the guess that statements like these are being made on the Soviet side only in an attempt to throw off guard the vigilance of the great powers of the West. But it is much more probable that Talensky's statements reflect the genuine view of the present Communist leadership.

This more probable view is supported by a passage in the "New Communist Manifesto" acknowledging that a Third World War would be tantamount to a catastrophe much more terrible than the First and Second World Wars.

Monstrous means of mass destruction and annihilation have been developed which, if used in a new war, can cause unheard-of destruction to entire countries and reduce key centers of world industry and culture to ruins. Such a war would bring death and suffering to hundreds of millions of people, among them people in countries not involved in it.

In other words, the Soviets acknowledge that under the present conditions of over-saturation with absolute weapons there will be no victorious, but only defeated, nations.

It should be evident from all this that the third condition (the relative strength of the parties must be such that one has reasonable expectation of victory over the other) is *not* present in the contemporary, international situation. However, it is also evident that this judgment is valid only as long as the leaders of the East remain realistic. In other words, it is *not* present as long as they continue to act not under the impulse of emotions, but guided by the cold logic of the situation. That they are realists in this sense is proved by the conduct of their foreign policy during the past thirty-five years, since the evaporation of the original revolutionary fervor. It was under this mistaken enthusiasm that they launched a number of ill-advised enterprises such as the eliciting of a communist revolution in Germany and in China (in this latter, they did it successfully in the forties but under quite different conditions). There is no reason to assume that now, almost fifty years after their original revolution, the Communist leadership will change its mind and act on the basis of some irrational faith in some irresistible force latent in Communist doctrine; they know from bitter experience that no such force exists at least not in relation to present day nations which would count in the eventual Armaggedon.[7]

There is another factor worthy of consideration in this question of victory—*morale*. The people of the United States have demonstrated, particularly during the Second World War, that when their personal liberties and the independence of their nation is at stake, they are capable of immense internal social solidarity. During peace time, and patricularly to outsiders, this cohesiveness seems very low indeed. But under stresses it reaches high intensity and results in the convergence of all forces toward the goal of victory.

Throughout their history the Russian people have also in general displayed similar tenacity and ability to unite to fight for common purposes. This would occur even when they had reasons to hate the political regime over them. But in the beginning of the Second World War certain phenomena contrary to this historical trend and ominous from the viewpoint of the Communist government began to appear. In many places the invader was acclaimed as the liberator with large masses of Russian soldiers gladly surrendering.[8] Had the German leaders correctly read the meaning of these symptoms and drawn the logical conclusions, the Soviet Union could perhaps have been really and irreparably defeated. But Hitler's political blunders, in addition to the purely military ones, saved the U.S.S.R.

The Soviet Union would never enter a war today without its satellites. But these satellites know well that each and all would easily be overthrown by an outside enemy were any important defeat suffered by the central Soviet. People in these satellite nations by and large hate the political yoke imposed on them, not by the Russian people, as Communist propagandists would have it, but by the *government* of Russia which has its power through subjugating both the Russian people and the peoples of the satellite countries. For the people of the satellites this is a double yoke: it is the yoke of a despotic power and a foreign yoke; for the Russian people it is only political.

The weight of this factor under consideration, i.e., morale, will be affected by the way in which an eventual Third World War may develop. Several modalities are possible. The one-sided destruction of the West would of course preclude all insurrections in the zone formed by the satellites. Another modality, the one-sided destruction of the East without substantial retaliation, would solve the problem from the viewpoint of the West, almost automatically. The peoples of the satellites would be left free to choose the governments and modes of life they want. They would almost certainly cede from any semblance of a Soviet dominated empire as the situation at present. The third modality would obtain if war would not be waged through massive thermonuclear means, but only by conventional techniques. If during such a war the forces of the West penetrate into the satellite zone, rebellion of the latter would most probably ensue followed by a realigning of the loyalties of the satellite armies with the forces of the West.[9]

All the alternatives under discussion cannot help but be well known to the leaders of the Soviet Union. They are undoubtedly taken into consideration when calculations of the chances of victory or defeat are made. As realists, they probably understand that the factor of morale is not in their favor.

Summary and Conclusion

The prognosis is therefore favorable. So long as the state of the present international system, as expressed in its relevant traits, remains unchanged, no Third World War is likely. To bring the motion from peace to war into reality, two changes are themselves first necessary. First, at least one of the parties must lose the hope to achieve his ends short of war, and, second, the relationship of the relative strength of the parties must become such that a fair chance of ultimate victory would be assumed to exist by one rather than the other of the two parties. Both at the present time are dominated by the fear of total defeat.

A real increase of the chances of victory of the Soviets would obtain if there would occur a rapid advance of the military and industrial potential of the Soviet, or if the same potential of the Atlantic bloc would proportionately decrease. Though the industrial potential of the Soviet Union is growing, the potential of the United States and the Western allies can balance these efforts through continued use of their own dynamism. As to China, her presentday position as of *tertium gaudens* is embarrassing for the two major powers at conflict, the Soviet Union and USA, but no more. China could use a Russo-American war to occupy some border provinces of the Soviet Union—but hardly could retain them after the defeat of one of the two major parties: the victor would be able to penalize China, in any case. If the Russo-American war would end in a deadlock, China would find herself in the same position in which it is today and the annexation of a few border provinces would not substantially improve her power position; there would be no major gains for her during a few years after the end of an eventual Russo-American war. The only danger for the U.S. is a very improbable change in the mentality and policies of America and its major allies.

Should America become complacent, should a demand for

a return to "normalcy" prevail, in other words, should any condition analogous to isolationism or aloofness to international commitments occur, the relative strength of these parties could move toward conditions of war. If nothing like these changes occurs, the political system of the world will remain, perhaps for decades, in the same state of acute tension in which it is now. Of itself an ideological war need never turn into a hot war.

How Probable is Revolution?

Revolutions are meant for the relaxation of tensions within the state as wars for relaxation of tensions between states. In our day, often enough, revolutions are associated with Communist activities and ideology. There are some exceptions as, for example, a disturbing revival of Fascism in Italy, and more minor, sporadic outbreaks of Naziism. But in Europe, west of the Iron Curtain, the attractiveness of Communist inspired revolution may be measured by the strength of votes gained by the Communist party. It is common knowledge that two major European nations, France and Italy, but few if any of the smaller nations, are tinged with Communist favor. The percentage of Communist vote in France and Italy is rather high and stable, reflecting active and acute tensions. Most of this has persisted since the end of World War II. But the other conditions for revolution hardly exist. The Communists and their fellow travelers have no reason to despair; sooner or later, they expect, through adroit maneuvers, subversive activities, perhaps eventually through war, the Soviet Empire will be expanded to receive these countries as companions. In France, this had been demonstrated in the expressed hopes of Communist party members even in the face of Pinay's bold offensive against them and by de Gaulle's rather general overhaul of the whole political system.

In Italy, de Gasperri and his successors have never doubted that they could crush an eventual Communist upheaval. And there, as in France, the economic texture of the country has been so strengthened by the Marshall Plan and its aftermath that the governments are obviously too influcntial for Communist leaders to subvert. This means that no matter how grave present tensions are internally, they are nowhere near strong enough to erupt into revolution.

In another place[10] we made the prediction that under the present situation a revolution is unlikely within the Soviet Union. Revolution could occur there only if the leadership was shaken deeply by a series of convulsions provoked by personal changes in supreme party leadership. The struggle "at the top" was minimal after the deaths of Lenin and Stalin. But for the first few weeks after Stalin's death the "collective leadership" which first took over did little to conceal their fear of grave disturbances. Negatively, there is nothing in the processes on-going in Russia to guarantee that when the top leadership changes over for a third and fourth time it will betray even greater weaknesses. Nothing seriously dangerous for the new supreme team, consisting of Brezhnev and Kosygin, has shown up.

Three other groups of nations, however, deserve much closer analysis. The probabilities of revolution are, or seem to be, relatively high in each.

The Latin American countries are all relatively unstable, and may be described as mixtures of small, wealthy, and well educated minorities living amid large masses in miserable poverty, filth, and illiteracy. The *pronunciamento* and other meaningless traditions are still there and often inhibit the more spontaneous functioning of democratic institutions. Fortunately, the tendency is for most of these countries to "lean toward" democracy, and much of the future will depend on the amount and the wise distribution of United States aid. Latin America will receive little support from elsewhere—except the Communists!

The social structures of the Arab nations and the newly arising nations of Africa are very similar to those of the Latin American countries—unstable and emerging. Africa does not have the problems of "wealthy ruling classes," but instead has the problem of white colonials who seemingly have done little to prepare native populations for democratic institutions. This leaves the tensions no less intense, but prediction in these cases is impossible.

13/Preventing
War and Revolution

IF WARS AND REVOLUTIONS can be forecast within limits, within similar limits they may also be prevented. This assumes, of course, the judgment that they *ought* to be prevented as something harmful.

Fifty years ago war was frequently considered as something desirable.[1] Probably, as is often the case, the real truth lies somewhere midway. It is proportionately as wrong to consider war as something desirable as it is to consider it something harmful and achieving nothing. The unifying of fractional political bodies into national states has been an important condition of progress increasing the areas of peace, and creating vast areas for economic and cultural exchange. Such unification could not have been achieved except by war. Very often, attempts at peaceful unification fell short of its goal because of the resistance of local dynasties or oligarchies and their vested interests. Wars of unification really settled something.

Some conquests were patently immoral, but lucrative for the conquerors and not without some advantages even to the conquered. Think away the British conquest of India, and a unified Indian nation endowed with many of the technical devices of Western origin and politically oriented toward the climate of freedom and democracy cannot be envisioned. On a smaller scale, the Russian conquest of the Caucasus and Central Asia has awakened these regions, liberated them from the plague of fratricidal feuds, and endowed them with many elements of Western technology. Much the same can be said of the role of France in North Africa.

Without the Mexican War, the United States would have been without access to the Pacific, and most probably would never have evolved into a "superpower," almost self-sufficient, but able and willing to assist the disinherited peoples of Europe and capable of standing for freedom against enslavement by totalitarian dictatorship and fascist strong men who ravaged so much of Europe in recent times.

At present, however, a new kind of situation has evolved. First, the cost of war in human lives and material goods has become prohibitive. Second, almost all the world is divided among nations of relatively high technological culture, or at least strongly influenced by such culture, so that the aftermath of a war cannot any longer signify the spread of such culture into areas not yet affected by it. Third, the movement of unification has been largely achieved, with exceptions possible only in the Near East, South America, and perhaps Africa.[2]

The only objectively valid war in our day would be a war to finally unify all mankind, as a means to eliminate war (war to end war). The prohibitive cost of war and the pitiful outcome of the two world wars which, once broken out, were waged for this noble goal, make the desirability of such a war highly doubtful. Especially for the technologically more advanced nations, war would mean a major catastrophe. But there is no universal agreement on the point.

Behind the Iron Curtain war may be pondered by some leaders as a means to unify the world around the Kremlin under the banner of Marxist philosophy. And local wars, e.g., between India and Pakistan, between Israel and her Arab neighbors, between some Central or South American states, or between African states, are not out of the question. But local wars may open the way to involving additional states and finally coalesce into a Third Global War.

This makes the problem of war prevention in our day one of paramount importance. Prevention may be attempted on two levels: concrete, the reversal of trends leading to a concrete war, and general, the uprooting of the cultural tradition of war.

Observation through history shows that attempts to prevent wars, without general plan and organization, fail. Counsels of moderation are rarely followed, and only concrete threats of violence, i.e., of war, or something close to war, may be effective. In 1875, Germany pondered another war against France to check her rapid recovery from the earlier war. A communication from the Russian Emperor to the German Emperor that, this time, Russia would interfere, stopped the development in the very beginning. In 1908, a Russo-Austrian war loomed on the horizon; Germany's declaration that she would fight on the side of Austria prevented further moves toward war.

A general mechanism for war prevention is possible to control those factors of interstate conflicts which normally lead to war. A special mechanism for the solution, for example, of territorial conflicts going much farther than the abortive means created by the Covenant of the League of Nations, would be a *must* as part of such a mechanism. It would be most important to grant a supranational organization, created for the purpose, a code of substantive rules. No existing state boundary should be considered sacrosanct. Of course, the role of the will of the people should be assigned high importance, but its elevation to the role of decisive factor, like any other monistic emphasis, is futile. "The will of the people" should be limited by the requirements of organized coexistence in the framework of a state. Similar mechanisms should be created to resolve economic conflicts regarding unequal distribution of raw materials, markets, skills, etc. The Charter of the United Nations and the activity of its Social and Economic Council are moving rapidly in these directions.

For the foreseeable future free migration seems to be the only effective remedy for wars arising out of population pressures. But this is only a very limited answer. The demographer sees very clearly that massive emigration almost never diminishes population pressure, since the numbers lost by emigration are commonly balanced by an increase of survivors through decline of the death rate. Moreover, massive emigration would soon result in the leveling of standards of living between the countries involved, and this, unfortunately, would mean lower levels for all concerned. Actually, this would mean a high price solution to population pressure on the part of the advanced nations, and finally for humanity as a whole.

Among the cultural precipitants of war, the phenomenon of oppressed minorities is the most crucial in war prevention. Since the elimination of domination-oppression between cultural minorities and majorities is very unlikely on the basis of self-determination, federation seems a more likely solution. Many oppressed minorities occupy territories basically too small, and too limited in resources, both natural and human, to exist as completely independent states. But a framework of culturally and geographically related ethnic groups, bound by constitutional ties, might lessen tensions—and ultimately— conflict between them. Another possibility is the exchange of minorities by states involved. This was characteristic of Turks and Greeks in the 1920's, under the auspices of the League of Nations.[4] This exchange strengthened each of the nations and allowed them to coexist peacefully. However, lately difficulties are apparent in the case of Cyprus.

These remedies presuppose the genuine and intensive will to keep peace on the part of all the nations forming a community. To the degree that this is not the case, they can help prevent only local wars among those members who share the goal.

Most difficult to control are the emotional factors involved in conflicts leading to war, especially the revenge and hatreds involved in international feuds. It is equally difficult to control such factors as the spirit of militarism when it permeates a whole nation, or when it motivates the rise to power of a war party. To overthrow such groups, a peace-minded state would have to wage war, and outside of the framework of an over-whelming international organization, the risk and cost of such a work to an individual state is a strong deterrent. Why should one state do what the community of states should do? There is no answer, and the task is not carried out, although the goal of eliminating warlords like Napoleon and Hitler played a contributory part in the genesis of several wars.

Remedies like these should not be neglected even though they obviously may not solve problems. The core difficulty lies in the fact that war is an inveterate complex in the culture tradition of a large community of the unorganized type, and that it is almost natural that such be its tradition. The corollary follows that structural change is needed.[5] The farthest reaching proposal is the formation of a super-state or world government. There would then be only one sovereign state and war with any other would be impossible. But in our day this seems a utopian ideal. A state presumes a community of values based upon a similarity of culture. But in the twentieth century there seem to be only a variety of value systems, some of them very wide apart, and actually or potentially, loaded with conflict. The clash between the values of Western society and Communist society is very open. The value systems of India, the Arab states, and of Latin America are far distant from the culture traditions of the Anglo-Saxon nations and their democratic allies. This is a situation quite at variance with the one which obtained when the American Union was formed, notwithstanding the naive references often made to that Union in discussing the proposal of universal federation.

A critical factor in any peace program at the present time will be Russia. If Russia succeeds in overcoming the Communist party dictatorship and returns to democratic processes for which her cultural elite struggled for a century and which she almost achieved between March and November, 1917, the goal would become much more easily attainable.

Even this would not settle matters overnight, and the pattern of world government would be adopted only with some difficulty. But world government is not a totally necessary prerequisite to enduring peace. The shift of pre-political society to political forms signified the emergence of an overwhelming drive toward law and order. In the case of the state this drive is realized through centralized power. In the international community, men may yet try the device of coordinated power; this is the principle behind the San Francisco Charter of the United Nations. After a sufficiently long period of enforcing the peace through the mechanisms of this Charter, we can expect the traditions of war to become weaker, and perhaps be forgotten, just as within the state, the traditions of private feuds become weaker and are then forgotten. Education which portrays peace as orderly progress toward more justice will strengthen and accelerate the program.[6] This must be done, however, through the community of nations, or it becomes criminal weakness, the basic error of the pacifists, weakening the power of resistance to war of those nations which sincerely wish to eliminate it, and granting advantage to those who would like to do away with war only after they have achieved their own egotistic goals at the expense of the rest of the world.

The functional prerequisite to permanent peace is the emergence of the corporate will of humanity to preserve peace. Since no such will is yet operative, we must humbly accept the probability that, in our day, complete elimination of war is out of the question. The only chance to keep the peace is to preserve the strength of peace-loving nations so high that all eventual aggressors will be deterred from launching into wars because of the conspicuous absence of any fair chance of victory. The presence of such a chance is, we know, one of the conditions of the movement of the political system of the international community from peace to war. This is the factor under control and, returning to what has been said in our discussion of prediction, it would be foolish, even criminal, to drop pressure on this decisive lever in the mechanism of the maintenance of peace.

The Prevention of Revolution

Obviously the prevention of revolution is analogous to the prevention of war. Is every revolution an evil, and therefore to be avoided? Historical experience shows that revolution is an expensive means of social change and that its outcome is quite unpredictable. Revolutions started for good causes have often brought about signal deteriorations of political, social, and cultural conditions in human existence.

Yet men resort to revolutions and hardly listen to exhortations to abandon this means of resolving intra-state conflict. There is the tendency for everyone to evaluate a revolution differently from others depending on differences in social ideals. A revolution striving for the overthrow of a dictatorship and the institution of a democracy will be heartily welcomed by the democrats of the world. Such was the instance in the Cuban revolution in its first stages when Batista's dictatorship was overthrown. But the revolution aiming at the establishment of a dictatorship in place of democracy will be perceived as a calamity.

Our discussion will be limited to discussing the prevention of revolution from the democratic viewpoint only. In other words: what can be done—what should be done—to prevent revolutions against democracy?[7]

A revolution presupposes the accumulation of social tensions reflected in the discontent and desire of rapid change, or a situation of *plasticity*. The leaders of a democracy should never allow such a situation to develop. To prevent it, they must understand that democracy is not only government of the people expressed in the majority rule. Democracies which do not go beyond securing the smooth unfolding of the political game, the voting stage, among selected party leaders, are vulnerable. Democracy is also government *for* the people. It is operative when it secures human dignity, participation of the rank-and-file members of the society in the economic and cultural achievements of mankind. Many nations are not yet able to give their citizens the same opportunities as the most advanced nations. But if the trend is obviously in the right direction, if today the citizens have more than they had yesterday and if they can reasonably expect that tomorrow will be still better, the danger of revolution is minimized.

Revolutions may still occur on the basis of new social ideals. At times these may be uncritical and foolish ideals, but they may still motivate men to revolt. They may mean a decrease in the chances of fuller participation in government on the part of many. But the minority instilling these ideals may organize itself using tactics to threaten democracy and frustrate the benefits enjoyed by the many. To prevent this the leaders of democracy must be aware of one of the propositions established as the roots of revolutions. A revolution may break out only if the leaders of the revolutionary movement may nurture the hope of victory through violence. This they may do only if the government is exceptionally weak. Hence the rule neglected by many democracies having succumbed to anti-democratic revolutions: the democratic government, being a government by and for the people, is also government of the people. In other words, it must actually govern, exert leadership, eventually resort to coercion. For a democratic government, this is a more difficult task than for a dictatorial one. But the respect for human dignity inherent in democracy cannot go so far as to allow the crystallization of movements striving for the overthrow of the rule of the majority, still less the outbreak of violence aiming at its overthrow.

The sad experience of many democracies which have succumbed to revolution, violence, then dictatorship, are witnesses to the necessity of these principles. In March, 1917, the author was appointed by the Provisional Government of Russia as a member of the Commission for the Adaptation of the Penal Law of Russia to the exigencies of the new regime. The commission entrusted to him the preparation of the draft of a section against subversive propaganda, a matter on which he was known to have worked over a period of several years. He submitted a draft which approximated the United States Act of 1940 (the so-called Smith Act). After some discussion with the commission, the section was incorporated in the draft which was submitted to the Provisional Government.

Here, one of the members, a Menshevik, strongly objected to the section in question. He asserted that democracy implied absolute freedom of speech, even direct incitement to violent overthrow of the government. The Provisional Government was a coalition government and accepted as a guiding rule the principle of *liberum veto,* meaning that the dissent of one member amounted to the rejection of the measure under discussion. So the draft was shelved.

This was in May, 1917. On July 5 (old style), the Bolsheviks made their first attempt to seize power by force; it failed because of the resolute resistance of Cossack regiments stationed in Petrograd. Then on July 6, the Government promulgated a decree enacting just one section of the draft on penal legislation, the section concerning itself with subversive propaganda. Events seemed to have taught a lesson!

But despite the law, the Bolsheviks continued their propaganda emphasizing the necessity of seizing power by force. Their best speaker, L. Trotsky,[8] spoke daily to crowds from the balcony of a palace once owned by a ballerina, but already "expropriated for revolutionary purposes by a group of anarchists." The author lived two blocks away from the palace and almost daily listened to inflammatory speeches advocating the violent overthrow of the Provisional Government. On October 22, he paid a visit to the Ministry of Justice with which he was continuing his work. He inquired of the director of the Department of Criminal Law why the law of July 6 was not being applied to Trotsky and many minor agitators. The director informed him that he had many times insisted on the arrest and indictment of Trotsky and his companions, but that the Minister of Justice, another Menshevik, had forbidden him to do so on the same grounds used by another member of the Government in May to veto the draft.

Three days after this meeting the Minister was in jail and Trotsky—a member of the "Workers' and Peasants' Government" under Lenin—was in power.

The attitude of the two members of the Provisional Government was not exceptional. After the communists had their *coup d'état,* most intellectuals with whom the author had the opportunity to discuss the situation believed that the rule of the party would last from three days to three months (opinions varied according to the temperament of the speaker) but would inevitably be destroyed by "the people" who, once they had gained liberty and democracy, would never tolerate the rule of usurpers.

The bitter experience of the past forty years has taught the world that this is not so; democracy can be overthrown by force, and like everything worthwhile, can be kept and extended only through continuous and careful attention.

When democracy is intelligently and effectively protected through measures consistent with its values and techniques, it is invincible, except when crushed by external forces, by wars of aggression, or through war-like intimidation. In this instance, to succeed democracy must be stronger than its destroyers; similarly, with regard to internal disturbances, ultimately revolution, a democracy must stand structurally strong—able to withstand internal deteriorations.

Power is frequently derided and, without discrimination, feared and rejected. It is true that power, especially political power, is dangerous and is often used for selfish purposes by those who hold it. But strength for the prevention of war and for the protection of democracy against subversion is strength in the service of justice and charity. Gathering and eventually displaying strength for these purposes is the prerogative of God-fearing and peace-loving nations.

Notes

CHAPTER 1

1. We can gain a preliminary insight into these two undulant processes (from peace to war and back to peace, and from order to revolution and back to order) by establishing, for a definite period of time and definite societies, the number of years marked by war and the number of years marked by revolution. Let us choose for illustration the history of England and France in the eighteenth and nineteenth centuries.

On the basis of enormous material collected by Pitirim A. Sorokin (*Social and Cultural Dynamics*, New York, American Book Co., 1937, Vol. III) and Quincy Wright (*A Study of War*, Chicago, University of Chicago Press, 1942), we can state that England was at war in the years 1701-13, 1715-19, 1743-48, 1755-65, 1775-83, 1793-1802, 1803-15, (1824-26), 1827, 1838-42, (1843-45), 1854-60, 1878-85, 1899-1900. Disturbances of inner order (all minor, but still covered by the concept of revolution) occurred in 1705, 1715-16, 1736, 1745-46, 1761, 1765, 1780, 1795, 1797, 1798, 1803, 1811-12, 1816, 1820, 1831-32, 1839, 1848, 1867, and 1886.

France was at war in the years 1701-13, 1718-20, 1733-38, 1741-48, 1754-63, 1779-1802, 1803-15, 1827, 1832, 1838-39, 1854-56, 1859, 1861-67, 1870-71, 1883-85, 1894-96, 1900. She was shaken by inner disturbances in 1702-10, 1719-20, 1740, 1744, 1776, 1789-99, (1803), 1815, (1816), (1820), 1830, 1831, 1832, 1834, (1839), 1848, 1851, (1852), (1858), 1870-71 and 1899.

In these lists some years appear in parentheses to denote that the classification of the corresponding events is dubious. The figures for England contain also years of strong unrest in Ireland, once part of the United Kingdom.

These lists of wars and revolutions have been checked against the somewhat narrower definitions of these phenomena used in this volume. Many sequences of war years correspond not to one war, but to several wars waged independently of each other. But the inclusion of a year into the number of years of war or revolution means only that during part of the year there was fighting with external enemies or between factions within the state. Therefore, one could not calculate the proportion of periods of war and peace, revolution and order, simply by subtracting from 200 the number of years appearing in the lists.

2. Cf. Pitirim A. Sorokin, *op. cit.,* pp. 352-360, for excellent evidence in support of this proposition. Quincy Wright is inclined to favor the thesis for periodicity.

3. For observational purposes this judgment will be further specified below.

4. The January, 1960 revolt in Algiers was vigorously suppressed by General Charles de Gaulle.

5. Pitirim A. Sorokin, in his analysis of revolution, actually operates with two definitions. First, revolution is an inner disturbance of some importance. "Quite insignificant disorders" have been omitted from this volume, the criterion used for judgment being the standard historical works of the country involved. The second definition is: revolution is

an attack against a substantial part of the population. While his political referents for the study of the frequency and movement of revolution deal with all the cases covered by definition one, Sorokin's presentation of uniformities in inner changes generated by the revolution deals with cases covered by the second definition.

6. This position is quite contrary to the theories of Hobbes, for example, or Gumplowicz, for whom conflict (or struggle) is the very basis for society to the exclusion of all other processes.

7. Cf. *infra,* Chapters 4 and 5.

8. Cf. *supra,* note no. 1.

9. Cf. Pitirim A. Sorokin, *Man and Society in Calamity* (New York, E. P. Dutton and Co., 1942).

10. This is, of course, not a moral judgment about the moral value or the political expediency of the intervention, but merely a statement of fact in terms of the definition already elaborated.

11. Cf. Pitirim A. Sorokin, *Social and Cultural Dynamics,* Vol. III, pp. 847-893.

CHAPTER 2

1. Karl Pearson, *The Grammar of Science* (London, W. Scott, Ltd., 1892).

2. Herbert Alexander Simon, *Models of Man, Social and Rational* (New York, John Wiley and Sons, 1957), pp. 39ff.

3. Werner Heisenberg, *The Physical Principles of the Quantum Theory* translated by Carl Eckart and Frank C. Hoyt (Chicago, University of Chicago Press, 1930). Heisenberg was intrigued by the apparent contradiction in the experimental evidence pointing to the nature of light. According to one set of evidence, light traveled in nearly straight lines, and they were to be regarded as streams of minute particles traveling at high speeds. Other evidence led to the designation of light as particles of matter moving at high speeds but in waves. From such experiments one could only conclude that matter and radiation seem to have a remarkable duality of character.

Heisenberg's solution to this duality involved his postulation of the principle of indetermination. *Two mental pictures* of light are formed depending upon the *conditions of experiment and observation.* Light itself is neither wave nor line, but indeterminate. The determinants are the conditions of experiment and observation.

4. George Andrew Lundberg seems most representative of today's neo-positive position. See especially his article, "The Natural Science Trend in Sociology," *American Journal of Sociology,* Vol. 61, No. 3 (November 1955), pp. 191-202.

5. Pitirim A. Sorokin, *Social and Cultural Dynamics,* Vol. I, pp. 10-13, 48, and 161-175; Georges Gurvitch, *Déterminismes sociaux et liberté humaine* (Paris, Presses universitaires de France, 1955).

6. Pitirim A. Sorokin, *Social and Cultural Dynamics,* Vol. I, pp. 72-101.

7. Cf. Robert F. Bales, *Interaction Process Analysis,* (Cambridge, Mass., Addison-Wesley Press, 1950). Here is another eminently logical discussion of the temporal dimension in the judgment of the observer. In the logic of Bales, the observer, the generalized other, sees all as present. The present as effect is past, as instrumentality is future. Causal relations are viewed by the observer as effect (past), as instrumentality (future) they can only be projected (in the present).

8. Cf. Gerard DeGré, "Freedom and Social Structure," *American Sociological Review,* Vol. 11, No. 5 (October 1946), pp. 529-536.

9. For an ex professo discussion of this position, cf. Ferdinand Töennies, *Community and Society,* translated and edited by Charles P. Loomis (East Lansing, Michigan State University Press, 1957). Several editions of this book have been published in Berlin under the title *Gemeinshaft und Gesellschaft.*

10. Cf. note no. 4 above. Also George Andrew Lundberg's "Some Convergences in Sociological Theory," *American Journal of Sociology,* Vol. 62, No. 1 (July 1956), pp. 21-27ff.

11. Pitirim A. Sorokin, *op. cit.,* Vol. IV, 1941. In *Sociocultural Causality, Space, Time* (Durham, N.C., Duke University Press, 1943), especially Chapter I entitled "Declaration of Independence of Social Sciences from Natural Sciences," Sorokin does not entirely deny the application to social phenomena of causal propositions, but only so far as physico-chemical and biological properties are concerned. These are modified and relegated to the second plane by propositions about the logico-meaningful relations obtaining in the system.

Notes

12. Robert Morrison MacIver, *Social Causation* (New York, Ginn and Company, 1942).

13. Basically this is the same position taken by Georg Simmel and used by him, consistently referring to form and content in social configurations. For an excellent discussion of Simmel and his works, cf. Rudolph H. Weingartner, *Experience and Culture* (Middletown, Conn., Wesleyan University Press, 1962).

14. Cf. N. S. Timasheff, "Sociological Theory Today," *American Catholic Sociological Review,* Vol. XI, No. 1 (March 1951), pp. 25ff.

15. For an explicit statement cf. Pierre Simon, Marquis de Laplace, *A Philosophical Essay on Probabilities,* translated from sixth French edition by Frederick Wilson Truscott and Frederick Lincoln Emory, with introduction by E. T. Bell (New York, Dover Publications, 1951).

16. A. Michotte, *La perception de la causalité* (Louvain, Éditions de l'Inst. supérieur de philosophie, 1946); English translation *The Perception of Causality,* trans. by T. R. Miles and Elaine Miles (New York, Basic Books, 1963).

17. György Pólya, *Mathematics and Plausible Reasoning,* Vol. I and Vol. II (Princeton, N. J., Princeton University Press, 1954).

18. Émile Durkheim, *The Rules of Sociological Method,* trans. by Sarah A. Solovay and John H. Mueller, ed. by George E. G. Catlin (Glencoe, Ill., Free Press, 1950).

19. Cf. Susanne K. Langer, *Philosophy in a New Key* (New York, Mentor Books, 1948).

20. Cf. note no. 3 above.

21. Cf. Felix Kaufmann, *Methodology of the Social Sciences* (New York, Oxford University Press, 1944). In this work the relationship between various laws of nature are too rigorously interpreted in a monistic conception of order.

22. Immanent causation seems central in Sorokin's theory. Cf. his *Social and Cultural Dynamics,* Vol. IV, pp. 590-92 and pp. 627-29. This, it seems to us, rests on the unwarranted attribution of causality to the time reference in which causes operate.

23. Cf. Chapter 11.

24. Cf. Ernest Nagel, *The Structure of Science* (New York, Harcourt, Brace and World, Inc., 1961), especially Chapter 15, "Problems

in the Logic of Historical Inquiry," for an extended discussion of this position.

CHAPTER 3

1. This chapter is a very generalized form of my "political sociology." For a more detailed discussion, see N. S. Timasheff, Paul Facey and John Schlereth, *General Sociology* (Milwaukee, Bruce Publishing Co., 1959). Also see S. M. Lipset, "Political Sociology Today," in Robert K. Merton et al. (ed.), *Sociology Today* (New York, Basic Books, Inc., 1959). Robert MacIver's *The Web of Government* (New York, The Macmillan Co., 1947) is perhaps one of the most extensive treatments of political sociology.

2. On the reality of social groups, see Timasheff, Facey and Schlereth, *op. cit.*, pp. 158-64.

3. For a much more complete elaboration of a theory of social power, see N. S. Timasheff, *An Introduction to the Sociology of Law* (Cambridge, Mass., Harvard University Committee on Research in the Social Services, 1939), and Robert MacIver, *op. cit.*, pp. 87-97.

4. Cf. Robert MacIver, *op. cit.*, pp. 314-59.

5. Cf. Gerard DeGré, "Freedom and Social Structure," in *American Sociological Review*, Vol. II, No. 5 (October, 1946), pp. 529-36.

6. Robert MacIver, *op. cit.*, pp. 52-55, 71.

7. This was probably the case of the Soviet Union after the Second World War. See N. S. Timasheff, "What Does This War Mean to Russia?" *Current History*, Vol. 8, No. 45 (May, 1945), pp. 426-430.

8. On the transfer of functions to and from the state, see P. A. Sorokin, *Social and Cultural Dynamics*, Vol. II, pp. 181-216.

9. The plan of the Abbé Sieyés (which was the first draft of the French Constitution of 1799) created two consuls, one of war and another of peace, whose activities would be coordinated by the Grand Elector (who would appoint and dismiss the consuls). In our day Gurvitch suggested the separation of political and economic power to be loosely coordinated by a system of arbitration. Cf. his *La déclarations des droits sociaux* (New York, Éditions de la Maison Française, Inc., 1944).

Notes

10. On the abuses of power and their combination, see N. S. Timasheff, "Totalitarianism, Despotism, Dictatorship," in Carl J. Friedrich (ed.), *Totalitarianism* (Cambridge, Mass., Harvard University Press, 1954), pp. 39-47.

11. Cf. Timasheff, *et al., General Sociology,* pp. 154-55 for a further discussion of this difference.

12. Cf. Chapter 13 of this work.

13. Cf. Timasheff, *An Introduction to the Sociology of Law,* pp. 260-63.

14. William J. Perry, *The Growth of Civilization* (New York, E. P. Dutton, 1924).

CHAPTER 4

1. Systematic and logically consistent studies of the social processes in general, and conflict in particular, still leave something to be desired. One of the best treatments, and still quite unsurpassed, is that of Georg Simmel, *Soziologie* (Leipzig, Duncker & Humblot, 1909), pp. 247-336. The English translation is by Kurt Wolff, *The Sociology of Simmel* (Chicago, Ill., Free Press, 1950). This chapter represents my own extension of many of Simmel's observations which I have already published in "Conflict," *Verbum,* Vol. 6 (March, 1949), Rio de Janeiro, pp. 3-31.

2. Cf. N. S. Timasheff, *Sociological Theory,* Revised Edition (New York, Random House, 1957), pp. 59-71.

3. Wilbert Ellis Moore, *Industrial Relations and Social Order,* Revised Edition (New York, Macmillan, 1951), pp. 338-39.

4. Leopold von Wiese und Kaiserwaldau, *Allgemeine Soziologie* (München, Duncker & Humblot, 2 vols. (1924-1929), available in an adapted English translation by Howard Becker, *Systematic Sociology* (New York, John Wiley & Sons, 1932), pp. 359-380.

5. Lewis A. Coser, *The Functions of Social Conflict* (Chicago, Free Press, 1956). Many penetrating judgments will also be found in Robin M. Williams, *Reduction of Intergroup Tensions* (New York, Social Research Council, 1947).

6. Coser, *op. cit.,* p. 49.

Notes

7. Alvin Johnson, *Encyclopaedia of the Social Sciences* (New York, Macmillan, 1930-35), Vol. XV, pp. 336-37.

8. New York Times, December 26, 1960, 1, 4.

9. The existence of "subcultures" in the framework of total cultures is now widely admitted. Cf. John Yinger, "Contraculture and Subculture," in *American Sociological Review*, Vol. 25, No. 5 (October, 1960), pp. 625-635.

10. The best studies on the causal background of race riots are to be found in Gunnar Myrdal et. al., *The American Dilemma* (New York, Harper and Bros., 1944), and Robin M. Williams, *Reduction of Intergroup Tensions* (New York, Social Research Council, 1947). Cf. also Brewton Berry, *Race and Ethnic Relations,* second edition (Boston, Houghton-Mifflin, 1958), Chapter 5.

11. This was one of the salient aspects of the Jewish *pogroms* in prerevolutionary Russia.

12. On strikes, see: Ernest Theodore Hiller, *The Strike* (Chicago, University of Chicago Press, 1928); Almont Lindsey, *The Pullman Strike* (Chicago, University of Chicago Press, 1942); Wilbert E. Moore, *Industrial Relations and the Social Order,* revised edition (New York, Macmillan, 1951); William L. Warner and J. O. Low, *The Social System of the Modern Factory: The Strike* (New Haven, Yale University Press, 1947); Robert V. Bruce, 1877: *Year of Violence* (Indianapolis, Bobbs-Merrill Co., Inc., 1959).

CHAPTER 5

1. No references to the literature on the subject are made in this chapter since this literature will be systematically surveyed and criticized in Chapter 11. The author's views on the subject were first published in an article "War or Peace," *Thought,* Vol. 25 (1950), pp. 393-411.

2. Cf. Chapter 11.

3. For the sake of brevity this term will be used often in place of "antagonistic process."

4. Cf. Chapter 6.

5. This is a famous statement by General Karl Clausewitz (1780-1831) in his treatise *On War*. Clausewitz was one of the authors

320

whom Lenin often consulted for guidance in his strategy of revolution.

6. Cf. Chapter 9.

7. Cf. Chapter 5.

8. Cf. Chapter 6.

CHAPTER 6

1. In contemporary sociology a procedure which may be called "quasi-experiment" has been developed, based on the certainty that no real experiment in sociology was possible. This quasi-experimental procedure is however applicable only on the level of "micro-sociology" (dealing with small groups), not of "macro-sociology" (dealing with large groups). The main premise of quasi-experiment, the finding of several social situations matching in all regards except the one under investigation, cannot materialize relative to states (nations) going to engage in war.

2. With the exception of the Korean and the Palestinian war, the statements in the text are based on extensive reading of standard works on general history and some monographs dealing with the particular wars. It was out of the question to make particular references to particular statements in these works—another volume would have been necessary.

3. See Chapter 8.

4. *Ibid.*

5. From this place on, the absence of normative inhibitions will be taken for granted. Therefore, the discussion of the causation of particular wars will be only three-dimensional, not four-dimensional, as has been done relative to the recent wars.

6. See Chapter 8.

7. After the success of the Dutch revolution, only its Southern part, roughly corresponding to contemporary Belgium.

8. See Chapter 7.

CHAPTER 7

1. No references to the literature on the subject are made for the same reason as explained in footnote 2 to Chapter 6.

2. III, 383-506 and 578-620. The data having served as background

for the generalizations in the text have been collected by Sorokin in cooperation with the present writer (see footnote on p. 383 of the volume quoted).

3. On the telling instance presented by the prelude of the Communist revolution in Russia (against the Provisional Government): see Chapter 12.

4. A conspicuous example can be seen in the stubborn resistance of the French government to negotiate with the leadership of the Algerian rebellion organized into a "government," in the earlier years altogether, later on, since de Gaulle's ascent to power, on the level of equality. After the plebiscite of January, 1961, further steps conducive to the recognition of that government have taken place.

5. The Belgian strike 1960-61.

CHAPTER 8

1. The material used in writing the case studies appearing in this chapter is analogous to that used in Chapter 6 (see footnote 2 to that chapter).

2. Cf. Chapter 10, Sect. 2.

3. During the abortive revolution of 1905, the Russian government headed by Count Witte made an offer of participation to a few among the most moderate leaders of the opposition. They declined the offer because they did not consider themselves representative enough. In 1906, Prime Minister Stolypin made a similar offer to a much larger group of leaders of the opposition. Again the offer was declined. This was probably one of the fatal mistakes which prepared the ground for the nefarious development of later years. During World War One, especially in 1915-16, a large number of the leaders of the opposition declared their readiness to join a government enjoying the "confidence of society" (in the specific meaning of the term then prevailing in Russia, connoting the totality of social organizations except those forming part of the government). Despite many advices of his own ministers and even of Granddukes, Emperor Nicholas II declined and thereby let go the last chance to save Russia (and himself with his family) from catastrophe.

Notes

4. As shown at the end of Chapter 7, this statement is tantamount to asserting the existence of all the conditions necessary and sufficient for the outbreak of a revolution.

5. The situation changed when President Hindenburg's dictatorship *de facto* replaced the constitutional powers. But this dictatorship lacked power to impose its decisions and therefore was unable to resist the rising tide of National Socialism.

6. The present author heard this proposition stated in 1918 by one of the vice-commissars for education, in an address to representatives of all the scientific institutions and institutions of higher learning of Petrograd (now Leningrad).

CHAPTER 9

1. Nicholas S. Timasheff, "The Postwar Population of the Soviet Union, *American Journal of Sociology*, Vol. 54, No. 2 (September 1948), pp. 148-55.

2. This line was first traced at the Paris Conference of Peace (1919) to separate areas inhabited predominantly by Poles from those where the Ukrainians and Byelorussians formed the majority. With slight changes it was used when partitioning Poland between Germany and the Soviet Union in 1939 and again by the 1946 peace settlement between the Soviet Union and Poland (represented by a Communist dominated government).

3. Cf. Chapter 8, Sect. III.

4. After Napoleon's defeat at Waterloo.

5. An enclave of the Pontifical State in southeastern France.

6. The endorsement by the people of the annexation of four German states by Prussia (1866) is dubious relative to the former Kingdom of Hanover where, until the First World War, a Hanoverian party survived.

CHAPTER 10

1. In contradistinction to war, stalemate in the course of a revolution is impossible: a government which succeeds in repelling a revolu-

tionary attack throughout the state's area has gained victory, even if the revolutionary forces have not been annihilated.

2. Charismatic leadership is a term introduced by Max Weber to connote leaders whose authority is based on the recognition of their extraordinary, almost superhuman capability of leadership. Cf. Nicholas S. Timasheff, *Sociological Theory* (Garden City, N.Y., Doubleday and Co., Inc., 1955), p. 179.

3. E. G., Edmund Aloysius Walsh, *Total Power* (Garden City, N.Y., Doubleday and Co., Inc., 1948).

4. See below, Chapter 13.

5. This was, however, not the case of the Russian revolutionary leaders who were confident that all the people were behind them; when this assumption proved to be false, they experienced a kind of "collapse of the universe."

6. This was the case during the first days of the March revolution in Russia; later on, leaders belonging to the sociocultural elite were called to form the Provisional Government, but true confidence between them and the real holders of power, the soldiers, never was established.

7. See above, Chapter 9.

8. Pitirim A. Sorokin, *Society, Culture and Personality* (New York, Harper and Bros., 1947), pp. 487-95.

Crane Brinton, *The Anatomy of Revolution* (New York, W. W. Norton and Co., Inc., 1938), pp. 25-26.

9. Which, however, often are not real revolutions as defined in Chapter 1.

CHAPTER 11

1. There are of course many *theories* of war causation, as we shall have occasion to see in this chapter. But the author is not aware of any causal theory of war where the theory is based upon *logically* integrated propositions. For a general discussion of logically integrated scientific theory cf. Ernest Nagel, *Logic Without Metaphysics* (Glencoe, Illinois, The Free Press, 1954), or the same author's *An Introduction to Logic and Scientific Method* (New York, Harcourt, Brace, 1934).

We are aware, as every scientist is, that this like any other theory is selective, i.e., abstracts only some from all possible relationships, to explain phenomena. In our present human condition and with our merely human means to know scientifically it cannot be otherwise.

2. Many if not most theories of social causation, including as we shall see, theories of war and peace, involve this reductionist process.

3. The assumption here of course is that social phenomena (e.g. war and peace) are natural phenomena, or phenomena in nature. For an ex professo discussion of these matters cf. Ernest Nagel, *Logic Without Metaphysics* (Glencoe, Ill., The Free Press, 1965), especially chapters 3 and 4.

4. Still another name for this kind of theory is *genetic* theory.

5. For a much more comprehensive discussion of the logical involvements of this cf. Ernest Nagel, *The Structure of Science* (New York, Harcourt, Brace and World, Inc., 1961), especially Chapter 15, "Problems in the Logic of Historical Inquiry."

6. Theodore Abel, "The Element of Decision in the Pattern of War," *American Sociological Review,* Vol. 6, 1941, pp. 853ff. Abel's study is based on observations covering twenty-five major wars which, however, he does not specify with the exception of the First Coalition War against France (1792), the Austro-Serbian War (a prelude to World War I), the Italo-Ethiopian War of 1935, and Hitler's all-out attack on the world around him. The presentation is in the form of a "natural history" with special emphasis upon analogies to the biological organism, i.e., references to specified stages.

7. Abel's phrasing here is such that it can be made readily applicable to revolutions as well.

8. Cf. B. Russel, *Why Men Fight* (1917), Sumner-Keller, *Science of Society* (1927), S. Steinmetz, *Die Soziologie des Krieges* (1927).

9. W. Waller, *War in the 20th Century* (1940).

10. M. A. May, *Social Psychology of War and Peace* (New Haven, Yale, 1943).

11. E. Walsh, *Total Power* (1948).

12. F. Schuman, *The Nazi Dictatorship* (1939), Alex Strachey, *The Unconscious Motives of War* (International Universities Press, Inc., New York, 1959), offers a somewhat less extravagant psychoanalytical theory. Here the state enables its members to gratify many of their

more infantile instincts by repressing others. Within the framework of the state fixation of some infantile dispositions takes place. But it is always probable that on some occasion a regression will take place. This is war. This theory sounds like a more sophisticated statement of the pugnacious instinct theory.

13. Other psychological and psychoanalytical theory will be found in the writings of O. Klineberg, *Tensions Affecting International Understanding* (1950), and the references given there.

14. This is the thesis of E. and A. Kulisher, *Kriegs und Wanderzüge* (1932), partly brought up to date by E. Kulisher, *Europe on the Move* (Columbia University Press, New York, 1948).

15. N. Berdyayev, *The Russian Idea* (1937), *The Russian Revolution* (Ann Arbor, Michigan, University of Michigan, 1960), *The Origin of Russian Communism* (Ann Arbor, Michigan, University of Michigan, 1960). All works published originally in Russian. Dates refer to recent English translations.

16. Two other writers might be mentioned in this context. F. von Schlegel (1772-1829) opposed degenerate Romans to virile Teutons so that the conquest of the Roman Empire by the latter was presented as a sign of progress. H. Treitschke (1834-96) developed the thesis that all nations except the Germans were deteriorating.

17. Russians whose armies had to cross over Germany during the Napoleonic wars unanimously reported their astonishment at the absence in Germany of any national sentiment. In 1831 a British Ambassador in Bavaria, Sir W. Hamilton, reported that the Germans showed a very weak sentiment of nationality. He does note their loyalty to local dynasties.

Prior to the wars of 1866 and 1870-1 Treitschke was a liberal. His conversion to nationalism is quite typical of the rise of a new spirit in Germany after Bismarck's victories.

German nationalism with emphasis upon *racial* aspects appears much later, and was probably imported into Germany through the works of A. de Gobineau, *Essai sur l'ingalite des races humaines* (1853-55) and H. S. Chamberlain, *The Foundations of the 19th Century* (1899). Neither of these authors is German.

18. L. L. Bernard, *War and Its Causes* (1944).

Notes

19. I have surveyed Sorokin's position(s) on the causality of war and revolution more fully in P. Allen (ed.), *Pitirim A. Sorokin in Review, The American Sociological Forum,* 1962, Volume I.

20. P. A. Sorokin, *Social and Cultural Dynamics,* (Boston, Sargent, 1957).

21. Pitirim A. Sorokin, "A Neglected Factor of War," *American Sociological Review,* Volume 3, 1934.

22. Pitirim A. Sorokin, *Russia and the United States* (1944).

23. Pitirim A. Sorokin, *Society, Culture, Personality* (1947), pp. 502-522.

24. Sorokin's study of revolution is based upon a survey of 1,622 revolutions. The survey was carried out by the present author and S. S. Oldenburg.

25. Pitirim A. Sorokin, "The Real Causes of the Russo-American Conflict," *World Affairs,* New Series, #3, 1949.

26. L. P. Edwards, *The Natural History of a Revolution* (1927).

27. Crane Brinton, *The Anatomy of Revolution* (New York, Vintage, 1957).

28. Quincy Wright. *A Study of War* (Chicago, The University of Chicago Press, 1942).

29. "The goal of causal knowledge is never attained, though our endeavors can bring us always nearer . . . we discover continuity in change, and change in continuity; we measure concomitances of factors and regularities of sequence; we infer the pattern of the scheme of values that every group sustains and forever reconstructs, adjusting means to ends, and ends to means through all the vicissitudes of its experience. As we follow these trails and indications, not in one instance but in multitudes, we gain a widening and deepening knowledge. From many angles we attack the problem of understanding human nature and its works. And if this human nature possesses any basis of identity through all its changeful manifestations these angles must converge towards a point they never reach, the goal of causal knowledge." Robert MacIver, *Social Causation* (New York, Ginn and Co., 1942), pp. 392-393.

Notes

CHAPTER 12

1. Cf. Chapter 9, Section 3.

2. Pitirim A. Sorokin and John A. Lukacs (*A History of the Cold War,* Garden City, New York, Doubleday, 1961) maintain, on the contrary, that the conflict is a traditional conflict between "paramount powers."

3. Robert Nigel Carew Hunt, *Marxism, Past and Present* (London, G. Bles, 1954), and *The Theory and Practice of Communism,* fifth edition, revised (New York, Macmillan, 1957).

4. Published in the *New York Times* "as provided in English by TASS," December 7, 1960, pp. 14-17.

5. This is a conspicuous example of the Communist manipulation of facts for propaganda purposes. Lenin's foreign policy was certainly *not* based on the principle of peaceful coexistence.

6. Reproduced in excerpts in the *New York Times,* October 13, 1960, 15, 4.

7. Nicholas S. Timasheff, *Great Retreat,* New York, Dutton, 1946.

8. The Russian defeatism of 1940 should not be exaggerated. Resistance to the German invasion was still formidable. An historical comparison points this up. In 1812 Napoleon crossed the Russian boundary at approximately the same time and place as Hitler did 128 years later. But on September 14, 1812 Napoleon's armies were in Moscow; in 1940-41 Moscow was never occupied by the invader, and the appearance of German detachments in the vicinity of Moscow took place only in October 1940. Remember, too, that Napoleon's armies advanced on foot or on horseback. Hitler's armies were highly mechanized.

9. An almost perfect demonstration of this general statement may be found in history. After the catastrophe of 1812 Napoleon fled from Russia with only 60,000 soldiers remaining in his Grand Army. What follows may be described as a process in reverse to that which had preceded Napoleon's invasion of Russia. Prussia, then Austria, changed sides. It was joined by Sweden, several secondary German states, the Netherlands (recently liberated by the allies from the status of a French province), and the Kingdom of Naples ruled by Napoleon's

brother-in-law, Marshal Murat. All these then brought claims on France (or other territories offered them as compensation by the major members of the anti-Napoleonic coalition). Gradually the conflict turned back to being mainly an ideological conflict, which it was in the beginning. The principle now guiding the allies was "legitimacy" (a term invented by Talleyrand), versus that of revolutionary change, later replaced by the principle of might, represented by Napoleonic France.

10. Cf. Chapter 8.

CHAPTER 13

1. Cf. Chapter 11.

2. It is probable that the Balkanization of Africa after the dissolution of the British and French colonial empires will not survive. There is no way of foreseeing what the mechanism of integration will be; but war is already, and probably will continue to be, one of the most likely modalities.

3. After the exhaustion of the expansion of the nomadic tribes of central Asia (the latest phases of whose invasions of Europe have been the Tartar invasion of Russia in the thirteenth century and the almost simultaneous invasion of the Near East and Byzantium by the Turks), population pressure has rarely played an important part in the emergence of conflicts conducive to war.

4. S. C. Ladas, *The Exchange of Minorities* (1932).

5. Cf. Chapter 3.

6. N. S. Timasheff, *The Great Retreat* (New York, E. P. Dutton, 1946).

7. Q. Wright, *The Conditions of War and Peace*, p. 323. The problem of prevention of revolution is thoughtfully discussed by G. Pettee, *The Process of Revolution* (1938), 161-4, but he discusses it, naturally, in terms of his own definition of revolution.

8. Many writers mention Lenin as the man having used the Kshessinka Palace. This was true during the late spring and early summer of 1917, but no longer in the decisive months preceding the coup d'etat. Lenin at the time was hiding in Finland.

Bibliography

THE BIBLIOGRAPHY presented here is (with a few exceptions) not repetitious of the references available in the footnotes. Its purpose is rather to serve as a guidance for further readings.

Alderson, Albert William. *The Only Way to Everlasting Peace,* London, P. R. Macmillan, 1960.

Arendt, Hannah. *On Revolution,* New York, Viking Press, 1963.

Boulding, Kenneth Ewart. *Conflict and Defense: A General Theory,* New York, Harper and Row, 1963.

Dennis, Lawrence. *Dynamics of War and Revolution.*

MacIver, Robert M. *Social Causation,* Boston, Ginn & Co., 1943.

Richardson, Lewis Fry. *Arms and Insecurity: A Mathematical Study of the Causes and Origins of War.* Edited by Nicholas

Rashevsky & Ernesto Trucco, Pittsburgh, Boxwood Press, 1960.

Schelling, Thomas C. *The Strategy of Conflict,* Cambridge, Harvard University Press, 1960.

Schoch, J. *Der Soziologische und Tiefenpsychologisch Aspekt des Krieges,* Zurich, Orell Fussli, 1955.

Sibley, Mulford, editor. *The Quiet Battle: Writings on the Theory and Practice of Non-violent Resistance,* Garden City, N. Y., Doubleday, 1963.

Simmel, Georg. *Conflict* (Translated by Kurt H. Wolff), Glencoe, Ill., Free Press, 1955.

Smelser, Neil J. *Theory of Collective Behavior,* London, Routledge and Kegan Paul, 1962.

Sorokin, Pitirim A. *Sociological Causality—Space—Time: A Study of Referential Principles of Sociology and Social Time,* Durham, N. C., Duke University Press, 1943.

Strachey, Alex. *The Unconscious Motives of War: A Psychoanalytical Contribution,* London, Allen & Union, 1957.

Waltz, Kenneth Neal, *Man, the State and War: A Theoretical Analysis,* New York, Columbia University Press, 1959.

Warner, William Lloyd and Lunt, Paul S. *The Social Life of a Modern Community,* New Haven, Yale University Press, 1941.

Wright, Quincy, Deutsch and Evan William M., editors. *Preventing World War III: Some Proposals,* New York, Simon and Schuster, 1962.

Wright, Quincy. *The Role of International Law in the Elimination of War,* Manchester University Press and New York, Oceana Publications, 1961.

Wright, Quincy. *The Study of International Relations,* New York, Appleton-Century-Crofts, 1955.

Wright, Quincy. *A Study of War,* Chicago, The University of Chicago Press, 1942.

Index

Index

DeGré, Gerard, 316, 318
Democracy, 10, 42, 91, 141, 154, 167, 209, 227, 228, 245, 261, 290, 300, 302, 308, 309, 310, 312
Dennis, Lawrence, 331
Dictatorship, 10, 14, 45, 141, 154, 302, 306, 308, 319, 323, 325
Dispute, 39, 67, 72, 78, 80, 84, 88, 89, 90, 91, 114, 139, 231
Durkheim, Emile, 29, 317

Edwards, L. P., 280, 281, 327
Einstein, Albert, 22
Enemy, 4, 88, 95, 125, 126, 127, 130, 168, 206, 211, 212, 214, 217, 219, 234, 274, 295, 314
Engels, F., 176
Equilibrium, 38, 47, 50, 51, 52, 53, 54, 58, 72, 81, 84, 95, 105, 116, 124, 136, 147, 220, 221

Facey, Paul W., 318
Feud, 50, 86, 97, 109, 112, 166, 175, 225, 234, 302, 305, 307
Fichte, J., 276
Fight, 6, 7, 64, 65, 68, 69, 74, 87, 89, 111, 126, 129, 139, 140, 165, 204, 233, 235, 237, 250, 254, 266, 295, 314
Foe, see Enemy
Force, 14, 39, 62, 63, 137, 148, 167, 168, 186, 190, 191, 195, 212, 221, 237, 240, 242, 259, 311, 312
Friedrich, Carl J., 319
Functions of state: 40, 41-46, 47, 50, 79, 84, 228, 318; coordination, 42, 43, 46, 146, 147; law and order, 13; self-assertion, 13, 42, 44, 45, 46, 48

Goal, 11, 39, 41, 43, 49, 51, 58, 61, 62, 63, 64, 65, 66, 71, 72, 74, 81, 84, 85, 86, 91, 94, 96, 97, 102, 103,
108, 112, 114, 137, 140, 158, 160, 178, 205, 210, 233, 235, 242, 243, 268, 283, 289, 290, 295, 302, 303, 305, 306, 307, 327
Gobineau, A. de, 326
Government, 7, 8, 9, 10, 11, 12, 14, 15, 40, 41, 42, 47, 50, 63, 73, 79, 80, 83, 86, 98, 104, 109, 112, 113, 122, 134, 139, 140, 141, 142, 143, 144, 145, 146, 147, 148, 149, 151, 152, 153, 154, 155, 156, 157, 159, 160, 162, 163, 165, 166, 169, 170, 174, 176, 180, 181, 185, 186, 187, 188, 191, 195, 201, 202, 203, 226, 236, 237, 240, 241, 242, 244, 245, 249, 251, 252, 254, 258, 261, 262, 265, 281, 286, 306, 307, 309, 310, 311, 322
Gumplowicz, 315
Gurvitch, George, 21, 316

Hegel, 276
Heisenberg, Werner, 20, 29, 315
Herder, J. H., 276
Hiller, Ernest Theodore, 320
Hobbes, 315
Hostilities, 103, 105, 112, 122, 125, 129, 130, 133, 191, 218, 220, 250, 273, 286
Hostility, 49, 51, 62, 122, 129, 173, 242, 274
Hunt, Robert Nigel Carew, 328

Ideology, 47, 81, 84, 85, 107, 120, 121, 123, 140, 143, 151, 183, 210, 287, 298, 329
Incompatibility, 11, 58, 61, 64, 68, 72, 74, 77, 79, 84, 86, 96, 102, 140, 160, 263, 278
Influence, 78, 82, 109, 116
Inhibition: 51, 52, 55, 68, 73, 74, 259; moral, 47, 73, 74, 87, 153; normative, 68, 72, 75, 86, 87, 88,

335

Index

96, 97, 101, 103, 104, 105, 106, 107, 108, 110, 111, 112, 116, 151, 153, 159, 160, 166, 265, 292, 321; social, 66, 69, 87

Johnson, Alvin, 60, 320
Justice, 144, 153, 254, 276, 307, 312

Kaiserwaldau, 319
Kaufman, Felix, 317
Klineberg, O., 326
Kulisher, A. and E., 326

Ladas, S. C., 329
Langer, Suzanne K., 317
Laplace, Pierre Simon, Marquis de, 317
Law: 10, 11, 13, 20, 24, 27, 30, 31, 38, 46, 48, 69, 98, 151, 152, 156, 165, 176, 195, 252, 307, 310, 311, 318, 319; international, 6, 14, 50, 52, 88, 221, 224, 233
Lindsey, Almont, 320
Lipset, Seymour M., 308
Loomis, Charles P., 316
Low, J. O., 320
Lukacs, John A., 328
Lundberg, George Andrew, 20, 316
Lunt, Paul S., 332

MacIver, Robert, 26, 317, 318, 327, 331
Marx, Karl, 176, 275, 288
Masses, 140, 143, 144, 149, 152, 155, 156, 158, 162, 164, 165, 168, 170, 177, 186, 244, 246, 247, 254, 255, 257, 259, 260, 261, 299
May, M. A., 274, 325
Mediation (see also Arbitration), 64, 66, 67, 73, 89, 90, 106, 112
Mendel, 29
Merton, Robert K., 318
Michotte, A., 28, 317
Militarism, 48, 55, 86, 97, 104, 105, 109, 275, 276, 305

Mob, 8, 11, 69, 70, 140, 246, 281
Monarchy, 12, 14, 117, 126, 141, 154, 163, 167, 170, 174, 178, 185, 186, 193, 194, 195, 257
Moore, Wilbert Ellis, 319, 320
Morale, 51, 210, 211, 212, 215, 217, 235, 294, 296
Myrdal, Gunnar, 320

Nagel, Ernest, 317, 324, 325
Nation, 4, 6, 49, 50, 55, 76, 77, 92, 112, 135, 139, 140, 146, 150, 172, 187, 202, 205, 207, 209, 210, 211, 213, 216, 220, 226, 229, 230, 232, 235, 241, 245, 247, 261, 273, 279, 280, 287, 290, 294, 295, 299, 302, 307, 308, 309, 312, 321
Nationalism, 44, 84, 112, 113, 114, 116, 168, 169, 170, 178, 179, 202, 255, 257, 276, 277, 326
Negotiation, 52, 64, 67, 70, 73, 89, 90, 100, 102, 104, 106, 107, 108, 110, 111, 114, 118, 124, 127, 128, 130, 136, 154, 155, 218, 219, 220, 287, 322
Neutrality, 6, 119, 125, 217, 242
Norms, 64, 66, 67, 70, 278

Oldenburg, S. S., 327
Operator, 32, 33, 34, 35, 36, 68, 69, 71, 75, 97, 98, 131, 133, 155, 159, 170, 174, 177, 235, 250, 265
Opposition, 11, 50, 65, 93, 94, 139, 140, 141, 142, 143, 145, 147, 149, 153, 154, 155, 156, 157, 159, 160, 162, 165, 166, 169, 170, 171, 172, 177, 181, 182, 185, 186, 196, 197, 203, 236, 237, 238, 240, 241, 242, 248, 249, 251, 322
Oppression, 71, 80, 143, 153, 158, 305
Order: concept and definition, 12, 21, 22, 24, 30, 52, 57, 317, 319, 320; maintenance of, 13, 46, 48,